TRAILS

Toward a New Western History

TRAILS

Toward a New Western History

Edited by
PATRICIA NELSON LIMERICK
CLYDE A. MILNER II
CHARLES E. RANKIN

UNIVERSITY PRESS OF KANSAS

Chapters 5, 6, 7, and 8 are reprinted by permission from
Montana The Magazine of Western History 40 (Summer 1990).
Chapter 9 is reprinted by permission from the October 1989
issue of *American Studies International.*
Chapters 10 and 11: Copyright by Western History Association.
Reprinted by permission. These articles first appeared in the
November 1989 issue of the *Western Historical Quarterly.*

Published by the University Press of Kansas (Lawrence, Kansas
66049), which was organized by the Kansas Board of Regents and is
operated and funded by Emporia State University, Fort Hays State
University, Kansas State University, Pittsburg State University,
the University of Kansas, and Wichita State University

Library of Congress Cataloging-in-Publication Data

Trails : toward a new western history / edited by Patricia Nelson
Limerick, Clyde A. Milner II, Charles E. Rankin
p.   cm.
Includes index.
ISBN 0-7006-0500-2 (alk. paper) — ISBN 0-7006-0501-0
(pbk. : alk. paper)
1. West (U.S.)—Historiography. I. Limerick, Patricia Nelson,
1951– . II. Milner, Clyde A., 1948–   . III. Rankin, Charles E.
F591.T683 1991   91-25640
978 '.0072—dc20

British Library Cataloguing in Publication Data is available.

Printed in the United States of America
10 9 8 7 6 5 4

To the memory of
Carey McWilliams

western public intellectual
of impeccable compassion and courage

CONTENTS

CONTENTS

III THE GLOBAL WEST

Photographs follow page 144.

PREFACE

THIS COLLECTION of essays originated in a project cosponsored by the Arizona, Colorado, New Mexico, Utah, and Wyoming State Endowments or Councils for the Humanities and funded by the National Endowment for the Humanities. The project centered on a twenty-four-panel exhibit called "Trails through Time." In September 1989, the exhibit was launched on its travels by a symposium called "Trails: Toward a New Western History." The first three essays in this collection were originally given at the Trails symposium: Donald Worster, "Beyond the Agrarian Myth"; Richard White, "Trashing the Trails"; and Peggy Pascoe, "Western Women at the Cultural Crossroads."[1] The fourth essay, Patricia Nelson Limerick's "The Trail to Santa Fe: The Unleashing of the Western Public Intellectual" is new, written for this collection, to explain the genesis of the Trails symposium and to reflect on the reactions and responses that followed it.

By the original plan for this collection, the presentations from Santa Fe were to form their own provocative, if slim, volume. Happily, the chance to join forces, by adding a number of other discussions of recent changes in the writing and teaching of western American history, came to the attention of the editors of the University Press of Kansas. This longer and more thorough set of reflections is the result.

The second set of essays was commissioned by

Charles Rankin, editor of *Montana The Magazine of Western History*. Rankin asked four scholars of western history to consider what the "New Western History" is, what its impact on western history has been thus far, and where it might lead as we move into the 1990s and beyond. Originally published in the summer 1990 issue of *Montana*, this second section includes Limerick's "What on Earth is the New Western History?"; Gerald Thompson's "Another Look at Frontier/Western Historiography"; Michael P. Malone's "The 'New Western History,' an Assessment"; and Elliott West's "A Longer, Grimmer, but More Interesting Story." The authors provide a range of views that clarify the changes in western history. Western history is getting its full share of the constructive tension of dissent, disagreement, and ferment. Scholars are subjecting the old and familiar to new assessments and exploring new and different horizons in all directions. As some scholars reevaluate the eighteenth- and nineteenth-century western experience, others lay the foundations for understanding the twentieth-century West.

The influence of perspectives originating in the 1960s is unmistakable. The new emphasis on ethnic and racial diversity in the past not only reflects the rejection of melting pot homogeneity, but also represents the logical extension of notions of social and cultural pluralism that first emerged to full political power in the decade of Kennedy and Johnson. Similarly, the new emphasis on humanity's historic interaction with the physical environment follows on the concern for ecological fragility and environmental exploitation that first surfaced in its contemporary form a quarter century ago. Likewise, the explosion of work in western women's history, which began in the late 1970s and gained momentum in the 1980s, can be linked to feminism's insistence since the late 1960s that women be recognized as active players in all facets of society. Consider the results. Women have become an essential part of the western story, as have ethnic and racial groups. Viewing the past from their perspectives, we find cultural and social complexity in place of archetypal white male simplicity. In fact, with this enriched and deepened perspective, that unitary term "the white man" dissolves, revealing a wide range of people with various ethnic origins, occupations, values, and characters. Rather than seeing a single Anglo wave moving west across a continent, we see one set of waves, predominantly but not wholly Anglo, encountering other waves: one Hispanic from the South, another Asian from the Far West, and amid it all, we find enduring yet dynamic Native American cultures. The environment, meanwhile, is no longer a resistant barrier to be overcome, but a vital historical component that itself changes with human interaction even as it shapes western economic and social patterns, not to mention the western imagination.

Perhaps most important, the New Western History offers a more balanced view of the western past. It includes failure as well as success; defeat as well as victory; sympathy, grace, villainy, and despair as well as danger, courage, and heroism; women as well as men; varied ethnic groups and their differing perspectives as well as white Anglo-Saxon Protestants; an environment that is limiting, interactive, and sometimes ruined as well as mastered and made to bloom; a parochial economy alternately fueled and abandoned by an interlocking national and world order; and, finally, a regional identity as well as a frontier ethic. Frederick Jackson Turner, father of the frontier thesis, comes in for hard criticism for having bequeathed what many historians regard as an interpretive straitjacket. We should remember not only that Turner was a man of his times but that he realized that fact. It was Turner, after all, who said that each generation interprets history anew, according to its own need for understanding. History thus can never be static, set down once and for all. One of history's highest goals is to make the past usable. If the New Western History does nothing else, it helps us consider the old and familiar in new ways. And, if we are fortunate, these new perspectives will be relevant to our times.

This second section concludes with Brian W. Dippie's "American Wests: Historiographical Perspectives." Originally published in the October 1989 issue of *American Studies International*, Dippie's essay has been included here with the *Montana* articles because, with its greater length, it adds depth to many of the issues raised in the shorter essays.

The third set of articles was originally brought together by Clyde A. Milner II, editor of the *Western Historical Quarterly (WHQ)*. For nearly twenty years, much that was new in the historical study of the American West crossed the desk of Charles S. Peterson. In 1971 Peterson joined the faculty of Utah State University as professor of history and associate editor of the *Western Historical Quarterly*, the newly founded scholarly journal of the Western History Association. In 1979 he became its editor. Peterson retired in July 1989, but his name remained on the masthead of the *WHQ* through the volume year. The November 1989 issue displayed his name for the last time. That issue attempted to capture the generous outlook toward western history that Chas Peterson had brought to the field in both his editing and writing. The *WHQ* staff called it informally the "Global West" issue, and the three essays published in it amply fulfilled their purpose. The essays honored Peterson, who had regularly advocated vital new directions in the study of the American West.

The writing of all three authors from the November

1989 *WHQ* is represented in this collection. Two of the original essays are republished here: Walter Nugent's "Frontiers and Empires in the Late Nineteenth Century" and Michael P. Malone's "Beyond the Last Frontier: Toward a New Approach to Western American History." William G. Robbins's essay for this book expands on some of the ideas he presented in his *WHQ* piece "Western History: A Dialectic on the Modern Condition." All three authors have built their essays from their own earlier works and from the give-and-take that characterizes scholarly inquiry. Walter Nugent's mastery of demography is evident in his examination of different forms of settlement across the planet. His essay first began to take shape as a major address that he delivered in Jerusalem. In similar fashion, Michael Malone's essay began as a paper presented at the national conference of the Organization of American Historians. Like Nugent, Malone has a global vision for western history. Malone encourages western historians to consider the ideas of "world historians" such as William H. McNeill, L. S. Stavrianos, Immanuel Wallerstein, and Theodore von Laue. In several essays, including his piece for the *WHQ*, William G. Robbins has advocated the end of the exceptionalist conviction in the "uniqueness" of the West's history. He has been especially perceptive about the dynamics of modern capitalism as it affects this region and the world. In his essay for this book, Robbins demonstrates how some scholars are expanding the understanding of the West's international connections through the study of subregions such as the Pacific Northwest and the Hispanic Southwest, areas where borders with Canada and Mexico are of vital importance.

Nugent, Malone, and Robbins are moving the intellectual boundaries of western history outward to a global perspective. Their provocative ideas remain a fitting tribute to the vision, at once inclusive and expansive, of Charles S. Peterson.

As readers will soon notice, this collection does not represent a new orthodoxy in the writing of western American history. The essays presented in the first section come the closest to agreement, but there are nonetheless subjects of hearty and productive disagreement among those four authors. The second and third sections include writers who are maintaining some cynical distance between themselves and the New Western History, while also keeping their ties to earlier schools of thought. What all the authors, as well as the editors, would agree on is this: The current disagreements and debates are not occasions for distress but are instead evidence of an era of great vitality in the writing of western American history.

We would like, most of all, to thank the authors whose work is assembled here. For their hard work on the Trails project, we are also in debt to Dan Shilling and Diane Facinelli of the Arizona Humanities Council, Jim Pierce and Jean Sharer of the Colorado Endowment for the Humanities, John Lucas and Valencia de la Vega of the New Mexico Endowment for the Humanities, Delmont Oswald and Brian Crockett of the Utah Endowment for the Humanities, Robert Young and Kelley Pellesier of the Wyoming Council for the Humanities, and John Meredith, program officer at the National Endowment for the Humanities. James Byrkit, Adrian Bustamente, Michael Cassity, Kathryn MacKay, and Charles Polzer, S.J., served as project scholars for the exhibit. In the preparation of the exhibit and at the symposium in Santa Fe, Cathy Lavender-Teliha played a key role in keeping things running smoothly. At the University of Colorado, Kim Gruenwald and Cathy Lavender-Teliha capably managed the manuscript, and Kenneth M. Orona tracked and corraled photographs. At the University Press of Kansas, Fred Woodward and Cynthia Miller expressed an early interest in this project, attending the conference in Santa Fe and remaining good-natured—and properly and helpfully impatient—through the process of getting this text assembled. Thanks also to the copy editor, Michele Kendall.

Patricia Nelson Limerick, Boulder, Colorado
Clyde A. Milner II, Logan, Utah
Charles E. Rankin, Helena, Montana

PART I

TRAILS

The New Western History

1

BEYOND THE AGRARIAN MYTH

DONALD WORSTER

COMING DOWN the Santa Fe Trail in the summer of 1831, a young merchant named Josiah Gregg brought a vision of the American West that must have seemed the only one there would ever be.[1] Raddled by years of consumption, he was rapidly restored by the bracing air and outdoor life. By the time he reached the vicinity of Council Grove, Kansas, he was able to ride a horse again, and it was about then that he was ready to raise his eyes to the surrounding countryside and contemplate its future. "All who have traversed these delightful regions," he writes in *The Commerce of the Prairies*, "look forward to the day when the Indian title to the land shall be extinguished and flourishing white settlements dispel the gloom which at present prevails over this uninhabited region."[2] That may seem a strange sentiment for a man whose life in the white settlements had been so sickly, but, feeling better the farther he got from home, Gregg became positively eager to forward the cause of United States expansion. Like so many other merchants and travelers of his day, all taking trails westward in search of profit or adventure, he expected to find more than the shabby little foreign town of Santa Fe lying at the end of his journey. The prospect of a bigger and broader America would be there too, of a na-

3

tion extending the blessings of its free institutions to the benighted Mexican and Indian peoples that it would conquer and subdue.

In his brief book on Gregg, the novelist Paul Horgan faulted him for being at times a humorless, cranky misanthrope and for showing little sympathy toward the Hispanic and Catholic civilization he encountered in the Southwest. But Horgan also admired in Gregg's narrative the great redeeming spirit of the western frontier—the work of a "great conquest" and the expansion of personal freedom that it was supposed to make possible.[3] I, on the other hand, representing a new generation of western historians, find it harder to take such a favorable view of Gregg's vision of conquest. That almost transcendental faith in American growth seems far from justified by the subsequent facts of history. At the same time, Gregg's misanthropy becomes a little more excusable with time, and I often nod in agreement at his acerbic comments on his fellow humans. In this reversal of assessment I am not alone. A growing number of citizens have become skeptical of where some of our national trails and ambitions have led.

For instance, a contemporary traveler to the West, Ian Frazier of New York City, expresses well our disenchanted mood toward the region, though he loves it as we all do. In his *Great Plains* (1989), Frazier recalls his rambles up and down the landscape but can summon none of the firm linear confidence of Josiah Gregg. His trail jumps distortedly from Glacier National Park in Montana to the black pioneer settlement of Nicodemus, Kansas, to the home of Lawrence Welk in North Dakota and then back to western Kansas and the home of the murdered Clutter family. Along the way he is sometimes filled with joy by the region's vistas—the "still empty land beyond newsstands and malls and velvet restaurant ropes"—but

4

it is a happiness edged with regret for the defeat of the Indian peoples, who finally for him are the lost essence of the land. The plains "are the place where Crazy Horse will always remain uncaptured. They are the lodge of Crazy Horse."

And then after so many miles on the road, so many roadside markers, so many sodbusters' tales, so many fields of cattle, dust, sorghum, finding himself at last standing before an ominous MX missile site in Montana, Frazier writes what he calls the "punch line of our two hundred years on the Great Plains" (actually more of a punch paragraph):

[We] trap out the beaver, subtract the Mandan, infect the Blackfeet and the Hidatsa and the Assiniboin, overdose the Arikara; call the land a desert and hurry across it to get to California and Oregon; suck up the buffalo, bones and all; kill off nations of elk and wolves and cranes and prairie chickens and prairie dogs; dig up the gold and rebury it in vaults somewhere else; ruin the Sioux and Cheyenne and Arapaho and Crow and Kiowa and Comanche; kill Crazy Horse, kill Sitting Bull; harvest wave after wave of immigrants' dreams and send the wised-up dreamers on their way; plow the topsoil until it blows to the ocean; ship out the wheat, ship out the cattle; dig up the earth itself and burn it in power plants and send the power down the line; dismiss the small farmers, empty the little towns; drill the oil and natural gas and pipe it away; dry up the rivers and springs, deep-drill for irrigation water as the aquifer retreats. And in return we condense unimaginable amounts of treasure into weapons buried beneath the land which so much treasure came from—weapons for which our best hope might be

5

that we will someday take them apart and throw them away, and for which our next-best hope certainly is that they remain humming away under the prairie, absorbing fear and maintenance, unused, forever.[4]

And with that Frazier's trail of adventure abruptly ends, not at the enlightened rule of peace, prosperity, reason, and liberty that Gregg envisioned but at the nightmare of institutionalized madness—the doctrine of Mutually Assured Destruction preached by today's military strategists, implanted in a West that now stands at the dead center of modern warfare. Of course, there are other roads and destinies in this region too, including more positive and optimistic ones; but Frazier feels compelled to end his journey with a dark vision of a people imprisoned in their own aggressive fear. It is a conclusion that other writers, including historians, share and that the public too is gradually coming to terms with.

A century and a half after Josiah Gregg's first exhilarating trip along a barely rutted path, the West looks unlike anything he could have foreseen. In the process of becoming what it is, the region has emerged from the old clouds of myth and romance and now seems for the first time honestly revealed. Today it looks a little smaller than it once did, though it is still notable for its amplitude of space and light. Now and then it can stir up the old indeterminate hopefulness in newcomers, but generally what people want out of the region is more practical and limited—a job, a home, a vacation. Liberty has turned out to be an ambiguous achievement and, in too many cases and mouths, is only a hollow phrase; westerners are more aware of that fact than ever before. Clearly, the grandiose history that white Americans once thought they were making out here in this land beyond the Mississippi River has come apart and does not compel belief as it once did. I think I know how that happened and want to claim some small credit for historians. For this region that was once so lost in dreams and idealization, we have been creating a new history, clear-eyed, demythologized, and critical. We have been rewriting the story from page one and watching it be accepted. That has been a slow, hard-won victory, and I think it is time we acknowledged the achievement.

The first bona fide revisionist, in a sense the prophet of a New Western History, was Henry Nash Smith, for it was he who first told us what was wrong with the old history and dared to call it myth. That was in 1950 with the publication of *Virgin Land*. By myth Smith referred to the grand archetypal stories of heroic origins and events that all peoples create for themselves, a kind of folk history written by anonymous minds. Myths tell us how things came to be, how they are and why they are, and, if the real world does not quite correspond to them, it may come closer to the ideal as time goes on; myths can mightily affect the course of events. In later years Smith admitted he had been a little too quick to dismiss myth as simple falsehood, when in truth popular belief and historical reality are joined together in a continuous circle, moving back and forth in a long, halting, jerky interplay. Still, it must be added that there is a lot of falsity in any myth, not excepting the one about the West, and such falsity can lead people into difficult, even tragic, situations.

We have had many myths about the West, but the principal one was a story about a simple, rural people coming into a western country—an ordinary people moving into an extraordinary land, as Robert G. Athearn has put it—and creating there a peaceful, productive life.[5] In this great, good place, human nature was supposed to rise out of its old turpitude and depravity to a new dignity:

7

Sturdy yeoman farmers would have here the chance to live rationally and quietly, free of all contaminating influences. By the millions they would find homes in the undeveloped vastness stretching beyond the settlements, bringing life to the land and turning it into the garden of the world. Never mind that much blood would have to be shed first to drive out the native peoples; the blood would be on others' hands, and the farmers would be clean, decent folk dwelling in righteousness.

From the beginning the agrarian myth was filled with all the unresolved contradictions of innocence. Civilization was to find in this region its next, higher incarnation, and in that expectation, the myth of the garden, writes Smith, "affirmed a doctrine of progress, of gigantic economic development." On the other hand, the West was supposed to offer a place to escape civilization; the myth implied "a distrust of the outcome of progress in urbanization and civilization."[6] Logic says you cannot have it both ways, physics that you cannot go forward and backward in the same moment. Yet the agrarian myth was able to hold possibilities together because it did not follow the rules of logical discourse; instead, it was a song, a dream, a fantasy, that captured all the ambivalence in a people about their past and future. Moreover, if your optimism is strong enough, you will believe that what is impossible for logic and physics is possible for you. No region settled in modern times has had so much optimism in its eyes as the West, an optimism that was all but blinding.

What people could not see was, in Smith's words, any possibility of "radical defect or principle of evil" in their garden. They knew there was plenty of evil in the world but supposed that it had all been left behind, and the people left behind were "by implication unfortunate or wicked." "This suggestion," Smith goes on, "was

8

strengthened by the tendency to account for any evil which threatened the garden empire by ascribing it to alien intrusion. Since evil could not conceivably originate within the walls of the garden, it must by logical necessity come from without, and the normal strategy of defense was to build the walls higher and stop the cracks in them."[7] The perfect society growing up in the West would be free of the problems found in the East or Europe: poverty; racial and class divisions; anger and dissent; bitter, intense conflict of the kind that had split the South from the North, that had pitted France against Germany, that had more or less been humankind's lot since the Fall in the original garden. This flawless West must be kept in precious isolation, removed from the contaminations of history and the world community.

One of Smith's most important insights was that the frontier thesis of Frederick Jackson Turner sprang directly out of the agrarian myth.[8] The first historian to undertake serious study of the westward movement, Turner never stopped believing that the old story was literally true. Returning to the wilderness, men could be restored to the innocence of their youth, sloughing off the blemishes of age. He handed on his faith to his disciples, and so western history was born. From the outset it was almost an oxymoron: "Western" and "history" were contradictory terms. What kind of history could be written about a people who had turned their backs on time? Certainly it could not be a history that looked anything like that of the Old World; therefore its historians would not have to pay any attention to that irrelevant experience. They would not have to pass foreign language exams, read works from abroad, or keep up with the Paris savants. They were excused from examining radical defects in the West, for there were none to be found.

It took a detached observer from Columbia Univer-

sity, Richard Hofstadter, to see what it was that eventually doomed Turner and his followers to national irrelevance: Turner was not "a critic of the human scene." He
often allowed his strong patriotic impulses to overrule his
brain. He lacked the "intellectual passion" of a critic,
sharpening his mind on the problems of his society. Gentle and humane in his personal relations, Turner had no
capacity to see the shameful side of the westward movement: "riotous land speculation, vigilantism, the ruthless
despoiling of the continent, the arrogance of American
expansionism, the pathetic tale of the Indians, anti-Mexi-
can and anti-Chinese nativism, the crudeness, even the
near-savagery, to which men were reduced on some portions of the frontier."[9] Such matters did not engage Turner's intelligence, and he could not fathom why anyone
would want to investigate them or would feel anguish
about them. In being so evasive he was not really lying
about the past as much as he was omitting whatever in-
terfered with what he regarded as the greater truth: the
genesis of a free people. The twentieth century has not
dealt kindly with Turner's reputation, and the reason has
more to do with the man's lack of critical acuity than of
hard evidence for his theories. As Hofstadter writes, "It is
the blandness of his nationalism that most stands out, as
it is the blandness of such social criticism as he attempted, the blandness indeed of his mind as a whole."[10]

The generation of western historians who were contemporaries of Henry Nash Smith and Richard Hofstadter, men and women who came of age in the 1950s and
1960s, began to lay the foundations for a different, more
academic style of regional history. They organized graduate seminars in which they trained hundreds of Ph.D.s in
the field. They sent them into the archives—to the
"sources," they said with solemn dignity—and taught
them to collect data and make footnotes. They launched

an industry of monographs. In October 1961, leaders of that generation came together in Santa Fe, New Mexico, to revive western studies in the wake of Turner's fall from authority; following that meeting they established the Western History Association and began publishing a scholarly journal, the *Western Historical Quarterly*. When those founders gathered around the banquet table, heads still bowed dutifully at the name of Frederick Jackson Turner, and a few still crossed themselves in reverence. The "westward course of empire" school still had its spokesmen in Ray Allen Billington and other frontier scholars. But for all those vestiges of piety, historians slowly began to conceive the West in post-Turnerian terms.

For the first time the West took on a clear, concrete shape, essentially the area from the Great Plains states to the Pacific Coast. But though they acknowledged that the West was an actual place, not that vague mythical landscape of pioneering that Turner had had in mind, postwar historians tended to downplay the idea that there was anything radical or distinctive about it. The story of their West was primarily the story of American economic enterprise written over and over again in new terrain—written in larger letters each time, written frequently with a heroic hand, but above all written in a familiar economic language. The key words for this postwar generation remained the standard national clichés of "expansion," "development," and "growth": growth in western transportation, growth in investment, growth in population, growth in statehood, growth toward an urban civilization.[11]

Growth had indeed been a prominent idea in the settlement of the West, and that idea was, by any cool, rational analysis, incompatible with backward-looking agrarian fantasies. The postwar generation faced up to that contradiction and threw the old mythic agrarianism out the window. Far from representing an escape from history, a place for idealists and romantics, they insisted that the West was urban and progressive to its core. By all the indexes of economic success, it began far behind the rest of the nation and long had to suffer as a mere colony of the East; nonetheless, it ran hard to catch up and become one with modern America. Thus the western story appeared to be not one of pioneers turning their backs on a spoiled past, but one of competitive, conformist drives to be in the national mainstream.

In reaction against Turner's theme of a primitive return in time, the postwar generation of historians, led by scholars like Earl Pomeroy and Gerald Nash, discovered the twentieth century. The West did not suddenly end in 1890, with the passing of the frontier, they declared, but was at that point only beginning its ascent to prominence. With the passing of the brief pioneer era, it entered into a new, open-ended period of expanding technology and enterprise that had no limits in sight. Historians were impressed by millions of new migrants coming into the region, and it was their experiences—their cities, work, leisure, and politics, their conflicts with and sources of capital in the East, their relations with the federal government, and especially their search for modern affluence—that increasingly came to dominate historical research. The legendary man on horseback fighting against a horde of menacing savages, the plowman toiling alone beneath a prodigious sky, all but faded away in this nonagrarian, professionalized, heavily footnoted, technology-centered, city-based redefinition of the region's past.

That is not to say there was no mythic element left in the postwar generation's writing. The old agrarian fantasy may have lost its hold, but there endured among many that old "doctrine of progress, of gigantic economic development," that Smith also identified as part of western mythology. We might call it the mythic world of the Chamber of Commerce, for whom the West will be an unfinished frontier until it is one with Hoboken, New Jersey, until we Americans will have written a saga of industrial conquest from sea to shining sea. Through the 1950s and 1960s not a few western historians acted as though they were charter members of the Chamber, and their books and articles could almost have been introductions to company reports or state tourist brochures trumpeting the arrival of a "New West."

One may, of course, find countless things to congratulate in the region, but is it the job of the historian to shout them up, to act as the Merv Griffin of the western game show? After all, there are plenty of well-funded agencies charged with that task. What the boosters will not do, and what the historian alone is in a position to do, is to examine those radical defects of society Hofstadter talked about. For a long time, even after it had left Turner behind, the academic history of the West did not make that examination. There was little interest in dwelling on the dark, shameful aspects of the region's past. Graduate students were not expected to emerge from their seminars with a critical perspective; on the contrary, they were commonly taught to be positive and hopeful, to believe in the essential goodness of their institutions, to avoid any expressions of radical discontent, and they dutifully did so. In that moral complacency, if not in all their theories, they remained true to the Turnerian spirit, and the history they wrote remained an exercise in blandness. While the rest of the world's historians were facing up to the horrors of the Holocaust, the infamy of southern slavery, the satanic mills of global industrialization, western historians continued to wear cheerful faces. Terrible things had happened elsewhere,

13

they knew, but on this happier side of the North American continent one could find only a little fraud and corruption in the land laws, only a few third-rate senators to decry, but no great evils to write about. A sense of tragedy had not yet made its way west.

One of the most important books produced by the postwar generation illustrates my point completely: Gerald Nash's *The American West Transformed* (1985). No one before him had demonstrated so compellingly the scope and promise of twentieth-century regional history. No one had traced the emergence of the New West of urban, industrial enterprise in more enthusiastic detail. And certainly no one could disagree with many of the conclusions he reached:

The American West emerged from the Second World War as a transformed region. In 1941 many westerners had feared that the expansion of the region had come to a close. The economy was stagnant, population growth had ceased, and the colonial dependence of the region on the older East pervaded most aspects of life. But by 1945 the war had wrought a startling transformation. Westerners now had visions of unlimited growth and expansion, a newly diversified economy was booming, a vast influx of population was changing the very fabric of western society, and the region had just witnessed a growth in cultural maturity which was totally unprecedented in its history. The West emerged from the war as a path-breaking self-sufficient region with unbounded optimism for its future. World War II had precipitated that transformation, and in retrospect constituted one of the major turning points in the history of the American West.[12]

14

Unquestionably, those words reveal a historical imagination that has gone well beyond the old frontier of Turnerian tradition, and they come from a historian who, with others of his generation, has reenvisioned the West in a fresh light.

But to my mind there are a few things missing from Nash's interpretation of the West, and they are serious omissions. How could one, for example, write about World War II's impact and leave out the glaring fact that the West henceforth would be dominated by the military-industrial complex, that its economic health would rise and fall with the prospects of the Pentagon and the cold war, a fact that is obvious today from San Diego's navy yards all the way to Montana's missile silos? Or how could one leave off that list of so-called achievements the doomsday shadow of the atomic bomb—the fact that the West has been forever poisoned by nuclear fallout and, since the war, has found itself sick and dying of radiation, beset by the problems of nuclear waste disposal, living in white-knuckled fear in the vicinity of Rocky Flats, Alamogordo, Los Alamos, Hanford, and the Nevada Test Site? Clearly there was more to the region than we had been told by either Frederick Jackson Turner or the postwar generation of Nash and others, but it would take yet another generation to see those darker aspects, to discover their roots, and to give them significance.

Around the year 1970 (the year when Dee Brown published his searing polemic against the United States military's aggression against Indians, *Bury My Heart at Wounded Knee: An Indian History of the American West* [New York: Holt, Rinehart, and Winston]) that untold side of the western past began to find its tellers. A younger generation, shaken by Vietnam and other national disgraces—poverty, racism, environmental degradation—could not pretend that the only story that mattered in the

15

West was one of stagecoach lines, treasure hunts, cattle brands, and wildcatters, nor for that matter aircraft plants, opera companies, bank deposits, or middle-class whites learning how to ski. What was missing was a frank, hard look at the violent imperialistic process by which the West was wrested from its original owners and the violence by which it had been secured against the continuing claims of minorities, women, and the forces of nature. That capacity for violence may be inherent in all people, but when it showed its ugly face among the respectable and the successful, it was called "progress," "growth," "the westward movement," "the march of freedom," and a dozen other euphemisms. It was time for historians to call such violence and imperialism by their true names.

During the past two decades a New Western History has appeared with the express purpose of confronting and understanding those radical defects of the past. This new history has tried to put the West back into the world community, with no illusions about moral uniqueness. It has also sought to restore to memory all those unsmiling aspects that Turner wanted to leave out. As a result, we are beginning to get a history that is beyond myth, beyond the traditional consciousness of the white conquerors, beyond a primitive emotional need for heroes and heroines, beyond any public role of justifying or legitimating what happened. Here are some of the most important arguments the new history has been making.

First, the invaded and subject peoples of the West must be given a voice in the region's history. Until very recently many western historians acted as though the West either had been empty of people before the coming of the white race or was quickly, if bloodily, cleared of them once and for all, so that historians had only to deal with the white point of view. They particularly ignored the continuing presence, the intrinsic value, and the political interests of the indigenous peoples, Indians and Chicanos.

All that has dramatically changed in the last few years. Today no historian who wants to be taken seriously would dare proceed without at least acknowledging the prior presence of nonwhite groups and their persistence into the present. Some historians, white and nonwhite alike, have gone even farther to attempt to rewrite the whole story from the point of view of the conquered peoples. I do not mean to say that this is the sole achievement of scholars under the age of fifty; on the contrary, many of that immediate postwar generation have also come around to a more pluralistic point of view. Gerald Nash again may serve as an example; three of the eleven chapters in his *The American West Transformed* deal specifically with the experience of blacks, Hispanics, Indians, and Japanese-Americans, and they are chapters filled with compassion and candor.

Nonetheless, it is the younger generation of the 1970s and 1980s who have made this new multicultural perspective their own. They have discovered not only that minorities have not always shared in the rising power and affluence of the West but also that they have in some ways thought differently about the ends of that power and affluence. As part of the reevaluation, we are increasingly asked to reexamine the process by which native peoples were dispossessed in the first place, to remind ourselves of the manner in which whites went about accumulating land and resources for themselves, and to uncover the contradictions in a majority, male-dominated culture that can in the same breath trumpet the idea of its own liberty and deny other peoples the right of self-determination. Further, we have learned to pay more attention to the substantial numbers of nonnative people of

17

color, people from Africa, the Pacific islands, and Asia, who have come into the garden of agrarian myth to live alongside the European settlers, making the West in fact a far more racially diverse place than the myth envisioned—more diverse indeed than either the North or South has been.

So we have arrived at an important truth that was long obscured by the old mythology: The West has not at all been a place to retreat from the human community and all its conflicts. On the contrary, it has been a place where white Americans ran smack into the broader world. It has been on the forward edge of one of modern history's most exciting endeavors: the creation, in the wake of European expansion and imperialism, of the world's first multiracial, cosmopolitan societies. That development has obviously been a terribly difficult one, plagued by racism, ethnocentrism, brutality, misunderstanding, and rage on the part of majority and minority peoples alike, but especially marred by oppression and exploitation on the part of those holding the whip hand. All the same the invention in the West of a diverse community has gone steadily forward, until today there exists in this region the potential for an enlargement of our several cultural visions that was inconceivable in the past.

A second theme in the New Western History is this: The drive for the economic development of the West was often a ruthless assault on nature and has left behind it much death, depletion, and ruin. Astonishing as it now seems, the old agrarian myth of Turner's day suggested that the West offered an opportunity of getting back in touch with nature, of recovering good health and a sense of harmony with the nonhuman far from the shrieking disharmonies of factories, technology, urban slums, and poverty that were making life in Europe and the East a burden to the spirit. That traditional faith in the region's natural healing power endures even now in the popular mind, which tends to think of the "real West" as a place without industry or cities, as an idyll starring Robert Redford in the role of lonely trapper wandering through an awesomely beautiful wilderness. Most of California, by that selective reasoning, is not in the West, nor are the open-pit copper mines of Arizona, or the labor union halls in Idaho, or the commuters wheezing and creeping along in a Denver freeway haze. Indeed, about the only real West we have left, according to the old mythic thinking, is the state of Montana, and Louis L'Amour's ranch in southwestern Colorado—last, fading sanctuaries where vigorous, independent men might live in the bosom of nature.

Here again truth is breaking in, driving out myth and self-deception, as we face unblinkingly the fact that from its earliest days the fate of the western region has been one of furnishing raw materials for industrialism's development; consequently, the region was from the beginning in the forefront of America's endless economic revolution. Far from being a child of nature, the West was actually given birth by modern technology and bears all the scars of that fierce gestation, like a baby born of an addict.

Agriculture was one of the first areas where this dependency on the global industrial economy appeared. Contrary to the agrarian myth, farmers in the West were some of the first agribusinessmen on the planet, and in places like the Central Valley of California (a part of the West long ignored by historians) the results of that fact in terms of labor oppression and class conflict, as well as environmental exploitation, have been open for all to see. Supporting the drive for industrial and capitalist development has been a powerful political apparatus in Washington, D.C., whose role has largely been to promote the pri-

vate accumulation of money through such public investments as water projects, mining leases, and military bases. That role is manifest all over the nation, in fact
throughout the global economy, but it may be the American West that best exemplifies the modern capitalistic
state at work.

Historians have more or less known this for a long
time, but until very recently they have chosen to downplay, or even disregard, its implications. They seldom un-
dertook to write about any of the ecological disasters and
nightmares that have occurred in the West—the pillaging
of public lands by oil companies and other energy and
mining entrepreneurs, the pollution of coastal waters and
pristine desert air, the impact of big-scale irrigation on
the quality and quantity of water, or the devastation of
wildlife habitat by the hooves and bellies of the fabled
cattle kingdom.

To be sure, older historians did not completely ignore
the devastation of the western environment that had
gone on. Often they took a stand in favor of "conservation"—meaning the careful, rational, utilitarian conver-
sion of natural resources into wealth. In that definition,
however, the historians marginalized more radical envi-
ronmentalists like John Muir, who had fought against
such materialistic resource management; if he appeared
at all in history texts, Muir was usually portrayed as an
impractical mystic or an "ecofreak." Yet it is Muir who
has turned out to be the most influential environmental
reformer of his day, and it is his radical embrace of the
nonhuman community that has gone out from the West to
win a global audience.

Over the past decade or two the neglect of industrial
capitalism's impact on the western environment has begun to be repaired, due to the fact that the study of the
West, more than of other regions, has come to be allied

with the emerging field of environmental history. This alliance has encouraged doubts about the role of capitalism, industrialism, population growth, military expenditures, and aimless economic expansion in the region and has questioned whether they really have blazed a trail to progress.

A third theme in the new history is that the West has been ruled by concentrated power, though here, as in other places, power has often hidden itself behind beguiling masks. The old "frontier school" liked to believe that the West did not have much of an internal problem with power and hierarchy. Power lay in the hands of easterners, while the West was a simple democratic place, unfortunately at the mercy of those outsiders but fortunately far removed from them physically. The postwar historians continued that fantasy by somehow writing about technology, growth, and urbanization without talking much about the knot of power gathering in the West. Now we can be more frank. The West has in fact been a scene of intense struggles over power and hierarchy, not only between the races but also between classes, genders, and other groups within white society. The outcome of those struggles has a few distinctive features found nowhere else in America—power elites that don't quite look like those in other areas, particularly those elites located at intersections between the federal land management agencies and their client groups—for example, the Bureau of Land Management and the various livestock associations, or the Bureau of Reclamation and western irrigation districts.

Though distinctive, the western elites have followed the old familiar tendency of those in power, to become corrupt, exploitative, and cynical toward those they dominate. Power can also degrade itself, as it degrades others and the land, yet it commonly tries to conceal that fact by laying claim to the dominant myths and symbols of its time—in the case of the American West, by putting on cowboy boots and snapbutton shirts, waving the American flag, and calling a toxic dump the land of freedom.

Perhaps the single most important, most distinguishing characteristic of the New Western History is its determination not to offer cover for the powers that be—not to become subservient, by silence or consent, to them. A rising generation of historians insists that its responsibility is to stand apart from power and think critically about it, as it is to think critically about western society as whole, about its ideals and drives, about the contradictions it has created, about its prospects for new identities, goals, and values.

This may be the hardest pill of all for more traditional historians to swallow. They may go so far as to agree that it is now time to talk seriously about admitting nonwhites to the conversation; perhaps it is even okay to use such hard but honest phrases as capitalism, conquest, imperialism, and environmental destruction to talk about the West. But for pete's sake, they add, don't talk critically (which is to say, hostilely) about those in power, for, after all, they are the great, necessary agents of progress and development. They make possible our universities, our salaries, our libraries, our history, and our museums. Don't knock them, and don't get the reputation of being a knocker. And if you must talk critically about power, or generally take a critical look at your society's past, don't show much passion or bite. Don't reveal that there may be important ideals that have been violated, or argue that there are new ones that we must discover; if you do you will be considered romantic, naive, biased, polemical, or ungrateful. You may even become "an ideologue" (a dreaded label that often is applied to any historian who doesn't take the dominant or official ideology for granted). In other words, keep western history, and the West itself, safe from controversy or radical challenge. Be sure to write in a style that is intellectually timid, long on footnotes and bibliography but short on original ideas, especially short on uncommon or unconventional ideas. If you have any such ideas, keep them to yourself or camouflage them with a dull gray prose so that no one will take them seriously.

History, insist many traditional western historians, is supposed to be an "objective science," intent only on collecting the pure, distilled, empirical truth. Nothing could be more misleading than that notion. The history of this region, if it wants to be vital and listened to, cannot be kept isolated from public controversy, struggles over power, the search for new moral standards, or the ongoing human debate over fundamental principles and values. Rather than claiming to be some detached laboratory technician, the historian ought to be unabashedly and self-confidently an intellectual whose express purpose and primary justification for being are that he or she lives to question all received opinions, to take alternative ideas seriously, to think as rationally as possible about them, and to work constantly to demythologize the past. When historians fail to see themselves as critical intellectuals, as I believe historians of the West have done, they become ideological in the most dangerous sense: They become prisoners of ideology rather than masters of it.

The New Western History insists that scholars must perform deliberately and thoughtfully the role of cultural analyst, even to the point of presuming now and then to be a self-appointed moral conscience of their society. While accepting membership in that society, being sympathetic to its needs and interested in its fate, historians must also be free to act like outsiders, as all intellectuals

23

do, free to transcend the common pieties of their region and explore freely the larger world of ideas.

In order to perform this complex role effectively and be true to their role as intellectuals, western historians must study and learn from other peoples, trying, for example, to look at the past through the eyes of an American Indian. Even more radically, they must try to examine human behavior from a nonhuman perspective—to look, as it were, through the eyes of the rest of nature.

That is often an unpopular stance to take, for the public does not find it easy to tolerate what may seem to be a betrayal of its interests. White intellectuals seem especially disloyal when they take the side of nonwhite minorities, minorities who can be as outraged as the majority by any criticism. Most minority history is still where Frederick Jackson Turner's history was in 1893: It is a celebration of "my people," a record of what "we" have accomplished, a lament for how "we" have been neglected or oppressed or underappreciated. Eventually, one supposes, that will change, as it has in the case of the dominant white majority, and Hispanic and Indian and Asian-American communities will find themselves confronting their own intellectual dissidents. Meanwhile, the white majority of the American West has reached the point where it ought to be secure enough in its power and wealth that it can expect something from historians besides the subservient role of cheerleader or defender. I believe we have arrived at that point—which is why a new generation of western historians has arrived on the scene, gaining national and international attention for the region, a generation indebted to the work of its predecessors but ready to perform a very different role in society.

Here then, as I see it, is the program of the New Western Historians:

To find ourselves prefigured in our ancestors and find

in them the origin of the problems and questions that plague us today;

To achieve a more complete, honest, penetrating view of those ancestors as well as of ourselves, including the flaws and ironies in their achievements, to question their and our collective successes, to explore other points of view, and to discover new values;

To free ourselves from unthinking acceptance of official and unofficial myths and explanations;

To discover a new regional identity and set of loyalties more inclusive and open to diversity than we have known and more compatible with a planetwide sense of ecological responsibility.

The New Western History is now setting the agenda of the field. Surely it has its own shortcomings, and they will become more apparent in the years to come. But if it delivers what it promises, the new history will help the American West to become a more thoughtful and self-aware community than it has been, a community that no longer insists on its special innocence but accepts the fact that it is inextricably part of a flawed world.

2

TRASHING THE TRAILS

RICHARD WHITE

FIRST OF ALL, I should make a disclaimer. The title—"Trashing the Trails"—is not mine. It is Patty Limerick's. I have, it is true, kept the title. I did so partially because Patty has been so publicly scornful of my own previous efforts at titles that I couldn't risk further humiliation. But I also kept it because garbage does give an entrée into my real topic: environmental history and the New Western History.

The following catalog of trash along the Oregon Trail is courtesy of one attentive, and presumably bored, army officer. He saw bar iron, large grindstones, and baking ovens dumped on the trail. He rode past cooking stoves, kegs, and barrels scattered among harnesses, clothing, bacon, and beans. Another traveler reported seeing a diving bell lying beside the trail. In a single 40-mile stretch of the Nevada desert in 1850, one migrant counted two thousand abandoned wagons. According to the standard account, the Oregon Trail had become by the 1850s a "wide and busy highway" so polluted with dust that "overlanders donned goggles to see." The debris, the dust, the manure, all of these things marked trails as an environment clearly shaped by human use.

In a sense, much of the difference between the New

and Old Western Historians is revealed by what they make of the garbage so lavishly strewn along the trails. Old Western Historians looked past the garbage and saw "nature." For them, untouched nature was preeminent. They wanted to see wilderness because from it they derived the culture of the West. Many New Western Historians—particularly environmental historians—see the garbage first. They see the cultural, and from it they try to explain the "natural." The New Western Historians—particularly environmental historians—have an affinity for trash as the evidence of human actions, the relics of culture. Where Old Western Historians see nature, New Western Historians see the debris and the consequences of human use.

When I use the term "environmental history," I mean specifically the history of the consequences of human actions on the environment and the reciprocal consequences of an altered nature for human society. Environmental history in this sense is not an invention of New Western Historians. In the best of the Old Western History—in Frederick Jackson Turner and Walter Prescott Webb—the environment was central to explanations of the history of the West. What distinguishes the New Western Historians from the Old Western Historians is not environmental history per se, but *the different way* the two groups of historians have formulated the role of the environment in creating a western region.

We can begin sorting out the differing uses New Western Historians and Old Western Historians make of the environment by asking two simple questions. First, how in dealing with the West do Old and New Western Historians divide the physical space of the place itself—the West of mountains, rivers, deserts, and plains? Second, what kind of stories do Old and New Western Historians tell about the movement of people through this space?

When do these stories begin, when do they end, who populates their narratives, what is their narrative line?

In the old history, Webb and Turner sharply bifurcated the physical West. They apportioned the West at any given moment before the magic date of 1890 between nature and culture; they called the dividing line the frontier. On one side of the frontier, nature reigned. Humans on that side of the line were, in Webb's words, "nature's children." Indians—and Hispanics—were children for Webb and Turner in an almost literal sense: They were people incapable of controlling their surroundings. Old Western Historians culturally coded this far side of the frontier as feminine: There Mother Nature took care of her children. On the other side of the frontier, there existed a much more complicated relationship. Humans had mastered nature, but nature, as it were, wrote the terms of surrender. Nature for these historians existed in much the same way women supposedly existed within a Victorian family: Limited to its proper sphere and fruitful within that sphere, nature yielded a proper economy and society. David Noble has insightfully commented that for Turner especially, nature was always feminine, always fruitful. Given this division and gender coding of the physical place, it was, of course, necessary that the land on the far side of the frontier be "virgin," awaiting its white American groom, and so it always was. Now with this kind of allocation of the physical space—and the rather obvious ways historians organized it in gender terms—those long trails entering the West have metaphorical connotations too obvious for comment. The people on those trails have to be virile, strong, and brave. They carry the seeds of a new society into the West. Given the initial division of physical space and its "genderfication," a whole series of cultural associations almost automatically group themselves around them. A story begins to appear that is culturally logical but not necessarily historically convincing.

Now compared with the Old Western Historians, who rode high in the saddle, New Western Historians tend to be kind of nebbishy. They're easy to ignore. Their division of the physical West lacks the bold lines of the Old Western Historians. When they look at the West at any particular time—say, the mid-nineteenth century—they see mountains, rivers, prairies, villages, and fields. They see various peoples—Indians, Hispanics, blacks, Chinese, various groups of European descent. These people are distinct, but they also shade into each other in important ways; each treats the land somewhat differently, but all of them, to varying extents, are modifying their environment. There is no sharp line between culture and nature. Wilderness—that is, land unaffected by human use—is rarely to be found. There is no obvious frontier except in the sense that in some places you run out of white people, which is of no particular concern to environmental historians.

Now remember, this is the same physical space that historians, old or new, are arranging and categorizing. In arranging this space, the New Western History stands in relation to the Old Western History as the Oregon Trail stood in relation to the Mormon Trail. The two trails paralleled each other, one virtually in sight of the other, along opposite sides of the Platte River. They were similar routes, traversing much the same terrain, but they yielded different experiences and wound up in very different places. Purely for purposes of illustration, let us say that the Old Western History heads to Utah—a beautiful, dramatic, but odd place where people hold certain social views that are now regarded as somewhat archaic. New Western Historians have decided, so to speak, to skip Utah. And to accomplish this, all they have to do is step across the Platte and pick up the New Western History trail.

In picking up this new trail, New Western Historians are still moving across the same land as Turner and Webb and the Old Western History wagon train, but they are seeing a different landscape. How you see, of course, in large part determines what you see, so it is no wonder that the landscape New Western Historians recreate is different. Things happen along the New Western History trail that don't seem to occur on the Old Western History trail. Present are aspects of western history usually missing from the frontier's nature/culture-wilderness/civilization dichotomy. Indians, for example, set prairie fires to get earlier growth of grasses in the spring. In 1850 Captain Howard Stansbury reported a 300-mile stretch of the Platte Valley burned in autumn fires. Lorenzo Sawyer, who traveled through the Platte Valley in mid-May 1850, saw the results of the previous year's burning: "Those portions of the valley which have been burnt over are covered with fresh, though short grass, giving them the appearance of smooth shaven lawns, while the portions still covered with old grass resemble thick fields of ripe grain waving in the breeze and just ready for the harvest."[1] The landscape Sawyer described was created by humans. Trees either died in the fires or were cut down by the Indians to get food for their horses. The horses themselves were representatives of one ecosystem that had made themselves at home in another. To make horses more comfortable, the Indians were busy modifying their environment, changing patterns of warfare and subsistence, and doing all kinds of interesting things supposedly reserved for whites.

But horses were only the biggest invaders to precede whites along the trails. Smallpox emptied Indian villages, and cholera wiped out whole wagon trains. This too is environmental change, change of the most significant kind. New Western Historians have just begun to rewrite the history of the region from the realization of massive Indian depopulation from exotic diseases. And they are still puzzling over why these diseases had differential impacts. Why, for example, did most groups decline from 50 percent to 90 percent while the Navajo population increased?

All of these things are visible on the New Western History trail rather than the Old Western History trail because New Western Historians have abandoned frontier blinders that restricted their view. The old frontier division into lands of nature and lands of culture made it very hard to see humans on the wrong side of the divide as anything but products of their own inability to cope with nature. But the classical notion of a frontier makes no sense if on both sides of the line people are modifying the environment. We can still talk profitably about different types of modification, different extents, different results, but we can't talk about nature versus culture. Similarly, diseases don't fit a frontier framework very well. If smallpox and cholera came but once, we might talk about disease frontiers, but they recur often. The West becomes a disease pool linked with other disease pools long before the frontier ever arrived. Anglo-Americans were thus not the initiators of linked environmental and social change in the West, although they certainly accelerated its pace.

Having set two such different stages, it is no wonder that very different narrative lines develop. The Old Western Historians usually write comedy, in the sense that they provide a happy resolution (even though many of them came to distrust it). This resolution doesn't come easily. Nature must be subdued and tamed, and "she" can only be subdued according to the terms "she" sets. Webb excelled at telling this story of culture's initial failure to conquer nature, but how, after changing to meet nature's terms, culture triumphs. Webb's western nature begins at the ninety-eighth meridian, which acts as an "institutional fault" line. "Practically every institution that was carried across it was either broken, remade, or else greatly altered." Old Western History, in Webb's writing, envisions a simultaneous institutional breakdown somewhere in the middle of Nebraska or Oklahoma. The wheels spin off the institutional wagons, the tongues break, the oxen die. Suddenly, in the metaphorical terms of the Old Western History, culture is impotent.

But nature provides therapy to those resourceful enough to learn (for Webb, this leaves out Indians, the Spanish, and the Mexicans). The pioneers regain their strength and ability. Webb introduces failure into western history, but it is only temporary failure. Now in its essence, this story of the western land and landscape, although told with far more sophistication and insight, is a narrative found in virtually all county histories or "mugbooks." In these books prominent citizens, from the vantage point of their late middle or old age, tell how they struggled to transform the West and how the very process of struggle taught them deeper lessons. They became better people than those easterners denied the frontier challenge. They changed the West, but the West left its imprint on them. This, then, is the narrative of the Old Western History: It is the story of a journey, a challenge, and a dual transformation of land and people.

What story can the New Western History tell to match this? One reason the New Western History has failed to displace the Old Western History in the popular imagination is that it lacks an equally gripping and ultimately satisfying narrative. Don Worster, who is the best environmental historian of the West, writes tragedies.

Things don't end well in the *Dust Bowl* or *Rivers of Empire*;[2] we confront our own fatal flaws. William deBuys's *Enchantment and Exploitation* is also essentially a tragedy.[3] The satisfaction we gain is the knowledge of our limits. New Western Historians may lean toward tragedy, but for most the logic of their own view of human-created environments diverts them. Unlike Worster, most end up with the far less satisfying mode of irony. Environmental historians are uncomfortable with easy references to the symbols that govern our perceptions of historical environments: wilderness, the agrarian garden. Trying to explain the logic of environmental change, they lose absolute reference points. They give comfort neither to those seeking the solace of the old story of progress nor to those who seek a return to some primal, beneficent nature, who seek to restore a "wilderness." New Western Historians find people attempting one thing and very often achieving another. Consequently, their interpretations, and their narratives, become ironic, for irony is that figure of speech in which the meaning of a statement is the opposite of that seemingly intended.

Let me give you an example of what I mean by ironic history by analyzing briefly two quotations by people directly involved in environmental change. One is a quotation I used in my doctoral dissertation and have tended to trot out with great regularity ever since. In the 1850s a farmer named Walter Crockett, upon settling in Washington Territory, had written home that his main object was "to get the land subdued and the wilde nature out of it. When that is accomplished we can increase our crops to a very large amount and the high prices of every thing that is raised heare will make the cultivation of the soil a very profitable business."[4] Where does the historian find irony? Well, the historian realizes, and poor Crockett doesn't, that the prairie Crockett is farming is an Indian

33

creation, shaped by Indian burning and use. It is not "wilde nature." The historian knows that Crockett is mistaking a complicated environmental process for a single-step process—nature to culture. In seeking to banish wild nature, poor Crockett is letting all kinds of things into his fields that he would rather keep out. For example, Canadian thistle came mixed with crop seed. Attempts to eradicate it were in vain, partially because one settler, taken with the thistle's flower, cultivated it. Tame pigs became feral, turning into ecological Frankensteins that did immense damage to the fields. Sometimes it seemed that the only thing that didn't get into Crockett's fields was profit.

But let me give you a second quotation; this one I owe to one of my graduate students, Mark Fiege. In 1907 R. H. Loomis was the first settler to prove up land under the Carey Act, and the *Idaho Republican* celebrated his success by proclaiming that Loomis had "left a nice home in Illinois to make a new home on this manless, homeless, weedless, bugless tract where he can put everything on the land just to his liking." The newspaper's dismissal of previous occupation of the land and attribution of an original condition of manlessness, homelessness, weedlessness, and buglessness to the place itself almost ensure that the environmental historian will interpret the quotation ironically. Environmental historians see the catalog of vacancies listed by the *Idaho Republican* not as the original condition of arid land but rather as the end product of industrial agriculture's attempt to put everything on the land to its liking.

But where does such irony leave us? Irony does a lot of things, but it doesn't stir people's souls. It can undermine the Old Western History's narrative, but it doesn't really provide one that matches its sweep, its drama, and its sense of triumph. At least it hasn't so far. Failing to find a story of the West as compelling as that of Turner and Webb, New Western Historians have, ironically, resolved the problem of regionalism that perplexed Turner and Webb. Turner and Webb were united not only by their devotion to the frontier but by their conviction that regionalism mattered greatly in American history. Trying to reconcile the frontier with regionalism created logical problems, but for both Turner and Webb the critical issue was not regionalism's past, but its future. They feared that a gray industrial homogeneity would eventually envelop the United States, obliterating all they valued about the country.

Both Turner and Webb tried in their scholarship to rescue the West—differently defined—as a distinct region. Although it seemed that the frontier and free land would create a homogeneous country, at least west of the Appalachians, Turner argued that other factors—slavery, "racial stocks," climate—would create regional variations on national traits. Webb refined this logic even more precisely. He isolated one distinctive factor—aridity—and used it to explain the uniqueness of the West. In one sense, Webb and Turner were emphasizing the diversity of the nation, but, more significant for the West, they emphasized western distinctiveness by imposing a homogeneity on the section itself. For Turner, the only legitimate diversity in the United States was regional diversity. For a legitimate regionalism, there had to be western types, western values, and western attitudes.

The Old Western Historians thus formulated what I'll call an essentialist West, a West that produced (again gender coding) men to match its mountains—that is, men able to overcome and dominate a feminine nature. From their domination they derived their distinctiveness. Now the problem with the essentialist West is that it postulated, at least partially, an environmental and social

35

homogeneity for what has historically been—and continues to be—one of the most diverse sections of the United States. Both Turner and Webb mistook homogeneity for distinctiveness. If there was going to be a western region, there had to be for them a regional type—there had to be a checklist of traits by which you could identify your real westerners, separate your buckaroos from your dimestore cowboys. But there has never been a regional type. Just as the Old Western Historians ignored the evidence of human presence that trail garbage represented, so they eliminated from their history as so much human garbage most of the diverse peoples of the West—Indians, Hispanics, Asians, and often ethnic Europeans—whose very presence endangered their regional homogeneity.

New Western Historians, by and large, do not seek essentialism. They do not search for the master traits and master factors of western history. They still assert that the West is a distinct region, but they define that distinctiveness in a fundamentally different way. They have what I'll call a relational outlook on the West. Now they certainly recognize distinctive attributes of the physical West—aridity, the only high mountains in the continental United States, vast tracts of largely unoccupied land, a general lack of navigable rivers. But unlike Turner and Webb, they do not see these environmental factors as translating automatically into a distinctive, essentialist western culture. How could they? Each successive group of immigrants has not confronted pure nature; they have confronted worlds created by people who came before them and in many cases continued to live alongside them. What made the West distinctive was not some direct communication of its life force, but rather a series of relationships established within that place which inevitably changed over time.

For many New Western Historians, the continuing essentialist interpretations that, in fact, govern much thinking about the West are important but silly. It is hard to escape such essentialism. Did you know that range managers consider 83 percent of the eleven contiguous western states to be range? Think about that. What if someone said parking lot attendants consider 83 percent of the eleven contiguous western states as parking lots? In a sense that's true. You probably can park a car on 83 percent of the West. But such statements confuse a potential use of the land with the intrinsic character of the land itself. Land is only range when you put livestock on it. Land is only parking lots when you put cars on it. Range is no more an environmental category than is a parking lot. It is a cultural category defined by how we intend to use the land. It is something we create. It is a relationship between us and the land.

There are numerous possible relationships between us and the land, and such meanings are contested. Despite multiple use, land cannot be simultaneously range, parking lots, and wilderness; discovering which perceptions and which uses of land prevail, and why, has become much of the subject matter of environmental history and the New Western History. Phrasing the study of the West this way turns the focus away from a homogeneous West and toward a West full of diverse interests and conflicts. In this West, not all groups enter the conflict with equal resources, nor do they have equal access to the levers of power that control land use. Environmentally, then, New Western Historians look initially at three things: first, the contesting groups; second, their perceptions of the land and their ambitions for it; third, the structures of power that shape the contest. All of these things are relational; all change over time.

The competing groups that historians concentrate on can be categorized in many ways. They can be economic or occupational groups: farmers, ranchers, miners. They can be ethnic or racial groups: Anglos, Indians, or Hispanos. In this area, changes in the landscape follow the ability of Anglos to wrench control of the land from Indians and Hispanos. The conflict can also be phrased locationally, as it often is today, with a division between the urban and the rural West. The competition can be between local capital and capitalists from outside. It can be class conflict.

One of the distinctive things about the West is the extent to which these contests have historically been structured through the bureaucratic agencies of the federal government. To a much greater extent than elsewhere in the country, the federal bureaucracy—the Bureau of Land Management, the Bureau of Reclamation, the National Forest Service, the military—becomes the locus for conflict. The way bureaucracy works—its own ties to other sources of institutional power, such as corporations, banks, and cities—often determines the outcome. The long history of the Bureau of Reclamation is a case in point.

For environmental historians, therefore, and for New Western Historians, the West is a legitimate and distinctive region not only because it is physically different but also because that difference is shaped by distinctive relationships between contesting groups, and conflicts are resolved through an institutional structure different in important ways from other parts of the country. There is no essentialism here; the relationships that set the West apart in the late twentieth century are not necessarily the same as those that set it apart in the mid-nineteenth century.

These relationships take us back to trails, because the whole relational logic of the New Western History forces attention to movement, to contact, to exchange.

38

The West—like all of us—is the product of relationships, either brief or prolonged. It is an historically derived, contingent place where one thing leads to another. Too narrow a focus on trails will, however, deceive us. For trails too readily bring to mind only the mid-nineteenth century trails—from the east, south, north, and west. They seemed to flow only in one direction: into the West. They were part of the great rush hour of western history, when new occupants, new diseases, and new plants and animals all flowed into the region.

But such trails were but a brief historical moment. We must concentrate on a more complex West in which the traffic out of the West—whether gold, silver, wheat, cattle, lumber, or people—mattered as much as the traffic into it. The trails in this West seem more a maze than a simple line from one point to another. They look more like modern Los Angeles than the Santa Fe Trail. And these trails lead to no happy and inevitable resolution, no essentialist West, but to a land and people constantly in the midst of reinvention and reshaping. The fate of this complicated relational West is contingent on what we do, on how we perceive each other and the land. And this West will always fail to conform completely to our intentions. It is this sense of historically derived relationships, and not preordained qualities of the land itself or the qualities of any single set of occupants, that is central to the regionalism of the New Western History.

3

WESTERN WOMEN AT
THE CULTURAL CROSSROADS

PEGGY PASCOE

PROBABLY NO ONE was more startled by the outburst of publicity about the New Western History than the scholars who assembled in Santa Fe, New Mexico, in September 1989, to offer their hopeful assessments for the field.[1] In the year since the Trails conference, the ideas presented there have been reported everywhere from the *New York Times Magazine* to the *New Republic* to the *Weekend Australian*. In a curious blend of scholarly debate and media hype, more ink than any of us could have reasonably predicted has been devoted to answering a single question: "What is the New Western History?"

As someone who specializes in the history of women, I have to admit that I find it very tempting to give the most obvious answer—that because the Old Western History paid little or no attention to women, everything written about women in the West must be part of the New Western History. At first glance, it makes a good deal of sense to emphasize the newness of women's western history. Practitioners of the Old Western History formed a more diverse group than the label "Old Western Historians" implies, but they were in accord on at least one thing: They saw no need to study women. Their neglect of the topic was so total that the first scholars who did study western women had to start out by convincing these doubting Thomases that there were women in the West to study at all. They were reduced to proving, sometimes by citing actual population figures, that there were enough women in the region—and enough primary sources about their lives—to justify spending time and energy to study them.

The first historians of western women, who were pioneers of a sort in their own right, launched an all-out search for primary sources; when they found dozens of diaries and travel accounts of women on the Overland Trail, they went to work on them with enthusiasm. Their goal was to determine whether or not the geographic move to the West had been a liberating experience for pioneer women. When the results were in, the already time-worn idea of the frontier as a place free from social constraints had taken yet another beating; most researchers concluded that the journey to the West isolated women from other women, heightened their vulnerability to men, and increased their domestic work load.[2] In this way, the subfield of women in the West cut its teeth by attacking two of the most cherished principles of the Old Western History: (1) the notion that it was white male pioneers who made up the "real" West and (2) the belief that the West was somehow freer, more democratic, more individualistic, and more egalitarian than the East.

The first historians of western women criticized not only the Old Western History but also the Old Western Popular Culture. If it was hard to find pioneer women in history books, it was a cinch to find them in the western novels, television shows, and movies that were popular well into the 1970s. But the pioneer women of popular culture were stock characters who fit predictable stereotypes. There were supposedly "good" women cast as helpmates on the trail, madonnas of the prairie, or civilizers of the Wild West (think of schoolteacher Molly in Owen

41

Wister's *The Virginian* [New York: Macmillan, 1902] or of any pioneer's wife in any television western). And there were the supposedly "bad" women who provided a hint of sexual intrigue before they were put firmly in their places (think of Kitty on television's "Gunsmoke"). Stereotypes like these provided the perfect foils for historians of women in the West, who delighted in cutting larger-than-life myths down to human size by contrasting each stereotype to the actual experiences of pioneer women.[3]

By pointing out the omissions of the Old Western History and by sweeping away the stereotypes of the Old Western Popular Culture, historians of western women made the topic of women in the West a legitimate subfield. They brought to life a new actor on the historical stage—the pioneer woman. In the 1980s the work of these historians spurred countless studies of frontier women—but it also elicited an increasing number of calls for a broader, more "multicultural" approach to the history of western women.

During the 1980s, the study of women in the West became something of a growth industry. Experts developed courses on the topic at universities across the United States and banded together to form a new professional organization, the Coalition of Women for Western History. Four conferences on the history of western women were held, and other are being planned. At least half a dozen review essays were published, and several anthologies of recent articles have appeared.[4] As a result, we now have enough—perhaps just enough—work on women in the West, so that I can avoid the temptation to claim that all of it is a part of the New Western History.

My own hopes for a New Western History range far beyond the debates about frontiersmen and frontierswomen—in fact beyond the concept of the frontier—that have so far preoccupied so many historians of women in the West. What I'd like to see is a Western history less concerned with defining the boundaries of its subfield and more concerned with connecting itself to the rest of American history. Western historians' obsession with defining our field seems to me to enclose us in ever narrower paths, almost as if we were circling our own pioneer wagons to fend off attacks from American historians all around us. But the sad reality of western history in recent decades is that American historians have been far less likely to challenge our conclusions than to ignore us altogether. So, on the principle that the best defense is a good offense, I think we should seize the initiative. By asking the questions that have been on the cutting edge of American historiography while centering our work firmly in the American West, we can, I think, open a dialogue between western historians and American historians that might be of value to both groups.

There is one part of the subfield of women in the West that I think has particular potential for contributing to that dialogue. So I'm going to skip over the most familiar studies of western women (women on the Overland Trail, frontier prostitution, and woman's suffrage in the West) and leave to others some of the topics just beginning to emerge (farm women's work patterns and the notions of gender embedded in depictions of western landscapes). What I would like to do instead is to build on the work of those historians—Betsy Jameson, Valerie Matsumoto, and Vicki Ruiz, among others—who have been calling for a history of women in the West that is multicultural, cross-cultural, and intercultural.

Taking their calls for multicultural history as my cue, I want to suggest that historians of women in the West replace the current emphasis on frontierswomen—mythic or real—with a new definition of our field and that we

43

learn to see our task as the study of western women at the cultural crossroads. The phrase "western women at the cultural crossroads" is deliberately broad. I hope it will prove malleable enough to sustain a variety of meanings and approaches, some of which highlight the distinctive aspects of the American West and some of which highlight the West's connections to American history in general. To show what I mean, I will explore some ways that developing the study of western women at the cultural crossroads might shape a New Western History.

Let me begin by drawing attention to the language of the phrase "western women at the cultural crossroads." Note that the word "frontier" is entirely absent. This is important, because shifting the frontier out of the limelight is the first step toward developing a New Western History.

As the outburst of publicity about the New Western History clearly indicates, moving the frontier out of center stage is no mean feat. A vocal and determined group of western historians remain wedded to the frontier as the central organizing principle of western history; indeed, many western historians have devoted their careers to fending off challenges to frontier scholarship by developing alternate meanings of the term "frontier." I hope no one writing today would defend Frederick Jackson Turner's definition of the frontier as the meeting point between savagery and civilization, but there certainly are historians who see the frontier as a geographical location, others who see it as a social process of creating new settlements, and still others who see it as a zone of interaction between different cultures.

Until quite recently, historians of women in the West have seen the frontier largely in geographic terms. Look, for example, at the titles of the best-known books on western women. Despite the calls for multicultural history, ti-

tles such as *Frontier Women, Frontierswomen,* or *Westering Women* abound.[5] In one sense, of course, these titles
are accurate descriptions of the subjects of their books;
that is, the books are primarily about mid-nineteenth-cen-
tury eastern women moving westward. In another sense,
the titles serve as clues that some of the same historians
who challenged the Old Western History for its exclusion
of women remained tied to the Old Western History notion of the frontier as the advance line of Anglo-American
settlement. In most studies of frontierswomen, the concept of the frontier is that of a road that stretches from
east to west, a one-way thruway for white settlers.

The main drawbacks of geographic conceptions of the
frontier are well known. Two of them are particularly
damaging: the identification of the frontier with movement westward and the assumption that once white settlers had arrived in the West (or perhaps as late as a generation after that), the frontier period was over. These
drawbacks make the frontier a particularly weak framework on which to build a multicultural women's history
of the West. They are so difficult to avoid that they seem
to undercut even the best intentions of scholars. Take, for
example, Sandra Myres's book on pioneer women, *Westering Women and the Frontier Experience, 1800–1915*
(1982).[6] In the book itself, Myres makes a far greater effort than most frontier scholars to include Hispanic as
well as Anglo-American women pioneers, but in the title
she lumps both groups together as "westering women," a
characterization that would no doubt have surprised the
Hispanic women pioneers who had moved north from
Mexico rather than west along the Oregon Trail.

What is needed, I think, is a vast re-imagination of
the West we study. In a multicultural western history,
neither the male frontiersman who took up supposedly
"free" western land nor that same frontiersman with a pi-

oneer woman at his side would occupy primary pride of place. We need to take as our starting point what ethnic studies scholars have pointed out again and again—that western land was neither empty nor free and that the white Americans who moved westward were never its only inhabitants.

To the extent that the frontier might remain a useful concept for western history, it would be as a frontier of interactions among the various cultural groups who lived in or passed through the area. In other words, we need to learn to see the frontier as a cultural crossroads rather than a geographic freeway to the West, and we need to focus on the interactions among the various groups of people who sought to control the region.[7]

If we thought of the frontier as cross-cultural, then expanding the focus beyond white pioneer settlers would be a logical necessity rather than a matter of good intentions. In order to tell the stories of all the participants in western history, scholars and students would have to learn about cultural groups other than Anglo-Americans. Just as important, a cross-cultural frontier would end only when cross-cultural contact did. It would not be solely a nineteenth-century phenomenon; in fact, it would last right up to the present and into the future. The range of topics and time periods for western history would expand enormously. A study of Hispanic women workers' struggles with Anglo factory owners in the 1960s would, for example, become a central contribution to western history. Even if its writer never invoked the ghost of Frederick Jackson Turner or mentioned the frontier, such a study would fit within the broad topic of western women at the cultural crossroads.

As this example suggests, learning to see the frontier as a cultural crossroads would mean abandoning the current preoccupation with "pioneer women," a term usually but not always used to refer to white women in the mid-nineteenth century, and developing instead a category that might be called "western women." This is, I think, the second step historians of women in the West should take in shaping a New Western History. If we adopt the goal of writing the history of western women at the cultural crossroads, we need to use the term "western women" to mean all women in the geographic region we now call the American West, from the period of Indian settlement to the present. Only by using the term in this way can we come to grips with one of the most distinctive aspects of the American West: its unique mixture of ethnic and racial groups.[8]

To many historians of women in the West, this argument will already seem "old hat," since leaders of the fields have been calling for more scholarship on women of color ever since the publication of Joan Jensen and Darlis Miller's influential review essay in 1980.[9] There has been some improvement on this score, most notably in the case of Hispanic women, where a number of new books have appeared and additional studies are in the works.[10] There is also a great deal of work in progress on Asian-American women, though most of the published literature remains in the form of articles rather than books.[11] The same is true of work on Native American women, which tends to be done by anthropologists rather than historians.[12] Prospects are probably most discouraging in the case of African American women in the West, where work has lagged far behind.[13]

In recognition of the promise of this new material, it is commonplace for historians of western women to divide review essays and course outlines into separate sections on white women, Indian women, Hispanic women, Asian-American women, Mormon women, and so on, in order to move, in Betsy Jameson's phrase, "toward a multicultural history of women in the Western United States."[14] But even the most determined of scholars must struggle against the discouraging fact that the preponderance of the literature on women in the West still focuses on white pioneer women.

This continued imbalance reveals the gap between good intentions and measurable results: At the moment, women's western history still suffers from what I think of as the dynamic of disappearing women of color. Once again, the evidence nearest at hand is in our titles. Take, for example, *Women and Indians on the Frontier* (1984).[15] Written by Glenda Riley, a well-known frontier historian, this book is a laudable attempt to explore cross-cultural themes in western history. It falls short, however, in displaying a title that highlights "women" and "Indians" but renders "Indian women"—perhaps the most interesting of all the actors in this particular cross-cultural drama—invisible.

As long as the dynamic of disappearing women of color continues to operate, the development of western women's history will suffer. Western history will, in fact, suffer far more than scholarship on women of color, for while western historians hesitate, ethnic studies experts rush to fill the gaps. Yet, ethnic studies scholars are authorities in social theory. They are far more likely to be trained as sociologists, anthropologists, or literary critics than as historians, so they have little reason to feel concern about the development of the subfield of women's western history, much less to care about building a dialogue between western and American historians. For this reason, addressing the problem of disappearing women of color should be the first priority for western women's historians. It is, I think, at least as important for our development today as the study of pioneer women was to the emergence of our subfield a decade ago.

If we placed the study of women of color at the center of the history of women in the West, we could find yet another meaning in the phrase "western women at the cultural crossroads." With only a little mental exertion we could conceive of the crossroads not only as a literal crossing of people's paths but also as an analytic crossing of three central axes of inequality—race, class, and gender—in American history.

To do this would be to take a giant step toward the cutting edge of American history, because over the past three decades, American historians have shifted their focus away from the powerful politicians, generals, and corporate leaders who were once considered its central actors and toward comparatively powerless groups such as women, racial/ethnic cultures, and working classes. Spotlighting the powerless instead of the powerful made it abundantly clear that hierarchies of race, class, and sex underlined the distribution of power in American history.

Following the lead of social scientists, American historians counted these factors, added them up, and ranked them on a scale of relative oppression. In early analyses of this type, white women were said to be disadvantaged on account of their sex (one oppression); white women factory workers were disadvantaged on account of their sex and their class (two oppressions); and black women domestic workers were disadvantaged on account of their sex, their class, and their race (three oppressions). Soon there were historians who specialized in studying each particular factor. Historians of women specialized in understanding sex; labor historians specialized in understanding class; and historians of slavery specialized in understanding race.

Along the way, the initial focus on the "factors" of race, class, and sex gave way to a much more sophisticated analysis of the social construction of race, class, and gender. Today, every major book in American social history has to pass muster as dealing with all three. In other words, race, class, and gender have become, as a somewhat disgruntled white male historian recently told me, the "holy triumvirate" of American social history.

I don't share his discomfort at this development, but I do think that his comment indicates the extent to which the study of race, class, gender, and the interconnections among them have become the central project of American social history. At the moment at least, attempts to explore the crossroads of race, class, and gender form the cutting edge of American historical writing. Taking on this project leads historians slowly but surely toward the study of women of color, because it is in the lives of racial minority women that the power dynamics of race, class, and gender are most clearly exposed.

At the moment, the hottest topic along these lines is the history of black slave women in the American South. So many historians are writing about slave women that they've started taking potshots at each other in book reviews, a sure sign that the topic is coming of age. There are several reasons for this fascination with the history of slave women. Historians of race are drawn to the subject because they tend to assume that studying race in America means studying the African-American experience, as if blacks were the only group branded as a "racial minority." Neo-Marxist historians use the topic of slave women to argue their point that slavery was as much a labor system as a system of racial discrimination. Historians of women are intrigued by the sharp contrast between the conditions of life for black slave women and the social code of white womanhood in nineteenth-century America. All have benefited from the rich tradition of regional history in the South.

But if there are several reasons why studies of the crossroads of race, class, and gender have so far been conducted primarily in southern history, there is no reason at all why they should not become a central project in western history. Indeed, the West provides new vantage points from which to consider the problem. The history of Indian women, Hispanic women, and Asian-American women is only beginning to be written. Yet the potential of the development has been demonstrated in three recent works. The first, Vicki Ruiz's *Cannery Women, Cannery Lives* (1987), explores a particularly successful attempt at labor organizing by Chicana cannery workers in mid-twentieth-century California.[16] Two others, by Sally Deutsch and Deena Gonzalez, examine the effects of the American conquest on Spanish-Mexican women in Colorado and New Mexico.[17]

All three authors explore the analytic crossroads of race, class, and gender that is now a central concern of American historians. Rejecting the assumption that because Hispanic women were "triply oppressed," they must have been pawns in the hands of the more powerful, all three writers emphasize women's innovative use of the cultural and personal resources they could command. In these studies, the dynamic of disappearing women of color vanishes, and in its place arise vivid stories of Hispanic women's efforts to control their destiny even while beset by the forces of economic power and social conquest.

In works like these we can see how the history of women of color reveals the crossroads of race, class, and gender. But this is not the only crossroads we have yet to examine. As we add new information about women of color to the backlog of information about white pioneer women—and, perhaps I should emphasize, *only* when we do this—we put ourselves in a position to study the relationships among diverse groups of women. This is yet another way historians of women in the West might shape a New Western History—by studying intercultural crossroads.

This too is a challenge currently facing the entire discipline of American history. In the mid-twentieth century, the average American historian could be content with understanding what was then called "American culture"; indeed, one such historian, Henry Nash Smith, turned his examination of the connections between American culture and the frontier into one of the best-known works in western history, *Virgin Land: The American West as Symbol and Myth* (1950).[18] But in the intervening years, historians have come to hold a new understanding of the term "culture." Nowadays, we're less likely to speak of "American culture" in the singular than we are of the "cultures" of various groups within the society of the United States. Today's American historian has to be familiar with a long list of these cultures, among them women's culture, working-class culture, and all the cultures of the various ethnic and racial groups, including African Americans, Asian Americans, Hispanics, and so on. It is in recognition of this multiplicity of cultures within American society that historians call for "multicultural" history.

Trying to write multicultural history is a challenging task. In the first place, it involves doing research on several groups instead of just one. In the second place, it involves finding a way to fit all the groups into a readable story. The most obvious way to do this is to try to grant every group equal time. For example, I might try to teach students about women in nineteenth-century San Francisco by assigning one article about middle-class white women, one article about Chinese immigrant women, one article about Jewish working women, then try to get the students to recognize the different experiences of each group. This is what we mean by emphasizing cultural diversity in history.

But this kind of multicultural comparison carries its own risks. As ethnic studies experts point out, it is all too easy for the process of emphasizing the differences between cultures to disintegrate into blaming some cultures for their relative powerlessness. To take an example from my own work, consider the history of Chinese immigrant prostitutes, who, for a short time in the nineteenth century, were a majority of the Chinese immigrant women in California. Chinese immigrant prostitutes were extremely vulnerable women who were held as indentured servants in a condition sometimes comparable to slavery. In trying to account for their position, should we look to the subordination of women in China as the root cause? If we do, we would miss the fact that Chinese prostitutes in China were far less vulnerable than Chinese prostitutes in the United States, and the reasons have as much to do with the racial attitudes of American citizens and the passage of American immigration restrictions as they do with Chinese ideas about women's place. In other words, we have to build our histories on intercultural relations as well as on multicultural diversity.

If, as Patty Limerick has convincingly argued, the central theme of the history of the American West is conquest, we need to come to terms with the ways that conquest shaped intercultural relations in the region.[19] Until recently, most discussions of conquest focused on incidents that were dramatic, violent, and led by men, events such as wars against the Indians. Women's experiences of these events were ignored or omitted. But as women's western history evolves, scholars are beginning to tell a different story of intercultural contact, one in which

53

women in general—and women of color in particular—are at the center.

Studies of women in intercultural relations have taken two general approaches. The first approach is to pose a question about attitudes, to ask: "Were frontierswomen more racist—or less racist—than frontiersmen?" To find out, scholars have read the diaries of pioneer women and charted their day-to-day interactions with the Indians they encountered on the Overland Trail or as neighbors in frontier settlements. Most writers have concluded that pioneer women were not as racist as pioneer men; they argue that daily experience with Indians led pioneer women to see Indians more kindly than the more militant pioneer men who rushed to battle along the frontier.[20]

This kind of analysis will, I think, ultimately be more important for raising the question of how a particular set of gender prescriptions shaped racial attitudes than for offering the answer that women were less racist than men. In fact, recent research on men who were army officers suggests that they also had peaceful day-to-day encounters with Indians, encounters that clearly did not prevent them from participating in or benefiting from white conquest.[21] Before concluding that frontierswomen were less racist than army officers, we need to examine the ways they too participated in and benefited from white conquest of the West.

It is important that we recognize that this question of "women's" attitudes toward race has a built-in blind spot. At base, it is really a question about *white pioneer* women's attitudes toward race. Because even the best answer to this question can only tell us about the attitudes of one group of women, it can't take us very far in understanding the larger process of intercultural relations. To do that, we have to pose a different kind of question.

54

For this reason, the most promising work has taken a different approach—that of focusing on women who were intercultural brokers, mediators between two or more very different cultural groups. Because this approach is grounded in all women's behaviors rather than in white women's attitudes, it brings to center stage a wide variety of women who have acted as cultural intermediaries. Two particular groups have been prominently featured in this kind of work: the Indian women whose marriages to white men created métis communities in the Upper Great Lakes region or ensured the survival of Indians in California, and the Hispanic women whose marriages and business contacts with white merchants shaped a unique society in the Southwest.[22] Perhaps the best-known study of this type, Sylvia Van Kirk's *"Many Tender Ties"* (1983), focuses on Indian women in Canada who, along with their white fur trader husbands, created a unique and rather precarious fur trade society, the dynamics of which shifted when white women entered the area sometime later. In this approach, women's lives became microcosms of the contradictions of conquest—embodiments of the relations of rebellion, cooperation, and subordination that underlay the massive changes conquest brought to the region.[23] Paying close attention to cultural nuance, these studies show the ways individual women of color shaped the historical development of their communities. If we are careful to keep a firm eye on the relative difference in power, the same set of questions can also be applied to sources left by white women—missionaries, field matrons, reformers, and travelers—who were also intercultural brokers.[24]

By asking questions like these, western history could put itself right in the forefront of the study of intercultural relations. Not only are there abundant sources from the region's eighteenth- and nineteenth-century history,

55

but twentieth-century demographics show the West to be the home base of the two fastest-growing racial/ethnic groups in the country—Hispanics and Asian Americans. There is every reason to believe that the twentieth-century West will remain a rich field for the study of intercultural relations.

Tackling the topic of women at the intercultural crossroads—and trying to face squarely the issues of power relations it raises—leads us from the uniqueness of western history right back to American history in general. American historians, nearly overwhelmed by the recent overload of information about disparate groups in American society, are currently preoccupied with the problem of how to synthesize their knowledge. Now that it is impossible to believe that there is only one cultural theme in American history, we're struggling to figure out how to write a history that does justice to them all. To solve the problem of synthesis, we need a history that is not only multicultural but also intercultural. To the extent that studies of intercultural relations centered in the West help American historians respond to this crisis of synthesis, they could advance American history in general. And not even American history is the limit, for, as any scholar who studies western immigrant groups quickly learns, the dynamics of conquest are played out in an international arena.

What I've tried to do, then, is to suggest that in at least four ways—by defining the frontier as cross-cultural rather than geographic, by focusing on women of color, by analyzing the crossroads of race, class, and gender, and by studying women at the intercultural crossroads—a New Western History could be organized around the concept of western women at the cultural crossroads.

I can't claim that the approach I'm advocating here is now the center of women's western history. Libraries are

still stocked with far more books on white pioneer women
than on their Asian-American counterparts, and students
seem as eager as ever to learn about the white pioneer
past they still envision as western history. The most immediate, if least encouraging, result of my own participa-
tion in the Trails conference was that I received a spate of
invitations to review new books, all of which turned out
to be about white pioneer women.

But the multicultural approach isn't a pipedream either. Change is visible on a number of fronts. The influential Southwest Institute for Research on Women (SIROW)
recently announced a two-year plan to focus all its interdisciplinary research on women of color.[25] *Frontiers*, the
women's studies journal that has been the most consistent outlet for western women's history, has adopted
multiculturalism as its goal. Historians who once might
have written studies of white male fur traders are now
envisioning more complicated stories of the relations between white traders, Indian wives, and the white women
who belatedly appeared on the scene. Researchers are at
work reinterpreting captivity narratives, missionary
journals, and ethnic community newspapers for the light
they throw on intercultural relations. Even the historians
of western women most dedicated to the notion of the
frontier are adopting a comparative approach that ex-
tends the range of their studies considerably; its best
practitioners (I think especially of Antonia Castañeda) focus on women of color and take up the question of intercultural relations.

For the moment, at least, the center of new research
is New Mexico, an entirely appropriate spot, given that in
New Mexico the paths of Hispanics, Indians, and Anglos
have crossed for centuries. It seems to me that when the
mention of western history brings to mind the complex
society of New Mexico as easily as the trappers, traders,

and soldiers of Turnerian rhetoric, our new approach will have come of age.

In the meantime, I think that adopting a focus on western women at the cultural crossroads has enormous potential. In addition to expanding traditional views of western history, it could be central to solving two challenges facing American historians today: the need to explore the interaction of race, class, and gender and to understand relations between the various cultures in American history. Whether this potential will be developed into a regional history strong enough to shape the contours of American history is very much up to us. In this sense, historians of western women face a crossroads of our own.

4

THE TRAIL TO SANTA FE
The Unleashing of the
Western Public Intellectual

PATRICIA NELSON LIMERICK

IN THE FALL of 1989, in Santa Fe, New Mexico, the "Trails through Time" exhibit began a well-received road tour, visiting towns and cities in Arizona, Colorado, New Mexico, Utah, and Wyoming. Launching the exhibit, the Trails symposium began tamely, but in terms of the level of media attention usually given the work of professors, it got wild fast.

The National Endowment for the Humanities had provided funding for the exhibit and for an accompanying symposium. As principal scholar for the project, I had considerable freedom to choose the subject of the conference. After months of reading on the routes and travels of Indians, explorers, traders, settlers, miners, soldiers, cattle drivers, urbanites, job seekers, and tourists, the idea of a two-day symposium on western trails struck me as too much of a good thing. "Let's keep the name 'Trails,'" I suggested, "but let's call the symposium, 'Trails: Toward a New Western History.' That way we can talk about how much Western history has changed in the last few years."

Once we had invited speakers for the conference, the preposition in the title began to wear on me. "Western historians," I thought, "are always calling for 'new

59

models' and 'new approaches'—and now, with this *'toward a New Western History'* phrase, we seem to be joining that chorus. We're always just starting the journey, always just on our way, always hoping that someday we'll arrive at a new way of thinking. When are we ever going to get there?"

When I was a child, my mother and father had infinite stamina as automobile tourists. Jumping off from Banning, California, our vacations echoed with a repeated dialogue:

> My sisters and I, from the back seat: "Aren't we there yet? Are we ever going to get there?"
> My father, from the driver's seat: "It's just a little further."

These latter-day "long drives" gave me early instruction in the vast spaces of the American West. But others might want to argue that those hours in the back seat finally bore their fruit in my impatience with the slowness of change in the field of western history. With the chorus of calls for new approaches and new models, my old lament, "Aren't we there *yet*?" had become an appropriate impatience. So I wrote the speakers and asked that we drop the word "toward" from the symposium title and proceed on the premise that we had *arrived* at a New Western History.

One of the commentators responded to my request by asking what this New Western History might be. It seemed a fair question. In answer, I wrote a one-page statement, "What on Earth Is the New Western History?" and circulated it to the participants and then to the audience in Santa Fe. It was not my intention to make this a party line—hence, the parenthetical phrase, "Not a Manifesto," after the title. The summation could serve, I thought, to focus discussion. People could agree or disagree with it as they liked, but at least we would have some terms of discussion in common. (See pages 85–87, where that statement is reprinted.)

Then, in Santa Fe, two unexpected things happened. First, several speakers used the phrase, "the New Western History," in a way that suggested that such a movement did exist. Second, several reporters covering the conference picked up my one-page summation and, quite understandably if also in defiance of its subtitle, treated it like a manifesto. T. R. Reid's article in the *Washington Post* and Mark Trahant's article in the *Arizona Republic* started off an improbable rush of media coverage. A variety of news organizations took up the story: the *New York Times*, the *Los Angeles Times*, the *Denver Post*, the *Boston Globe*, the *Christian Science Monitor*, *U.S. News and World Report*, the *New Republic*, the *Chronicle of Higher Education*, and National Public Radio. Even if the phrase was sometimes surrounded by cynical quotation marks, the New Western History had come to exist.

Typical of historians, who have never shown much talent as prophets, I did not see this coming. If I had, would I have chosen another name for the movement? Certainly "New Western History" has some of the qualities of a showdown, with the Old and the New taking aim at each other from opposite ends of Main Street. Premised on the existence of an "Old Western History," this now well-entrenched phrase has set off a debate over what ideas qualify as New and what ideas get stuck with the status of Old.

In his *Great Plains* (Lincoln: University of Nebraska Press, 1981; reprint of 1931 edition), for instance, Walter Prescott Webb was decidedly New in his emphasis on the West's limited water and decidedly Old in his patronizing treatment of Indians and Hispanics, in his celebration of the late-nineteenth-century cattle kingdom, and in his conviction that, at long last, thanks to the persistence and adaptability of Anglo-Americans, the Great Plains finally bowed to their masters.

In the same way, Frederick Jackson Turner's 1893 essay, "The Significance of the Frontier in American History," has remained the cornerstone of the Old Western History. Nonetheless, in the years after 1893, Turner sometimes sounded considerably Newer than many of his mid-twentieth-century followers. Consider the observations in his essay "The West and American Ideals," delivered as a commencement address at the University of Washington in 1914. "The federal government has undertaken vast paternal enterprises of reclamation in the desert," Turner noted, acknowledging a crucial post-1890 form of western economic expansion. Or consider his appraisal of the struggles of mining workers in the Rockies: "Like the Grand Canon, where in dazzling light the huge geologic history is written so large that none may fail to read it, so in the Rocky Mountains the dangers of modern American industrial tendencies have been exposed." With these observations, Turner seemed to be casting his lot with the speakers who would gather at the Trails conference in Santa Fe nearly sixty years after his death. Turner was, after all, one of the historical profession's most consistent spokesmen for the necessity of updating our thinking about the past in response to current events. "It is important to study the present and the recent past," he wrote in 1910, "not only for themselves, but also as the source of new hypotheses, new lines of inquiry, new criteria of the perspective of the remoter past."[1]

In 1973, visiting Madison, Wisconsin, my architect-husband and I wrote our most memorable piece of doggerel verse. Originally written to capture the spirit of the

Taliesin Fellowship's devotion to Frank Lloyd Wright, it applies as well to twentieth-century Turnerians:

> The Master informed us, "Find a new way;
> The styles of the past are dated and gray.
> Do not with tradition continue to stay,
> And that is, of course, why we do things *His* way."

The contradiction between Turner's demonstrated flexibility and the comparative inflexibility of his latter-day defenders directs us to a central fact about the Old Western History: It should, more accurately, go by the title the Restored Old Western History. Quite solidly trounced in the 1930s and 1940s, the frontier model presented in Turner's 1893 address might have faded quietly and gracefully from the scene. The frontier thesis, one might have expected, would have remained a subject of study for historians interested in the intellectual climate of the 1890s, but it would yield ground to more inclusive models for the teaching and writing of western history.

Instead, the diligent labors of Ray Allen Billington and his allies in the mid-twentieth century rescued and refurbished Turner's 1893 ideas. The result of that labor is visible, particularly in the standard western history textbooks. However they might tinker with the Turner thesis, the authors remain fixed on the model of a westward-moving frontier that ended somewhere around the turn of the century. In both *Westward Expansion* (1982) and *America Moves West* (1971), the point of view was firmly set in the East, with English-speaking white males holding a firm grip on the status of main characters.[2]

This restoration of the Old Western History carried an enormous irony of timing. Well-adapted for carrying the ideological freight of the cold war, the revamped model of the frontier pulled out on the road again—just in

63

time to run full tilt into the 1960s. An attempt to incorporate Indian, Hispanic, Asian, and black peoples, as well as women of all ethnicities, into the Restored Old Western History could not go much beyond the "conjunction school of historical revision." The conjunction school responded to the fact of western ethnic and gender diversity with the liberal use of the word "and," as in "and women," "and Hispanics," or "and Asian Americans." With a few added paragraphs, or perhaps even a chapter or two, these "others" remained distinctly peripheral to the main story of the male Anglo-American advance across the continent.[3]

The Restored Old Western History was having an equally tough time incorporating the events of the twentieth century in western America. It was a widespread article of faith that the frontier had closed, sometime around 1890, and fractured western American history into two parts. Indeed, since the word "West" often served as a synonym for "frontier," by the grimmest interpretation, the closing of the frontier ended western history entirely. But demography spoke loudly on behalf of the twentieth-century West; the westward movement of this century, in sheer numbers, far outweighed the westward movement of the nineteenth century. Reckoning with the reality of a century of western history after 1890, conventional historians could offer only a puzzling distinction between a "frontier West" and a "post-frontier West."[4]

Following Thomas Kuhn's model of paradigm shifts, by the late 1970s, the pressures had built up on the fault lines of the old paradigm and something had to give.[5] Sometimes restrained in voicing their discontent, any number of western historians chafed under the dominance of the Restored Old Western History. Many books, by professional scholars as well as by journalists, told stories set in western America that could find no home in the standard western history textbooks.[6] Quite a few of the writers of these books, in fact, simply chose not to identify themselves as western historians. Even though their studies made direct contributions to an understanding of the American West, they preferred to call themselves Indian historians or ethno-historians, Chicano historians, Asian-American historians, women's historians, environmental historians, legal historians, social historians, urban historians—anything but western historians. But whatever they called themselves, their work was the principal force heightening the abundant tensions along the fault line of the frontier model.

Responding to these pressures, I and a number of others would have been eager to consult the manual that Thomas Kuhn did *not* write to accompany his *Structure of Scientific Revolutions*. That manual, tentatively titled *How to Shift Your Paradigm Smoothly*, is a publishing opportunity still open to an enterprising writer. In its opening chapter, the manual would have to take up the vexing question of objectivity in historical writing. In the early 1970s, when I started graduate school, the whole business of emotional involvement, ideology, and objectivity was in a very confused state, with two exactly contradictory ways of thinking available to us and no visible way to reconcile them.

According to one theory, historians were purely objective assemblers of data. Historical books should sound as if they had been written by a computer or a committee. Conviction and feeling should play no part in professional work. The worst kind of conviction was concern for the present; historical studies should be conducted solely on their own terms. Presentism, the exercise of connecting the past to the present, was very bad indeed. In classes where these laws were promulgated, I used to sit with some anxiety, feeling like a thinly disguised criminal in a school for law enforcement officials, expecting that the first course assignment would be the arresting, charging, trying, and punishing of me.

But then, by a second theory, these laws of objectivity had dissolved and left us all to live in a shifty, relativistic universe. The notion of hard, set facts, of an objective reality "out there" waiting to be discovered and transcribed, was an illusion. *Everything* was a matter of point of view and interpretation.

One of my professors told a story that summed up this relativistic model, a story that drove the objectivists to despair and distraction. It seems that a marriage counselor was being observed by a student in training. At this particular session, the husband came in first and explained how everything that had gone wrong with the marriage could be traced to the wife's flaws. The marriage counselor listened and then said, "You know, I think you're absolutely right." Then the wife came in and told a mirror image of the husband's story, in which everything was *his* fault. The marriage counselor listened to her and then said, "You know, I think you're absolutely right." So the wife left, and the marriage counselor turned to the student who had been observing and said, "Well, what do you think?" "To be honest," the student said, "I think that was a mess. You listened to two completely contradictory versions of the problem, and you said both were right, and now you've made an even bigger mess of things." And to that, the marriage counselor replied, "You know, I think *you're* absolutely right."[7]

So that was what we had to choose between: a rigid discipline of giving "just the facts" and nothing but the facts, on one side; and, on the other side, a model that offered a universe of relativistic mush, in which there were no facts but only points of view.

Thank heavens, the years pass and the things that made one's head spin in graduate school lose much of their power to terrify. Consider, for instance, the question of just how well the guardians of objectivity were doing in meeting their own standards. The answer is, "Not very well at all," and many of the Restored Old Western Historians were a case in point. Although they thought of themselves as rigorously neutral, without ideology or bias, they had in fact placed their sympathies with English-speaking male pioneers and then called that point of view objectivity.

Western historians, in other words, have usually written with emotion, subjectivity, point of view, and sympathy. It is, after all, a characteristic of human beings to have individual voices and individual points of view, and there is no particular need—and no viable way—of escaping that fact. No one is omniscient; everyone draws his or her conclusions from the lessons learned from an individual set of experiences; and that is no occasion for shame. Emotions and values are wired into our heads, and putting those emotions and values on record is the best, indeed, the only workable way to deal with them. We never fully capture the past, but the discipline of examining as much evidence as possible, considering as many points of view as possible, and then thinking as hard and as rigorously as possible (the stage, in the anecdote, that the marriage counselor skipped) leads to worthwhile results, results that may well be modified and reinterpreted by later historians but that are still worthwhile for both writer and reader.

With the mystique of objectivity dispelled, *How to Shift Your Paradigm Smoothly* could move on to the real action, a process of rethinking that often begins in one's own classroom. Teaching my first lecture course in 1980, and without this manual at hand, I took students on a tour of western history that included Indian, Hispanic, Asian, women's, and environmental history. At the end of the tour, I instructed them at the final exam, "Reinterpret the 1893 Turner Thesis in light of new information in western ethnic and environmental history." The students were, as they all must be at final exams, compliant and they did their best with this improbable question. Not a one took the risk of writing the obvious answer: "None of this stuff has any bearing on the Turner Thesis, and vice versa." The question was, after all, as improbable as a science exam that asked students to reinterpret particle physics in light of Darwin's *On the Origin of Species*. A very creative student might be able to make something out of it, but the intellectual play of comparing two completely unrelated things cannot appeal to many.

I blundered on for another year, leading the students in a mad chase around the continent, from Santa Fe to Quebec, Jamestown to Sitka, pursuing the manifestations of a process that we could not name or define. We could call it the "frontier" if we liked, but attempts to define that term only delivered us over to another set of unrewarding and very abstract final exam questions.

When someone does write *How to Shift Your Paradigm Smoothly*, that useful manual will be a tribute to the necessary role of teaching in scholarly thought. "In order to realize how completely you are entrapped by traditional thinking," the manual will say, "you must entrap yourself repeatedly in front of a group of eighteen-to-twenty-two-year-olds. If you are a decent and fair teacher, then eventually you will no longer feel comfortable at imposing on their deference. At a certain point, you will finally have to say to them (and, more important, to yourself), 'What I am offering you in the way of a big interpretation does not make very much sense.' "

That is the key moment in the paradigm-shifting business: You recognize that the old model is even more irrelevant than it is wrong. With the full recognition of women, minorities, and the actual physical environment, there was no longer any point in trooping off to the Turnerian wars. There was no longer any reason to risk injury—or more likely, boredom—in fighting for or against the propositions of 1893 in either their original form or in the form recarved into stone by the Restored Old Western Historians.

It was, after all, the perception that western American historians devoted most of their interpretative activity to debating the Turner Thesis that had given the field its low status in the appraisal of many other scholars. I remember, for instance, the opening question at a job interview in 1979: "Why, Patricia, did you choose to go into this backwater of a field?" I remember, as vividly, a conversation six or seven years later in Boulder, with an American studies scholar who had just gotten a job at a prestigious southern university. "Now that I'm moving to the South," he said, "I'll have to do a lot of reading in southern history and literature." I, in turn, asked, "When you moved to Colorado, did you have to do a lot of reading in western history and literature?" The response was hearty laughter, conveying his conviction that I had just made an intentional, and pretty funny, joke.

Quoted in the *New York Times*, Yale western historian Howard R. Lamar noted that the New Western Historians have "a 'ferocious' regional pride."[8] That appraisal hits the nail on the head. The old frontier model relentlessly trivialized the West, ignoring the enormously complex convergence of diverse people, rendering the nineteenth-century past irrelevant to the twentieth-century present, and treating actual western places only as stage settings for the repeated sequential performances of the frontier play. The frontier model, in other words, worked against a recognition of the American

West as a real place, as a region of significance with a serious history.

Traditional western historians were, curiously enough, quickest on the draw with objections to any definition of the West as a region. The West, they would argue, does not have the coherence necessary to qualify as a real region. Trying to answer that objection was the intellectual equivalent of trying to join a club where the membership standards were constantly rising—rising high enough to disqualify most of the already admitted members of the club. The West, said the strict enforcers of the admissions requirements, could not be a region because it had too many different subregions; especially in the cases of California and parts of the interior, the West had too great a difference in prosperity and poverty; residents of the West did not have a consistent and coherent sense of themselves as westerners.

Would the West be admitted to the club of American regions? Application denied, on the basis of insufficient internal homogeneity and coherence.

Judged by equally stern standards, very few regions—and fewer nations—would qualify as genuine units of society or units of study. Certainly the differences between the states of Nevada and Washington, for instance, are considerable. But so are the differences between South Carolina and Arkansas, and yet both are commonly and justifiably referred to as southern states. For all the examples of heterogeneity between the ninety-eighth meridian and the Pacific Coast, it is indisputable that much of the West shares common characteristics:

1. It is more prone to aridity and thereby more difficult to conquer;
2. It contains more Indian reservations and more visible, unvanished Indian peoples;

3. It has more land still in federal control;
4. It shares a border with Mexico;
5. It is closer to the Pacific than the rest of the country is;
6. It underwent Anglo-American conquest at a time when the United States was a fully formed nation, providing, thereby, a more focused and revealing case study of how the United States as a nation conducted conquest and especially how the federal government adopted a central role for itself;
7. As a result of all these factors, it is a region particularly prone to demonstrate the unsettled aspects of conquest, to show in the late twentieth century more than its share of the evidence that the conquest of North America came to no clear, smooth end.[9]

Although there is no reason to argue that residents of the West now live with an enlightened regional self-consciousness based on these elements of commonality, there is also no reason to argue that they could not or should not. In the months since the Trails conference, thanks in large part to the labors of journalists, the public has heard a lot about the changing fortunes of western history. The response has been one of remarkable receptivity. Far from closing ranks against the debunkers of old western myths, westerners have seemed quite willing to give us a hearing. In speaking engagements throughout the West, I and others have road tested and field tested the New Western History, with happy results. In the most gratifying cases, discussion goes on long after the speaker leaves; in Casper, Wyoming, for instance, a friend told me that during the next week, his garage mechanic, his dental technician, and his hair stylist all discussed my speech with him.

On these occasions, westerners give every sign of eagerness to let lessons from the region's past contribute to their understanding of the region's present. In fact, the picture of the West offered by the New Western History is often a very close match to the lived experience of western public audiences. As one man in Sacramento, California, put it, "I enjoyed your speech, but since I'm not a western historian, everything you said was obvious to me." Any number of westerners, like this man, live with a daily recognition of the region's ethnic diversity as well as with a recognition of the unsettled issues of conquest.

One of the most heartening responses to the changes in the field came from the Western Governors' Association (WGA). *Beyond the Mythic West* (1990), a collection of essays commissioned by the WGA, got an enthusiastic hearing from the governors at their July 1990 meeting in Fargo, North Dakota.[10] For public officials coping with the uncertainties of boom/bust economies, ongoing Indian-white friction, the dilemma of nuclear waste disposal, and conflicts over public land management, the Restored Old Western History was decidedly irrelevant. The New Western History, on the other hand, has a direct bearing on the issues these men and women encounter every day.

Generally willing to give these ideas a try, western audiences do sometimes seem surprised by their own amiability. The way in which they express their surprise follows very closely on the pattern of a story told by the great desert writer Joseph Wood Krutch. In 1929, long before he had taken up nature writing as his profession and passion, Krutch published *The Modern Temper*. This glum book explored the ways in which science and rationality had stripped faith and meaning from modern lives. On a promotion tour for *The Modern Temper*, Krutch was scheduled to speak in Detroit to a women's club. Arriving at the train station, he waited for the woman who was to meet him: "She approached me only after every other descending passenger had left the platform. 'Are *you* Mr. Krutch?' 'I am.' Her face fell. 'But you do not look as *depressed* as I expected.' "[11]

In the last few years, I have accumulated a substantial collection of similar remarks: "You do not seem as glum, as bitter, as angry, as negative, as I expected," to which, I guess, one is supposed to reply, "Thank you."

What I value especially in Krutch's telling of the story is the way he captures the woman's actual disappointment: "You do not look as *depressed* as I expected" could almost be translated as, "You do not look as depressed as I *hoped*." Audiences can arrive at a lecture with the expectation that the New Western Historian will treat the defenseless, much-loved Myth of the West much as Margaret Hamilton handled poor Toto. For those who came expecting the Wicked Witch of the West to ride up, cram the myth into her bicycle basket, and pedal away cackling malevolently, the actuality—of a New Western Historian presenting a realistic but still compelling story of a complex region—can be a bit disappointing.

Once the disappointment wears off, audiences may well wonder where their expectations of negativity and gloom came from. Journalists bear some of the responsibility for giving the New Western History its aura of grimness. The pressures of telling a complicated story in a few hundred words may well force newspaper writers into presenting the contrast between the Old and New Western History as a contrast of light and dark, cheer and gloom, optimism and pessimism. But why some professional historians, under no obligation to paint complicated pictures in simple lines, have adopted the same characterization remains a puzzle to me.

The New Western History, according to some of these curious statements, is a steady flow of tears and lamentations. With our attention focused on the "dark strains" and "splatters of mud" in western history, we offer "a picture of unrelieved bleakness," "a somber West, devoid of light, marked by hardship, suffering and failure," peopled "by victims of institutionalized brutality and avarice." We judge western history to be "a profoundly disturbing and negative aspect of the nation's past," a "most destructive heritage of which Americans should be ashamed."[12]

My own appraisal of these matters is quite different. I have never known any way to divide human experience between the light and the dark, the positive and the negative. Human character and human life are, at virtually every moment, a muddled mixture of qualities, and that proposition applies fully to this region. The American West has the same moral complexity as every other part of the planet. If you said that the American South was a place of moral complexity or if you said that the urban Northeast was a place where progress came mixed with costs and injuries, it is hard to imagine anyone crying in response, "How glum, how disillusioning!" But if you say those same things about the American West, then everyone with a heavy emotional investment in the mythic West of innocence and fresh starts will immediately break into protest—"How depressing, how negative, how dark, how 'devoid of light.' "

For people with strong, often unexamined emotions about the West, the phrase "New Western History" has become a kind of well-publicized ink blot or Rorschach test. When someone looks at the picture we present and says, "How deeply depressing and gloomy," there is no particular point in correcting them. It is, indeed, a great deal more interesting to explore this misprision, to respond, "How fascinating that you would see this version of western history as so negative. Shall we talk about *why* you feel that way?" If, in other words, the New Western History must for a time carry the label "disillusioning," then this is surely a tribute to how much illusion had accumulated in the region's historical accounts.

Anyone reading this collection straight through will know that, on this question, I am offering my own convictions and not a party line. Donald Worster, for instance, is quite willing to say that the darker side of western history should indeed be our topic; and both he and Richard White are happy to charge me with wimpiness and punch pulling on this subject. In the same vein, the most energetic dispute at the Trails symposium was a disagreement between Worster and White over the degree to which nature in the West has been fundamentally shaped by human action. Is there any longer such a thing as intact, self-governing nature? One said yes, the other said no. As that exchange made clear, the New Western History is fundamentally a free-for-all, not a party line of "political correctness."

Indeed, one key reason for printing this collection is to give the whippersnappers in the field something to use for target practice. Graduate students and scholars with new Ph.D.s give every sign of having been productively stirred up by the debate in the last few years. Far from trying to create a new academic orthodoxy to take the place of the Restored Old Western History, I fully recognize that the outcome of the debate is, finally, in the hands of these whippersnappers. Whether or not the revitalization of western American history proves to be something more than a short-lived media event is up to the scholars who will publish their first books in the next decade. If this collection of essays gives those young scholars the intellectual equivalent of a poolside to push off from, it will serve one of its primary purposes.

Santa Fe, New Mexico, proved to be an ideal location

for the Trails symposium. It is, in fact, the core of my hopes for western American history that any future models for the field will be inclusive and expansive enough to take places like Santa Fe into account. The old concept of the frontier—that bipolar opening-and-closing operation—never looked sillier than it did when applied to New Mexico. When, for instance, would one say the frontier opened in what would become New Mexico? When the Athapaskan Indians came into Pueblo territory? When Coronado made his failed exploration in the 1540s, or when Oñate planted his precarious colony in 1598? Did the successful Pueblo Revolt of 1680 close the frontier or prolong it? Or does the concept of the frontier require the presence of Anglo-Americans? Then did the frontier open with the Santa Fe Trade in 1821, and close with the conquest in 1848? Or did the frontier close with the arrival of the railroad in the 1880s, or with statehood in 1912, or with the attempt to establish comprehensive control of the Mexican border with the immigration law of 1986?

Pitted against the complexity of New Mexico, the Restored Old Western History totters. Embracing the complexity of New Mexico, the New Western History is in its element. Whatever the whippersnappers do with the field in the future, it is my hope that they will not turn back on the trail leading western history to a full reckoning with Santa Fe.

In nearly every field of academic inquiry, the twentieth century has seen a retreat to the university. Professors write for other professors; specialization, jargon, and academic timidity have placed a canyon between public audiences and intellectuals. The Trails symposium, and the improbable publicity that followed it, built a bridge across that canyon. And that is my principal hope for the future of western history: that we will maintain that bridge and keep two-way traffic flowing over it. All around the West, the public is eager to join in this discussion, giving western historians in the late twentieth century the finest opportunity imaginable to revive the role of the western public intellectual. The New Western History is part of a much broader regional movement: In fiction, in poetry, in landscape photography, in painting, in architecture, in legal thinking, and in environmental sciences, westerners are taking the West seriously, putting together a firm, grounded sense of where we really live, how we got here, and on what terms we can continue to live here in each other's company. The 1990s stand a good chance of being a crucial decade in western American history, a decade in which westerners might become settlers, and not unsettlers, of the region. Myths of the lost glory of the old frontier aside, we are far from running out of opportunities for courage and heroism in the West today.

PART II

APPRAISING THE TERRITORIES

Old and New Western Histories

5

WHAT ON EARTH IS
THE NEW WESTERN HISTORY?

PATRICIA NELSON LIMERICK

I AM FROM Banning, California, a town on the edge of the desert, 80 miles southeast of Los Angeles. When I grew up there, cattle grazed at the Brinton Ranch north of town, and once a year we celebrated Stagecoach Days, commemorating Banning's location on a principal route of travel into coastal California through the San Gorgonio Pass. Forest fires sometimes consumed the mountains on either side of the pass; I remember Mount San Jacinto in flames, with the sky glowing in that weird way that only a forest fire produces.

Banning was, from its aridity to its mountain setting, a world apart from Portage, Wisconsin, the hometown of Frederick Jackson Turner. Turner grew up in a place with plenty of water, a place remote from the Pacific Coast and the Mexican border. Indian people, French Canadians, and a variety of people of northern European background played their role in the area's history. But on this count, too, Banning was a world apart—with Cahuilla Indians from the Morongo Reservation on the edge of town; Hispanic people of varying origins, long-term residents of the United States as well as more recent immigrants; African Americans; Filipinos; and "white" people, with all the range of backgrounds that that odd category carries.

There has been a grand tradition in western American history, a tradition in which I am proud to play a small part: taking one's home seriously. Turner took Portage seriously; Walter Prescott Webb took his Texas plains home seriously; and after a spell of wondering why I had to grow up in a town that seemed so far from the main course of American history, I ended up taking Banning seriously.

Take Banning seriously, and you find yourself immediately in the role of rebel against the standing models of western history. Tailored to fit Portage, Wisconsin, Turner's frontier theory simply won't fit Banning, regardless of how you trim and stitch, tighten and loosen. Western American historians with backgrounds like my own had the choice of accepting the standard Turner-derived interpretations of the field and discarding our own personal experiences or trusting our experiences and discarding the old theories. It is a tribute to the power of tradition that so many western historians submitted to the first option so long and chose theory over experience.

Conventional frontier theory never made much room for the West beyond the ninety-eighth meridian. Any number of central characteristics of that region played either a limited role or no role at all in Turner's thinking. Western aridity is only the most obvious. The continued presence and resistance to conquest of Indian peoples; Spanish settlement in the Southwest preceding Anglo-American settlement anywhere in North America as well as the continued give-and-take between Latin America and Anglo America; the industrial reality of much western mining; Asian immigration and the West's involvement in the Pacific Rim; ongoing disputes over the ownership and management of public lands; the existence of something other than the ideal pioneer democracy and equality in western state and local governments—most of these central items found their homes on the edges of the field, if they found any home at all.

Just as important as Turner's lack of attention to the Far West was the accumulation of a century's worth of history since he made his major statement on the meaning of the frontier. A man of considerable intellectual courage, Turner said that the frontier ended in 1890, and he made this claim a bare three years after 1890. In this willingness to assess the currents of his own time, Turner was virtually kin to the John Naisbitts and Alvin Tofflers of our own time, standing on the edge of the future and forecasting megatrends.

Certainly courageous, Turner was also, on this count, wrong. If the "frontier" meant, in one of its many and changeable definitions, the discovery of new resources and the rush of population to exploit those resources, then 1890 was no deadline. Homesteading persisted into the twentieth century; rushes to pump oil or to mine coal or uranium punctuated the 1900s. In sheer numbers, the westward movement of the twentieth century far outweighed the westward movement of the nineteenth century. Moreover, the cross-cultural encounters and conflicts engendered by the "frontier" are still with us in 1990; the population of western America shows few signs of turning into a blended and homogeneous whole.

Personal experience had taught me a great deal of this, long before I had any professional interest in western American history. In the 1940s, in the process of moving from Los Angeles to Banning, my parents had given my older sister Ingrid an early and perhaps excessive exposure to the language of that archetypal figure of westward expansion, the real estate agent. On one outing, Ingrid woke from a nap in the backseat of the car, looked out the window, and asked where she was. "In Temecula," was the answer, and Ingrid then solemnly declared: "I think Temecula is going to grow and grow and grow."

In my own childhood, we laughed at this story because Temecula did not grow. But then, in the 1970s, my sister's long-term gift of prophecy became clear. Temecula grew and grew and grew, and we stopped laughing and started wondering why Mother and Father hadn't had the sense to borrow money and *buy* Temecula in 1950. But encased in this piece of family folklore was an essential message about the unpredictability of western American life and about the folly of believing that any "end of the frontier" had put to rest these matters of regional growth and instability.

By the 1980s, the field of western American history was ripe for major change. Not only was there evidence, in Temecula and elsewhere, that life in the region had not settled into a post-frontier sameness, there was also a wonderful accumulation of innovative, scholarly books in the fields of environmental, ethnic, community, and women's history as well as social, economic, and political history. Much of the content of those books strains the limits of Turnerian frontier models; indeed, by the early 1980s, it seemed to me that the accumulation of new studies had burst through those limits entirely. But we had no book reuniting these scattered subfields into one whole model.

It was my enormous good fortune to be seized by a spirit of daring and, under its influence, to resolve to write a book offering a new synthesis. Writing such a book offers the author opportunities to feel deep and compelling anxiety. For virtually every paragraph, the writer recognizes five or ten experts who know the subject in considerably greater depth than any synthesizer possibly could. But each of those moments of high anxiety is counterbalanced by much longer spells of excitement and satisfaction. Writing *The Legacy of Conquest*, I was in daily face-to-face contact with the breadth, drama, and power of western American history, even when I was not entirely succeeding in capturing those qualities in prose. Published in 1987, *The Legacy of Conquest* (New York: W. W. Norton) has had a remarkably happy career, passionately loved by some, passionately hated by others, and creatively revised and responded to by many more. Publishing a book can sometimes feel like shouting in a sound-proofed room, but *Legacy* has been heard in a way that has exceeded my wildest dreams, back in Banning, that I might someday be an author.

What, then, is the essence of this emerging way of looking at the western past? Preparing for a symposium called "Trails: Toward a New Western History" (held in Santa Fe, New Mexico, in September 1989), one of the participants quite sensibly wrote me to ask what "New Western History" meant. In response, I wrote a summation, a one-page text that has had a prosperous career in copying machines and appears here in print for the first time:

New Western Historians define "the West" primarily as a place—the trans-Mississippi region in the broadest terms, or the region west of the hundredth meridian. The boundaries are fuzzy because nearly all regional boundaries are.

New Western Historians do see a "process" at work in this region's history, a process that has affected other parts of the nation as well as other parts of the planet. But they reject the old term "frontier" for that process. When clearly and precisely defined, the term "frontier" is nationalistic and often racist (in essence, the area where white people get scarce); when cleared of its ethnocentrism, the term loses an exact definition.

To characterize the process that shaped the region, New Western Historians have available a number of terms—invasion, conquest, colonization, exploitation, development, expansion of the world market. In the broadest picture, the process involves the convergence of diverse people—women as well as men, Indians, Europeans, Latin Americans, Asians, Afro-Americans—in the region, and their encounters with each other and with the natural environment.

New Western Historians reject the notion of a clear cut "end to the frontier," in 1890, or in any other year. The story of the region's sometimes contested, sometimes cooperative, relations among its diverse cast of characters and the story of human efforts to "master" nature in the region are both ongoing stories, with their continuity unnecessarily ruptured by attempts to divide the "old West" from the "new West."

New Western Historians break free of the old model of "progress" and "improvement," and face up to the possibility that some roads of western development led directly to failure and to injury. This reappraisal is not meant to make white Americans "look bad." The intention is, on the contrary, simply to make it clear that in western American history, heroism and villainy, virtue and vice, and nobility and shoddiness appear in roughly the same proportions as they appear in any other subject of human history (and with the same relativity of definition and judgment). This is only disillusioning to those who have come to depend on illusions.

New Western Historians surrender the conventional, never-very-convincing claim of an omniscient, neutral objectivity. While making every effort to acknowledge and understand different points of view, New Western Historians admit that it is OK

and the frontier process still seem to have the upper hand. Those who dispute regionalism declare the West to be a vast, divergent place that will not hold together as a unit. The extremes of geography, climate, ethnicity, and economy are well known, but the dissenters from regionalism postulate that forces of disunity are stronger. Subregions seem to fare better; the Great Plains, the Pacific Northwest, the Pacific Coast, the Rocky Mountain West, the Great Basin, and the Southwest coalesce well as distinct climatic and economic places. But how can a scholar unify an area containing Salt Lake City, Des Moines, and Los Angeles? Diversity is not the cement of regionalism.[5]

There is also a vagueness about the West's location. Where is it? Is Dallas in the West? Hawaii? What about those older places that were once the West like Illinois or Louisiana? Martin Ridge declares that "There is a psychological and not a physiographic fault line that separates regions." He adds, "There is a culturally defined public entity with geographic boundaries that is a part of the larger national whole to which it contributes and with which it interacts in a significant fashion." Ridge argues that what holds the West together as a distinct region is a shared series of "special experiences" that, when assembled, produce "a cultural basis not only for fixing boundaries of the West but also for giving it meaning and significance."[6] But what are the cultural values and shared experiences that hold the region together?

If the West as a region is unfocused and vague, the definition of frontier is equally imprecise. When and where does the process commence and terminate? Do we use Walter Prescott Webb's "Great Frontier" thesis and start with Renaissance Europe? Many of Turner's and Webb's disciples believe that, above all else, the frontier was an economic evolution that explained American growth in the nineteenth and twentieth centuries. But within this Turnerian framework is an explicit rise-and-fall syndrome, a sort of nascent Marxism, that has caused more than a few frontier scholars, including Turner and Webb, to take a dim view of America's future. In contrast, Limerick looks back at a negative historical experience but seems to face the future with optimism, creating an almost perfect mirror image of Turner.

If the frontier has ended in the United States and the American economy entered into a twilight of decline, what has become of the capitalistic frontier? Logic dictates that it can be found in Singapore, Hong Kong, and South Korea. But this conception of the frontier as a synonym for "modernization" is so far-flung as to be almost meaningless. Scholars who subscribe to this view usually refer to a developmental thesis and avoid using the word "frontier." Although this ethereal world of frontier theory makes for heady reading, it falls to earth when confronted with the economic vitality of the Sunbelt since World War II. Decades ago, Turner's theories about democracy stemming from the frontier were attacked, and now many of his economic ideas seem equally outmoded. Assuming a close relationship between Marxist economic beliefs and the frontier thesis, the movement of socialist and communist countries away from Marxism bodes ill for the longevity of the traditional frontier process. The frontier thesis may well survive, but it will surely need significant rethinking.

The frontier can be seen, however, as a process, occasionally violent, that extended Western civilization into the Far West. Limerick is correct in part that it was conquest, and Turner would agree. In his essay "Pioneer Ideals and the State University," Turner wrote: "The first ideal of the pioneer was that of conquest. It was his task to fight with nature for the chance to exist. . . . Vast forests blocked the way; mountainous ramparts inter-

posed; desolate grass-clad prairies, barren oceans of rolling plains, arid deserts, and a fierce race of savages, all
had to be met and defeated."[7]

But Turner's conception of the frontier can be distinguished from Limerick's in an analysis of the overall
results that flowed from the conquest. Despite his concern
for a frontierless America, Turner never doubted that
something better followed for most individuals and the
nation, and his contention would seem to have held true.
Envision the possibility of California and the Southwest
having remained a part of Mexico. The advantages to
both conqueror and conquered would at least seem argua-
ble. Do the millions of illegal aliens who have crossed the
southern border in recent years come to live their lives as
a conquered people? Without doubt, Native Americans
suffered the most from the frontier process, but few Indians have been willing to abandon the material advantages of Western culture. This was even true of the earliest contacts between Native Americans and Europeans
when tribes possessed genuine independent existence.
Furthermore, Native Americans have commenced the
process of obtaining legal redress for cases of past
victimization.

Capitalism, of course, arrived in the trappers' saddle-
bags and pioneers' wagons, but to argue that the West's
economic history has been largely negative because of it
flies in the face of the reality of our regional history.
Moreover, the frontier was also legal, political, religious,
philosophical, and artistic. Thus a more modern usage of
the word "frontier" carries far less economic connotation
than it did for Turner and comes closer to what others
like Martin Ridge have called a cultural frontier—Western civilization in all its varied aspects.

From the vantage point of 1990, the closing of the
frontier is a far less distinct event than it was for Turner.

Common sense indicates that as the United States ages, the importance of the nineteenth-century frontier as a vehicle for self-definition will diminish. Still, most psychologists, like most historians of an earlier generation, recognize that formative experiences have a great impact upon the nature and character of the adult. As scholars, most of us have learned to cast a skeptical eye on autobiography, but we continue to think we can define ourselves with total objectivity. Less partial observers do a better job, and when one looks at how others define Americans, he or she finds that the American image abroad is drawn in large measure from the frontier. Tribal myths, the myths that create national character, are formed when nations undergo the creation process—they arrive early in the life of a people, a tribe, or a nation—and they last as long as the people themselves last, far beyond the actual conditions that create the mythology. There can be additions or subtractions, but national mythology remains constant at the core. Critics might rail that the frontier myth is dangerous and destructive, but based upon the history of other nations and cultures we would seem to be stuck with it. Like an unsavory relative, it's ours for better or worse.[8]

Unlike the frontier, the West as a region lacks an overreaching historical or cultural experience that crystallizes its identity. Only two regions have such precision: the South, whose identity is delineated by slavery, secession, and defeat; and New England, whose identity is defined by Puritanism. One cannot find such common cultural underpinnings in the West. Instead, the West would seem composed of a series of overlapping characteristics that must be taken as a unit to fix the general location.

I asked my students at the University of Toledo, "What comes to mind when you think of the West?" Their observations were written on the blackboard, and in about fifteen minutes we had an interesting definition of the West, one that reflects the frontier image.

COWBOYS. What Donald Worster calls the pastoral West. Cowboys represent an ongoing economic activity from the earliest days that includes sheep raising.

INDIANS. The living presence of Native Americans in significant numbers with an accompanying lifestyle that retains strong elements of traditional culture.

ARIDITY. Particularly as defined by John Wesley Powell and Donald Worster. True deserts are only found in the American West.

MOUNTAINS. Mountains that are geologically young. They have always been part of the public's image of the West, whether in the days of Thomas Jefferson, or John Muir, or David Brower.

HISPANIC INFLUENCE. Like Native Americans, the presence of Hispanic peoples in the West in significant numbers with a visible culture and influence.

SPACE. Those parts of the West with fewer than six persons per square mile.

MINING. The image of the mining West remains strong even though mining's importance in the region has declined in recent decades.

FEDERAL GOVERNMENT. States with 50 percent of their land base controlled by Washington.

LONG TERRITORIAL EXPERIENCE. States that acquired statehood after 1861 and whose lengthy territorial experience was often colonial in nature.

URBANIZATION. The West is the most urbanized part of the United States.

Students also often mentioned certain intangibles such as individualism, freedom, and violence, but I refrained from including these characteristics because they are subjective and cannot be mapped. Each factor was put on an overlay and then the overlays were put together. Although the edges lacked convergence, the process produced a western core, or "Heart of the West."[9]

Whatever inability we have in defining the frontier process or the region itself, however, there is no malaise in western history. When historians can engage in such fundamental debates over self-definition as we have witnessed in the last few years, one must conclude that extraordinary scholarly energy exists here. Consensus might well be an undesirable goal that is about as useful to historical creativity as a desert mirage. Moreover, western history and frontier history, like the region itself, have plenty of room for divergent opinions and multiple approaches to the subject. Recent discussion and argument are signs of intellectual vitality and should surely be encouraged.

7

THE "NEW WESTERN HISTORY," AN ASSESSMENT

MICHAEL P. MALONE

A FRIEND OF mine who is a theologian once said that his is the only discipline in which the very existence of the subject matter is open to dispute. Similarly, it is truly questionable whether there really is a "New Western History." In the sense of a genuinely defined school of interpretation, there probably is not. The New Western History can claim no precise definition to match that of the revisionist school of diplomatic history introduced by William Appleman Williams and others three decades ago, nor even as much precision as that claimed by the celebrated *Annales* group of "nonevent-oriented" history. In fact, it would seem to lack even the coherence of that generation of American historians who, three-quarters of a century ago, called for a "new" or "progressive" orientation toward the study of the past.

Yet, in broader perspective, the main currents of western historiography have shifted remarkably both in direction and in velocity during the past two decades and especially in the past few years. It seems warranted, therefore, to conclude that though there is no narrowly defined school of New Western History, there is indeed a broad reconfiguration of this subdiscipline of American history emerging that might be so labeled. The correct question then is: What is the nature of this reconfiguration?

This question begs another: What is the "Old Western History?" That one is easy enough to answer. The traditional western history is essentially frontier history, focusing upon a *to-the-region* approach and featuring a heavily romanticized preoccupation with wilderness, Indians and pioneers, and the adventure of conquering one new land after another.

As most everyone knows, the conceptual lodestone of this frontier/western historiography was provided by Frederick Jackson Turner, who began in the 1890s to describe the frontier experience as the forge of American national identity and the font of such enduring national traits as individualism and democracy. Turner was not a historian of the West but of the frontier. Arguably, the greatest of the true western regionalists was the Texas historian Walter Prescott Webb, who saw in the abiding aridity of the West the main shaping force of its regional identity. But Webb too preoccupied himself with frontiering, and his writings reinforce the Turnerian/frontier bent of western studies rather than challenge it.

Thus the classic paradigm of western history emphasized the frontier, the Americanization of the land and its peoples, and the early eras of land and resource taking. Conversely, of course, it neglected the postfrontier eras that followed the 1890s, the diversity of peoples outside the Anglo/white mainstream, and the women and children who less frequently wielded rifles, plows, and axes. Also neglected were the cities with their industries, professions, and life experiences that seemed alien to an agrarian frontier even when cities arose before farm economies.

On the one hand, western history's preoccupation with the frontier has produced some of the best narrative writings in all of Americana, from Francis Parkman to Bernard De Voto and Robert Utley. Historians of the West have held the popular audiences that most of their colleagues have lost. This important fact should not be disregarded, nor should the ever greater numbers of excellent and sophisticated frontier histories that appear yearly. But the truth is inescapable that preoccupation with the frontier in western history has tended over the years to stigmatize it as romantic, antiquarian, and—worst of all— irrelevant to achieving a true regionalism.

Whether we choose to call the remarkable enrichment of the field during the past quarter century a New Western History or not, the fact is that the timeworn themes and preoccupations of the Old West have been visibly crumbling recently in the face of an unprecedented surge of scholarly vitality. In large part, this surge is simply the predictable result of mainstreaming the western subdiscipline by applying to it trends in the broader field of American history and American studies.

A closer look tends to reinforce this judgment, for the main thrusts of the New Western History are generally those of modern American historiography itself. The campaign to pay attention to western women, for example, led by historians like Julie Roy Jeffrey, Sandra Myres, and Glenda Riley, now has many supporters. Another example is the ever greater attention Francis Paul Prucha, Lawrence Kelly, and others are paying to western Indians and Indian policy and to other regional minorities, particularly Hispanics and Asians. Still other examples include the new urban history of the West, particularly the Southwest; the profusion of writings about all aspects of the western environment; and the increasing application of quantification and the new social history to western topics.

Conversely, the New Western History has had the least impact in precisely those areas of emphasis that the new American historiography itself has slighted—

namely, the prosaic but fundamental mainstays of human activity and history: the economy, the political-governmental order, and the major events of day-to-day life. Consequently, as the New Western History tends to be less political and economic and more socially oriented, it runs the risk of losing its relevance and appeal to the broader literate public. This is what has happened to the wider field of history in general.

The subfield of western history still maintains its distinctiveness within the larger field of American history, however, as a visit to any annual conference of the Western History Association quickly makes clear. This distinctiveness serves to remind us that there is more to the New Western History than simply the regional application of national trends. The West as a field of Americana still appeals to the broader public, not just because of the frontier mystique but also because of the public's fascination with the West as a place, a unique place. The most subtle challenge to contemporary historians of the West is to make the field relevant while not losing the attention of the literate public.

To do so, they must not only maintain the humanism and attention to well-crafted narrative that are the essence of any truly societally based history. They must also join in the search for a new paradigm upon which to base a genuine regionalism. Without such a reconceptualization, historians of the West must either continue to follow the threadbare environmental determinisms of Turner and Webb or follow the unrewarding practice of simply interpreting national events and trends in unexplored regional settings.

During the past decade, historians of the West have made considerable progress along new lines of thought. Some of the most thoughtful of them, particularly historians of cities, women, and minorities, have simply dismissed the older approach of Turner and Webb as irrelevant, or at least outmoded, and moved on to address their subjects in the best ways possible. For example, Earl Pomeroy, the dean of western historians, has discarded the frontier orientation in favor of an interpretation that stresses continuity of development and the role of cities. Pomeroy also eschews lively narrative in favor of close analysis.

However much the new regional history accomplishes through scholarship that broadens and deepens the field, it still must come to terms with the search for regional identity. Once it does so, the old problem of dual identity between college courses on the frontier and those on the West will fade. Frontier, or *to-the-West*, courses will still be taught, but they won't be confused with *in-the-region* courses that are the natural counterparts of regional offerings on the South, New England, and the Midwest or courses that address similar global regions such as the Russian steppes or the African savannas.

To my mind, the most interesting facet of current western historiography is this search for a post-Turnerian paradigm for regional study. Three scholars associated with the distinguished Yale University doctoral program in western studies—a program so prolific that some consider it to *be* the New Western History— offer three separate approaches to this end.

Patricia Nelson Limerick, for one, attempts to establish a "legacy of conquest" to replace the Turnerian frontier approach. Though stimulating, her interpretation seems not really to address the West as place. William Cronon ingeniously argues that the new environmental history is the natural modernization of Turner's environmental interpretation. And Donald Worster argues, quite convincingly, that the true essence of western history is, as Webb said, its aridity and basic reliance upon fragile water systems.

Personally, I believe that the new regional paradigm must be multifaceted, not singular. The enduring impact of both Turner's frontier and Webb's aridity must be taken into account. Equally important, however, are other regionally binding factors such as the federal presence in the region, the special importance of extractive industries, and the continuing process of integrating the West into the global economy. This latter process is one in which the resource-reliant West lies on the cutting edge of America's ongoing factoring into what Immanuel Wallerstein calls the "world-system."

Thus the search for a new regional paradigm need not mean an outright rejection of Turner and Webb's frontier preoccupation, but it certainly does require a broadening and enrichment of a focus that by itself is too narrow. This is clearly happening. Whether or not one chooses to term this flowering of regional writing a New Western History, it is truly the birth of an authentic *regional* historiography, and the phenomenon is indisputably genuine. I hope that out of the current multiplicity of gender and ethnic studies, community and city histories, and economic, policy, and political histories, our first real comprehension of the West-as-region will emerge. That will be something to celebrate.

8

A LONGER, GRIMMER,
BUT MORE INTERESTING STORY

ELLIOTT WEST

I HAVE FRIENDS who say that a lot of the "New Western History" is not really new and that much of what is new is not really history. I disagree. It is true, I admit, that many new trends were anticipated by earlier writers. And certainly today's historians are borrowing from several disciplines, including anthropology, economics, psychology, environmental science, literature, and art. Nonetheless, something new is definitely happening in the history business. The metaphors are tempting—our angles of vision are shifting, our embrace widening. However we describe it, the prevailing view of the western past has changed more in the last ten years than in the previous ninety.

This change is coming about through three lines of investigation. First, writers are reexamining the broad, overarching themes that explain the "what" and the "how" of the West and its past. Just what are our region's defining traits? What have been its most revealing developments, and how can we best understand them?

The theme seekers have worked with two quite different goals in mind. Some have tried to isolate those elements that have made the West and its history unique. There are some obvious candidates, beginning with the weather. Western aridity tells us much about our development (and lack of it), our politics, and distribution of economic power. The West is different, others say, because of the extraordinary range of ethnic groups that have met (or rather collided) there. Still others point to the dominating presence of the federal government.

Complicating things has been a growing appreciation for the region's geographical and historical diversity. The Willamette Valley and Tucson, the Texas panhandle and the Wind River Mountains—these places have less in common than, say, the Tennessee hills and the Green Mountains of Vermont. Does it make sense, then, to speak of "the West" as a region at all? At the very least, say new historians, we need to define more precisely our subregions and how they fit together.

Other writers argue that we have spent too much time thinking of the West as a place apart, a land with a setting and a story that can be understood only on its own terms. We should turn away from this old "exclusivist" approach, say writers like William Robbins, and pay more attention to the ways western history has been one result of developments that have transformed the nation and much of the world during the past few centuries.[1]

Many of these historians focus on one event in particular—the rise of a global capitalist economy. The dynamics and motives associated with capitalism can explain much about the West, past and present, from the restless and exploitive urges of pioneers, to the control and manipulation of resources by centers of corporate power, to the erratic, depression-prone economy of today.

For all their differences, these theme seekers have a couple of things in common. They play down, or deny altogether, the significance of the frontier, that European-American pioneering experience that has dominated almost utterly the earlier tellings of western history. Now the frontier is at most a chapter in a longer, more complex, and more interesting story.

Western history also feels different, for want of a better term, when told through these new themes. Under the older frontier interpretation, the story shimmered with a romantic, heroic glow. Suffering and tragedy were redeemed by the glorious results presumed to have followed—the nurturing of American individualism and democracy and the coming of a civilized order into a wilderness. The new themes, by contrast, emphasize a continuing cultural dislocation, environmental calamity, economic exploitation, and individuals who either fail outright or run themselves crazy chasing unattainable goals.

A second line of investigation proceeds from the bottom up, taking a fresh look at particulars. It is a reconstruction of the basics, starting with the "when" and the "who" of western history. At what point can we say that the story of our region begins? Just who has shaped it and how? As a social historian with a nagging curiosity about how people have muddled through their days, I think the works in this second category are especially fascinating. They are also important because, like the new themes, they challenge what has passed for generations as basic truths.

By the traditional view, for instance, western history basically begins with Lewis and Clark and ends with the Populists, and virtually everything in between is accomplished by adult white males. Recent scholarship is changing that perspective. Because of a prodigious outpouring of work on women's history, the story of settlement is finally going coed. Single women homesteaded, ranched, and ran businesses in the infant towns; wives played essential roles in their families' economic survival.

More fundamentally, these writers are telling us that we can best understand westward expansion not in terms of the bold and intrepid pioneer man but of his family (including, I should emphasize, his children). Families, it seems, were a key not only to economic transformations but also to social and even political changes, including the making of communities and development of labor unions.

Once we begin to retell part of the story, inevitably the rest begins to change. Women's historians, for example, have shown how the first white fur trappers and traders relied on Indian wives both as laborers and as essential liaisons in their first contacts with Native American societies. In time many of those Indian women were caught in the middle, without a place in either their original societies or the white communities then beginning to dominate the West.

Their dilemma in turn suggests another lesson taught over and over in the new history. Just as westward expansion cannot be understood solely from the perspective of adult white males, so the long-term story of the West is hopelessly distorted if we consider only the actions and interests of Anglo-American pioneers.

We are learning the Law of the Country Club. If you lower just one barrier and let someone new in, suddenly everyone else is crowding in. The dilemma of those Indian women reminds us that our history will be hopelessly distorted unless we include all ethnic groups as well as both genders and all ages. For one thing, the pioneer invaders were not all blue-eyed sons of Albion. Our region, in fact, was the most polyglot of the republic during those years. Recent issues of *Montana The Magazine of Western History* have showcased the new work on ethnic history with articles on, among others, the Irish, Chinese, Basques, French, Slavs, Finns, and Nova Scotians.

More fundamentally, we are obliged to study everyone who has ever lived in the West—and for the length of time they have lived there. That sounds obvious, but in fact the story of many peoples have been told only in relation to the frontier epic of the last century. Reading older texts, for example, it is easy to get the impression that Indians and Hispanics were significant only as barriers to the bold frontiersmen who pushed beyond the Missouri after 1820. One wonders how the Nez Percé and Navajos survived the boredom of long centuries waiting for invaders from the East to show up.

But now, as we expand our vision of the "who" of western history, the "when" is stretching with it. The new history proposes that we think of the West instead as a land washed by successive waves of immigrants who have been moving, settling, and adapting to the country for at least twenty-five thousand years. The story does not stop with the homesteaders. Yet another wave, this one from the south, is rolling into the country today.

The nineteenth-century frontier was certainly one of the most important of those immigrant waves, but when we study it, we should include its full implications for those already there. Seen this way, the pioneer era was not all draped in glory. It brought a variety of disastrous changes. Consider, for instance, those familiar images of the pioneers: The plowman busting sod; bullwhackers driving their straining teams; cowboys watching over contented herds. These heroic portraits in fact depict an economic system that required a profound ecological transformation. We cannot say these changes were imposed unilaterally on those already living in the West; Indians rather eagerly took part in some of these enterprises, most obviously the fur trade.

But the expanding economic system triggered a sequence that was finally fatal to native independence. As they exploited western resources, the invaders reshaped the environment. Those changes in the land undercut older native economies and left no alternative to the new ways of living. Living those new ways, Indians found themselves economically subjugated to their new military and political masters.

But there is more to the story than that. Indians and Hispanics may have been militarily subdued, but when we start to reconstruct the details, we find that, contrary to the usual "triumphalist" view, those cultures have been remarkably resilient. If much has been lost, much has survived, and there has been a vigorous exchange between the conquered and the conquerors, a cross-fertilization of customs, ideas, material culture, language, and worldviews.[2] A dozen other examples could be offered, but these are enough to make the point. Reflecting the fresh themes of western history, the details of the story are being reconstructed.

There is a third perspective of the new history. This line of investigation is still rather unfocused, and it has drawn less attention than the first two. But it is full of promise. This perspective considers the emotional and psychological dimensions of western history, the human responses to the peculiar physical and social settings of the West. Whereas the other approaches consider western history from the top down and the bottom up, this one looks from the inside out.

The history of the West is partly that of perceptions. The same could be said of any region, of course, but given the new approaches to our story, human impressions take on an extraordinary significance. The West has been a place of very different peoples bumping into one another, of centuries of immigrants confronting the unexpected and trying to adjust to a demanding, changing environment.

Besides, people act according to how they see things around them. We cannot possibly grasp the Indians' resistance and accommodation, for instance, without some understanding of how they perceived the changes triggered by the coming of the Europeans. Nor can we explain the making of modern western institutions without some account of how their builders saw the country, its limitations, and their own roles and prerogatives.

As historians come to recognize the great diversity of the western historical experience, they have begun to reconstruct what its various peoples have seen and what they thought about what has happened. Ethnohistorians, for instance, are starting to answer some of western history's most intriguing questions: For example, how did the Euro-American invasion appear to Native Americans, and how did their vision of the world change in response to those traumatic events?[3]

As for the pioneers, from their first glimpses of the West, their impressions were far more diverse and complex than typically described. Women viewed the prospect of uprooting and resettlement with far greater trepidation than men. Men usually initiated the move west, but they too had their reasons for finding the change emotionally troubling. And the children, who were just learning to understand their surroundings, viewed the new land differently from adult men or women.[4]

Nowhere is this perceptual approach more helpful (and the older approach more worthless) than in charting the emergence of a modern regional identity. It is a commonplace that "the West is a state of mind." There is some truth behind the cliché; any region is, in part, what its people think about it. Westering settlers arrived with varied perceptions. During the years that followed the pioneers' arrival, many elements of western society engaged in a reckoning—native peoples with their new status; newcomers with the land's possibilities; everybody with ecological, social, and economic transformations as profound as any at any time in American history.

Making some sense out of this is one of the most formidable challenges to confront western historians today. Two recent books by Robert Athearn and Patricia Nelson Limerick have given us some cues.[5] In many ways these books could hardly be more different, but they have some things in common. Their historical terrain is that stretch of generations from the end of the last century until today. Between them Athearn and Limerick write of the persistence of old dreams of development and of recasting earlier, simpler myths into new forms. Most of all, they are concerned with what the West has meant to people, how those impressions have and have not changed, and how it all has made for westerners' sense of themselves and their place.

Several notable books have approached these same questions from other angles. To understand the modern West we need to consider the region's literary and visual iconography. So some writers have studied the evolving images and impressions of the past century or more. Their sources have ranged from accounts of early explorers and travelers to the complex vision of contemporary novelists and artists.[6]

There is, in fact, a "new fiction" that has grown up alongside the new history. The novels and short fiction of Douglas Unger, James Welch, Patricia Henley, Craig Lesley, Kent Haruf, William Kittredge, Louise Erdrich, and David Quammen are stories of disappointment and persistence, grudging accommodations, the ghosts of traditions. Just as the new historians look hard at the romantic idealism of earlier works, these writers break with the easy heroism of the traditional western novel. There is little about promise but much about costs. Dreams have become obsessions and comic lusts. The characters—whether snake-farm proprietors, rodeo Indians, or over-mortgaged turkey farmers—are bound to the country by a bitter affection, a connection that is hard earned and as inescapable as blood kinship.[7]

Novelists take liberties that historians are not allowed, of course. But these stories speak of emotional insights quite in line with recent historical works. They should remind us, I think, that the new history really is part of something larger. It is a maturing understanding of the West, a comprehension that takes into account the full length of its history, its severe limitations and continuing conflicts, its ambivalence, and its often bewildering diversity.

That still leaves room enough and more, of course, for other ways of looking at the western past. Certainly those who are fond of more familiar topics can still find plenty new to read. After all, two of the most successful books of the past few years have been Robert Utley's fine biographies of George Custer and Billy the Kid.[8]

9

AMERICAN WESTS

Historiographical Perspectives

BRIAN W. DIPPIE

WESTERN AMERICAN history today, like the West itself, is not what it used to be. The old themes are fading, the old chronology crumbling. We are now within easy striking distance of one hundred years since Frederick Jackson Turner, following the lead of the Superintendent of the Census, proclaimed the end of the frontier and with it "the closing of a great historic moment": "The peculiarity of American institutions is, the fact that they have been compelled to adapt themselves to the changes of an expanding people—to the changes involved in crossing a continent, in winning a wilderness, and in developing at each area of this progress out of the primitive economic and political conditions of the frontier into the complexity of city life." Then, in 1890, it was all over.[1]

Turner, a young professor at the University of Wisconsin, delivered his paper on "The Significance of the Frontier in American History" at the 1893 meeting of the American Historical Association in Chicago. The setting gave point to his observations. Chicago was hosting a gargantuan fair, the World's Columbian Exposition, commemorating the four-hundredth anniversary of Columbus's discovery of the New World. The session at which Turner spoke met on the exposition grounds where build-

ings, coated in plaster of paris, formed a White City sym-
bolizing civilization's dominion over what in a human life
span had been a wilderness on the shore of Lake Michigan. Chicago's magical growth was, in microcosm, the
story of America. Four centuries since Columbus and a
century since white settlers began occupying the interior
of the continent, there was no frontier, no vast reserve of
"free land" to the west.

Turner's timing was acute, the psychological moment
perfect to find symbolic meaning in recent events. The
Ghost Dance with its vision of a rejuvenated Indian
America, the arrest and killing of Sioux leader Sitting
Bull on December 15, 1890, the culminating tragedy at
Wounded Knee two weeks later—all attested to the fact
that the "winning of the West" was no longer a process
but a fait accompli. Indian wars, a fact of American life
since the first English colony was planted at Jamestown,
were finished. There was no longer an Indian domain to
contest by resort to arms; apart from scattered reservations, it had evaporated, along with the Jeffersonian vision of an agrarian democracy resting on an abundance of
cheap, available land. Whatever else farmer discontent
represented in the 1890s, it manifested an awareness of
the new urban-industrial order. America's twentieth-century future was reaffirmed in Chicago the year after the
exposition when labor unrest erupted into violence and
troops that had served on distant frontiers taming Indians were shipped in to tame Chicago's unemployed instead.

When Turner read his paper, then, portents were
everywhere. Buffalo Bill's Wild West was camped near
the exposition grounds offering the public its immensely
popular version of the frontier experience. Sitting Bull's
horse and the cabin from which the chief was led to his
death were both on display. Frederic Remington, the art-

ist most responsible for the public's perceptions of life in the West, was on hand to tour the midway and take in Buffalo Bill's show; a year later he was back in Chicago to cheer on the troops against the mob—"the gallant Seventh" of Indian war fame, as he put it, against "the malodorous crowd of anarchistic foreign trash." It did not take a prophet to discern a pattern in all this, but Turner reached beyond the obvious. Frontiering, he argued, was not just a colorful but ultimately inconsequential phase of American history. It had actually shaped the American character. On the frontier, environment dominated inherited culture, forcing old customs to conform to new realities. Circumstances promoted individualism, self-reliance, practicality, optimism, and a democratic spirit that rejected external constraints. Taken together, these qualities, reinforced on each succeeding frontier, defined the American. In Turner's reading of United States history, then, the significance of the frontier was simply enormous. Whatever distinguished Americans as a people could be attributed to the cumulative experience of westering: "What the Mediterranean Sea was to the Greeks, breaking the bond of custom, offering new experiences, calling out new institutions and activities, that, and more, the ever retreating frontier has been to the United States." To understand American history, one had to understand western history.[2]

Turner's audience in Chicago received these ideas with polite indifference; in time, however, the frontier thesis gained influential adherents. For almost half a century it served as the master explanation for American development. Problems in facts and interpretation were acknowledged. But Turner's essay offered a coherent, self-flattering vision of the American past, and it seemed prophetic in anticipating American involvement abroad. It would be "rash," Turner wrote, to "assert that the expansive character of American life has now entirely ceased. . . . [T]he American energy will continually demand a wider field for its exercise." Cuba and the Philippines provided early verification. Like any good historical explanation, the frontier thesis seemed to account for past and future. Finally, its sweeping imagery and elegiac tone nicely matched the nostalgic mood that, in the twentieth century, would make the mythic Wild West a global phenomenon. To this day, Turner's frontier thesis remains a primary document in the case for American exceptionalism and a touchstone for students of American culture.[3]

The frontier thesis's inadequacy as an explanation for the complex industrial civilization that suffered through the Great Depression and the rise of the United States to world power outmoded it by the 1940s. But if American history was only temporarily under Turner's shadow, western history has never quite emerged. Turner's West was a fluid concept, an advancing frontier line and a retreating area of free land. If one instead defined the West as a geographical entity—that old standby "the trans-Mississippi West," for example—then over half of western American history proper has transpired since Turner's 1890 cutoff date. What the Louisiana Purchase inaugurated in 1803 is an ongoing story of growth and change. The boundaries of this geographic West are usually set at the forty-ninth parallel to the north, the Mexican border to the south, the Mississippi to the east, and the Pacific Ocean to the west, though historians have found each of these too arbitrary. Some see these boundaries as too inclusive to be meaningful, others as too restrictive. A fur trade historian might want to embrace all North America, a borderlands historian all Mexico, a student of outlawry the Old Southwest, a student of the Indian wars the Old Northwest. Some students contend that the Pacific slope represents a distinct region (certainly it fits least comfortably into general interpretations like Turner's), others that the definition of the American West must be expanded to include Alaska and Hawaii—and beyond.

Periodization has been equally problematical. Turner's frontier West ended with the nineteenth century. To effect a revolution in western history one need simply move forward into the twentieth. Immediately, most of the familiar signposts are missing: fur trade and exploration, Manifest Destiny (overland migration, war with Mexico, Mormonism, the slavery expansion controversy), gold rushes and railroad building, Indian wars, vigilantism and six-gun violence, trail drives and open-range cattle industry, the farmers' frontier, and the Populist revolt. Beyond 1900 a different West emerges, a hard-scrabble land rich in scenery and resources, perhaps, but thinly populated for the most part, chronically short of capital and reliant on government aid, a cultural backwater whose primary appeal nationally is as the setting for a romantic historical myth. (Such is the thrust of Robert G. Athearn's bittersweet meditation *The Mythic West in Twentieth-Century America* [1986]). A romantic myth that is untrue for the present is probably untrue for the past as well. By redefining western history's subject matter, a twentieth-century perspective facilitates reassessment of the nineteenth century too. In 1955 Earl Pomeroy at the University of Oregon published a breakthrough essay, "Toward a Reorientation of Western History: Continuity and Environment," that pulled together many of the dissatisfactions with the frontier thesis and offered a persuasive alternative.[4]

The crux of Pomeroy's revision was in that word "continuity." "America was Europe's 'West' before it was America," a pair of literary critics once observed. Frontiering was a global phenomenon, as old as the idea of the

West, which, Loren Baritz has reminded us, was freighted with significance even for the ancient Greeks. More than a direction or a place, the West was a cultural ideal signifying quest and the prospect of fulfillment in some elusive Elysium. To the west, then, myths ran their course, and America was simply a recent stage in an older dream. Turner was responsive to this enlarged vision, as was the distinguished Texas historian Walter Prescott Webb, who in his 1952 book *The Great Frontier* widened the scope of inquiry to embrace four hundred years of European expansion. But Webb will always be most closely associated with an earlier work, *The Great Plains* (1931), and its compelling case for aridity as the controlling factor in settlement west of the ninety-eighth meridian—the ultimate argument for environmental determinism of the sort Turner had anticipated when he wrote: "The frontier is the line of most rapid and effective Americanization. The wilderness masters the colonist." Thus when western history developed into a separate field of study under Turner's tutelage, it involved isolating not a portion of America from the rest but all America from Europe. Webb carried this a step further, defining a distinct western past determined by a permanent environmental condition. Pomeroy's proposed revision consisted of restoring the severed connections between West and East by demonstrating that most of what passed for western history was better understood as a continuation of eastern development.[5]

Charging the Turnerians with a "radical-environmental bias," Pomeroy argued for the persistence of inherited culture. Indeed, cultural continuity, imitativeness in everything from state constitutions to architectural styles, a deep conservatism only intensified by the process of moving away from established centers, and a constant drive toward respectability and acceptance—

these, not individualism, inventiveness, and an untrammeled democratic spirit, were the real characteristics evinced by the West historically. "Conservatism, inheritance, and continuity bulked at least as large in the history of the West as radicalism and environment," Pomeroy wrote. "The westerner has been fundamentally imitator rather than innovator. . . . He was often the most ardent of conformists." In lieu of the West as path breaker for the nation, Pomeroy substituted the West as a kind of colonial dependency, an area dominated by eastern values, eastern capital, eastern technology, eastern politics. To understand American development, one need no longer look west; but to understand western development, one *had* to look east. That was the essence of Earl Pomeroy's reorientation.[6]

To historians born in the twentieth century, Pomeroy's version of the western past seemed much nearer the mark than Turner's. Moreover, Pomeroy reinvigorated western history by suggesting subjects outside the frontier thesis that merited investigation. An expert himself on the territorial system—closely allied, as he pointed out, to the British colonial system and thus the institutional basis for the colonial relationship between the federal government and the West—Pomeroy urged further study of frontier justice, constitution making, politics, and parties. His call was answered, most notably, by Howard Lamar at Yale, who sought to rectify the historical neglect of the later territorial period with *Dakota Territory, 1861–1889* (1956) and *The Far Southwest, 1846–1912* (1966). In *The Far Southwest* Lamar remarked on the inadequacy of environmental interpretations to account for the varied experiences of New Mexico, Colorado, Utah, and Arizona. Clearly, "artificially drawn boundaries" were historically important. This contradicted Webb's Great Plains hypothesis in the Southwest, as Paul

Sharp's *Whoop-Up Country* (1955) did for the northern Plains. Borders, internal and international, mattered. If Pomeroy's example influenced both Lamar and Sharp, it directly inspired Lewis Gould. In *Wyoming* (1968), Gould argued that the economic priorities of Wyoming citizens overrode social concerns and fostered a "symbiotic relationship" with the federal government, characteristically western, that "put a premium on conservatism and stability."[7]

Territorial studies have remained a staple of revisionist western history. So too, as Gould's argument implies, have economic studies emphasizing the West's dependence on eastern investment capital. In his 1955 essay Pomeroy wrote that the economic history even of "the pre-agricultural frontiers" would come to rest "on the cold facts of investment capital." However, he commented, "we still know the homesteader better than the landlord, the railroad builder better than the railroad operator. The trapper, the prospector, and the cowboy, moving picturesquely over a background of clean air and great distances, hold us more than the tycoons and corporations that dominated them." The revisionists had their work cut out. The fur trade had long been accepted as part of business history. But, in William Goetzmann's memorable phrase, even the trappers, those legendary embodiments of wanderlust, were Jacksonian men, expectant capitalists out to make their fortune. In *Bill Sublette, Mountain Man* (1959), John Sunder detailed one entrepreneurial success story frequently reliant on eastern capital or credit. According to legend, cowboys were second-generation mountain men, fiddle-footed wanderers with guns on their hips. Their status as seasonal agrarian workers might be obscured by romance but, Lewis Atherton noted in *The Cattle Kings* (1961), cowboys were simply hired hands who lived with the environment while their employers, the ranchers, were businessmen out to dominate it. Profit was their motive, and as Gene Gressley showed in *Bankers and Cattlemen* (1966), profit rested on the flow of eastern money into western ranching during the last three decades of the nineteenth century.[8]

The prospector was the third type Pomeroy mentioned whose myth had obscured his economic reality. Nowhere was eastern domination more evident than on the mining frontier. Gold rushes thoroughly disrupted the stately progression of Turner's frontier line, making a shambles of his East-West advance and the stages of social evolution preceding urban civilization. Western urban development had never conformed to Turner's theory, according to Richard Wade, who began his history of early Pittsburgh, Cincinnati, Lexington, Louisville, and St. Louis, *The Urban Frontier* (1959), with an assertion that inspired a literature of its own: "The towns were the spearheads of the frontier." Mining was a case in point. "On the mining frontier the camp—the germ of the city—appeared almost simultaneously with the opening of the region," Duane Smith wrote in *Rocky Mountain Mining Camps* (1967). In California, the flood of gold hunters created an overnight urban civilization with eastern values unaltered by an intervening frontier phase. In his history of the Far West, *The Pacific Slope* (1965), Earl Pomeroy noted that in 1860 California had a population three times that of Oregon, Washington, Idaho, Utah, and Nevada combined and an economy thoroughly integrated into that of the Atlantic Seaboard. A network of eastern merchants and inventors supplied the California miners through West Coast middlemen, a theme in Arthur Throckmorton's *Oregon Argonauts* (1961). In all this, the individual prospector was quickly eclipsed. As men dug deeper, overhead soared and the need for capital with it.

British investors contributed so heavily they made the Far West part of Britain's "invisible empire" and provided the leadership to draw out more-cautious American investors as well, explained Clark Spence in *British Investments and the American Mining Frontier, 1860–1901* (1958). Since 1955, studies of the "cold facts of investment capital" have been prominent in western history. One thing they share in common is the premise that the West was never economically self-sufficient.[9]

In advocating a reorientation, Pomeroy had suggested various paths western historians might follow to discover East-West continuities. The study of frontier justice would open into an examination of western legal history, and precedents would reveal themselves. Inquiry into frontier religion, literacy, education, and architecture would establish the westerner's cultural conservatism. The army in the West should be considered only intermittently a fighting force but continuously a visible manifestation of the federal government and its role in promoting western development. Pomeroy cited W. Turrentine Jackson's *Wagon Roads West* (1952) as a model of what he had in mind. Forest Hill's *Roads, Rails, and Waterways* (1957) and William Goetzmann's *Army Exploration in the American West, 1803–1863* (1959) answered the challenge. Goetzmann went on to refocus the history of western exploration from the exploits of hardy individuals to a collective, nationalistic enterprise in which the federal government played a decisive part, the theme of his Pulitzer Prize-winning *Exploration and Empire* (1966). Western historians have never abandoned the Indian wars, but the army has increasingly been studied in terms of its administrative structure and as a federal partner in the unlocking of western opportunity. Western communities exaggerated the Indian threat in order to enjoy the benefits—payrolls, improved transportation and communication facilities, even an enhanced social life—that an army presence brought. Contractors of every stripe vied for the military's business. The link between East and West, metropolis and hinterland, federal government and frontier citizen, was everywhere a fact of western life.[10]

Pomeroy in 1955 warned western historians against exchanging "new narrowness for old." "An appraisal of western conservatism and continuity," he insisted, "must leave ample room for qualification." But just as Turner had found his attempt to downplay inherited culture construed by others as a denial of inherited culture, Pomeroy's case for continuity over environment has rigidified into a new orthodoxy. The obligatory chapter on the nineteenth-century West in a 1989 United States history text bears the telltale title, "The Trans-Missouri West: Another Colony?" Of course, new orthodoxies elicit new challenges. By submerging regional in national concerns, Pomeroy's colonial interpretation makes western history as such of limited significance. Regional histories are predicated on the assumption that there are meaningful differences between local and national developments. For example, C. Vann Woodward contended that the South was distinguished from the rest of the nation by a unique past marked by the un-American experience of guilt arising from slavery, military defeat, and occupation. History, more than any other factor, accounted for southern distinctiveness. Similarly, in making the West synonymous with frontiering, Turner had established fluid boundaries in time and space whereby all America was once the West, and the last area to experience frontier conditions was the most American of all. Thus a region roughly corresponding to Webb's Great Plains was characterized as the last frontier. Pomeroy's model robbed the West of its distinctiveness, making it simply an appendage of the

East that was neither exceptional nor especially consequential historically.[11]

Opposition to Pomeroy's colonial thesis has usually
worked some variation on the exceptionalist premise. In
his essay, Pomeroy had made a pitch for twentieth-century western history: "The historian cannot easily ignore
the challenge to explain this new present in which he
lives and works, a present in which West and East are visibly more alike than they were in Turner's day." Gerald
Nash, the first to attempt a synthesis of twentieth-century western history, rejected Turner's frontier chronology with its 1890 terminal date and accepted colonialism
as a feature of western life well into the twentieth century. But, Nash maintained, World War II liberated the
West from its political, economic, and cultural dependency on the East. The year 1945 became a new dividing
line in western history, signifying the moment not when
the frontier passed into oblivion but when the West
passed out of colonialism to become "a pacesetter for the
nation." However, it is only by focusing on the Sunbelt,
and especially southern California—that historical
"great exception" with its population still out of all proportion to that of the surrounding states—that Nash was
able to make much of a case for western pacesetting. As
William Robbins has written,

> The question remains whether southern California
> and the urban Southwest are an appropriate model
> for explaining structural alterations in the relation-
> ship between East and West. The focus on "trendset-
> ting" and California "lifestyles" emphasizes the su-
> perficial and ignores the persistence of fundamental
> problems—of race and class inequality, of unre-
> stricted industrial and urban growth, and of the in-

creasing hegemony of those urban power centers over much of the West.[12]

One needs to be cautious in making parts of the West synonymous with the whole and, out of regional pride, discarding too readily the unflattering fact of western dependency. Such caution informed Patricia Nelson Limerick's provocative new synthesis *The Legacy of Conquest* (1987). Limerick was much less sanguine than Nash about the evidence for western trendsetting, arguing instead for a continuity in western history uninterrupted by any turning points. It is *this* continuity—not links to the East but the defining western experience "of a place undergoing conquest and never fully escaping its consequences"—that validates a regional approach, investing the geographical West with a historical imperative akin to Woodward's burden of southern history. A legacy of conquest, of course, is consonant with Pomeroy's colonial model. But Limerick in effect viewed the East-West relationship from a western perspective rather than a national one. "With its continuity restored," she wrote, "Western American history carries considerable significance for American history as a whole. Conquest forms the historical bedrock of the whole nation, and the American West is a preeminent case study in conquest and its consequences." By insisting that the American West is significant both in national terms and on its own terms, Limerick reclaimed a prominent place for its history even while rejecting the frontier thesis. She titled her introduction, "Closing the Frontier and Opening Western History." It is time for historians to put away the toys of childhood and get on with the sterner duties of adulthood.[13]

The nature of popular western frontier history is behind much of the uneasiness Limerick articulates. Western historians regularly berate themselves for failing to keep up with trends in the discipline. The field has been characterized as glorying in narrative at the expense of analysis, in the colorful and peripheral to the neglect of the ordinary and substantial. In his revisionist critique Pomeroy conceded that too often the "flabbier minds" among graduate students were drawn to the field because it was considered intellectually undemanding. In short, hard riding makes for easy reading, and the very qualities that explained the public's love affair with the West also explained western history's decline in academic circles. Michael Malone and Richard Roeder, in a 1969 anthology, *The Montana Past*, observed that frontier historians of the state had "concentrated less upon the historically significant than upon the romantically colorful—road agents, vigilantes, cowboys and Indians." In the interpretive history of Montana they coauthored a few years later, Malone and Roeder noted: "Seekers after 'Wild West' lore will find nothing here about such Montana favorites as Calamity Jane, Liver-eating Johnson, or Kid Curry. We have focused instead upon the shaping of present-day Montana." Either western history matures like the West itself or sinks into irrelevance.[14]

Suggestions for revitalizing western history have been pretty conventional: Find out where everyone else is going and follow suit. In particular, there has been much handwringing over a perceived tardiness in adopting "new history" agendas. "If present historians fail to shift their focus, emphasis, and interest to issues not considered to have been of major significance a century ago, then the field will follow the dinosaur and the dodo down the path to well-deserved extinction," Roger Nichols warned in the introduction to *American Frontier and Western Issues* (1986). Of course, the same warnings were issuing forth about *all* history a few years ago: Learn to quantify, adopt social science methodologies, and realign the very nature of historical inquiry and expression or fade into academic oblivion. Intellectual history was put on particular notice: Shape up or suffer the consequences. But western historians should proceed cautiously in this latest reorientation. The most extravagant claims for the new social history, for example, have been recanted, and dire predictions about the early demise of "old-fashioned" history have failed to materialize. It is apparent now that too often new history's advocates adopted the strategy of Melville's lightning-rod salesman and sold fear rather than necessity.[15]

Nevertheless, western history has been continually exhorted to get on track, and Nichols ticked off some possibilities: comparative and interdisciplinary history; geographic, economic, and social mobility and the processes of community building; class, race, gender, and ethnicity; corporate activity and labor issues—the stuff of the new social history. Others have mentioned educational, family, environmental, technological, recreational, and legal history as areas worthy of more study. The proliferation of possible subjects is evident in every issue of the *Western Historical Quarterly*, the journal of the Western History Association. The table of contents, a running record of recent articles topically arranged, and the book review section serve as sensitive barometers of recent trends in the field. To date, the net effect of the new history revolution has been new topics rather than a consistent new direction for western history, fragmentation rather than synthesis. Although "urban and social historians have succeeded in calling into question the dominant conceptual framework," Spencer C. Olin, Jr., has written, "they have not yet substituted a new one." Instead, they have leaned rather heavily on an old one, Earl Pomeroy's colonial model. Nor have they entirely rejected Turner's frontier thesis, paradoxical though that seems.[16]

Turner's thesis is now notorious for excluding women and everyone whose skin was dark or language was not English. Indians were obstacles handy for demarcating the frontier line and eliciting pioneer traits in the white men who would overcome them; women apparently stayed in the East until the frontier had passed and the land was tidied up and made presentable; Mexicans and other ethnics never existed. In truth, Pomeroy's reorientation was not especially concerned with these lacunae in western history either. Pomeroy was out of sympathy with the emphasis placed on "local foreign groups" and cited the role of Spanish culture in southwestern history as having been exaggerated. But the ineluctable Hispanic fact in the West, coupled with academic interest in ethnicity, multiculturalism, and social structure, has made the Mexican American more prominent than ever in the literature on western minorities. The twentieth-century orientation of many studies fosters the impression that some of what passes for social history is pure sociology. Mario Barrera's *Race and Class in the Southwest* (1979) announces itself as an extended historical and interdisciplinary case study, but description of the colonial nature of Hispanic economic exploitation is subordinate to the amplification of a theoretical model. Sarah Deutsch's *No Separate Refuge* (1987) is a veritable compendium of social history themes. "By tracing the transformation of work, family, and community roles of Chicanas from 1880 to 1940 through patterns of migration, organization, and interaction," she noted, her book "reveals the nexus of culture, class and gender in a new light."[17]

Indians stand outside ethnic history as a field unto themselves. In 1955 Pomeroy had been more concerned with downplaying Indian wars and the like than with advocating new approaches, though his own study of the territorial system related to the formulation of federal Indian policy and the local administration of Indian affairs. Both subjects remain important to students of Indian-white relations, who have followed another trend in western history by placing much greater emphasis on twentieth-century developments. But policy and administrative studies have been labeled old-fashioned by partisans of ethnohistory, a fusion of anthropology and history intended to break free of the habit of viewing Indians as obstacles to white advance or as helpless victims of white avarice by presenting them instead as major actors in a cultural interchange affected by a multitude of variables, many of them Indian centered. Pomeroy's colonial model has been of interest primarily to the historians of Indian-white relations who have become increasingly aware of the possibilities offered by comparative studies—the Sioux and Zulu wars, for example—and the direct applicability of the government's Indian experience to problems in overseas colonial administration.[18]

The colonial interpretation has proven most influential in western women's history, which, despite all the nay saying, has flourished of late. Substantial monographs on women in fur trade society, army wives and daughters, women teachers, women on the overland trails, farm women, prostitutes, divorcées, widows, and urban women have forever altered the sentimental stereotypes of sunbonneted pioneer mothers and soiled doves with hearts of gold. Pomeroy's argument for cultural continuity has been echoed in discussions of one key issue: Did the move West liberate women from conventional sex roles? John Mack Faragher concluded *Women and Men on the Overland Trail* (1979) with a flat negative: "The move West called upon people not to change but to transfer old sexual roles to a new but altogether familiar environment." Although confessing that she had hoped to find otherwise, Julie Roy Jeffrey in *Frontier Women* (1979) was forced to agree: "The frontier experience served to reinforce many conventional familial and cultural ideas. . . . The concept of woman as lady, the heart of domestic ideology, survived."[19]

Jeffrey did detect some changes in women's roles attributable to frontier circumstances: Prostitutes, for instance, were treated as individuals in the West rather than simply as a class. Polly Welts Kaufman in *Women Teachers on the Frontier* (1984) also strained against the limitations implied by the colonial interpretation, noting that the decision of the two hundred fifty women who went west to teach for the National Board of Popular Education before the Civil War was influenced by a desire for independence and control over their lives, though she conceded that teaching was among the few occupations that met "society's expectations for women." Liberation plays an even larger part in Paula Petrik's *No Step Backward* (1987). Her examination of a range of women's roles in a single setting—Helena, Montana—led to the neo-Turnerian conclusion that the move west did change things for some women, at least during the frontier period. Challenges to Pomeroy's model have been advanced by scholars working in other new areas as well. Imitativeness would seem axiomatic in western legal history, for example, but innovativeness, according to Kermit Hall, was often necessitated by local social and economic conditions in the West. Challenges aside, however, colonialism appears pretty much entrenched as the explanation of choice for western historians.[20]

There is another current strain of western historical scholarship that holds particular promise for students of American culture: It makes the western myth itself its subject. Americans have loved the myth with an abiding, though some say waning, passion. It has circled the globe in its appeal. To its critics, it is an invitation to the wrong set of values. It embodies an essentially conservative ethos—rugged individualism, stern justice, indifference or hostility to women and ethnic others, exploitation of the environment, development at any cost. It also embodies the core of the American dream, the polestar for generations of immigrants who sought a greater measure of human happiness in a land of unrivaled wealth and opportunity.[21]

Long before Henry Nash Smith's *Virgin Land* (1950) opened a fruitful avenue of inquiry in American studies, Walter Prescott Webb observed that the Great Plains had touched the popular imagination as a setting for romance and adventure. Distance made the mundane magical, the ordinary exotic. Indeed, Webb pointed out, the image of the Wild West is largely the work of outsiders meeting outside needs. There seems no escaping eastern domination. Pomeroy himself traced an aspect of this cultural imperialism in his imaginative *In Search of the Golden West* (1957). The West, he found, became whatever the eastern tourist wanted it to be: "For sixty or seventy years . . . tourists had to be reassured, and westerners felt that they had to assure them, that the West was no longer wild and woolly—until fashions changed and it was time to convince them that it was as wild as it ever had been." A parallel argument is advanced in Goetzmann's *Exploration and Empire*, where the explorer is characterized as culturally programmed to find and to see certain things and not others. Thus perception is critical to understanding the explorer's achievement. Similarly, the myths and legends surrounding certain individuals become ways of understanding American culture.[22]

Casting about for examples of how western history

might successfully merge "into the mainstream of American history" and "rejoin the rest of the profession," Roger Nichols suggested that instead of asking, "Who shot first at the OK Corral," one could ask, "What social or economic forces led to community violence and the temporary breakdown of law and order that incident illustrates." One could also ask why a relatively minor incident like the shootout at the OK Corral has seized and held the American imagination for over a century, and why figures like Wyatt Earp and Doc Holliday still command attention. There is an established tradition in western history of separating fiction from fact to get at the truth behind such storied individuals and episodes, epitomized by the cranky, opinionated and readable bibliographies of Ramon Adams. Don Russell's *The Lives and Legends of Buffalo Bill* (1960), Joseph Rosa's *They Called Him Wild Bill* (1974), William A. Settle, Jr.'s *Jesse James Was His Name; or, Fact and Fiction Concerning the Careers of the Notorious James Brothers of Missouri* (1966), Robert De Arment's *Bat Masterson* (1979), and Jack Burrows's *John Ringo* (1987) are good examples of this approach to biography. Kent Ladd Steckmesser's *The Western Hero in History and Legend* (1965) covers a clutch of key figures—Kit Carson, Billy the Kid, Wild Bill Hickok, and George Armstrong Custer—all of whom have received individual attention. For example, Ramon Adams was assiduous in exposing the legends surrounding Billy the Kid in *A Fitting Death for Billy the Kid* (1960). But cultural historians find the legend more arresting—and revealing—than the facts. Strip Billy the Kid of his myth and little of historical consequence remains, as Robert Utley has ably demonstrated. But the mythic Billy the Kid is full of interest, for reasons Stephen Tatum explained in *Inventing Billy the Kid* (1982). Tatum's approach accepts myths and legends as facts for a different kind of history—the study of how people conceive the past in mythic patterns that define a culture and its value system.[23]

Since cultural values shift over time, myths, in order to remain relevant, shift their meanings as well. If, as most would agree, the major challenge facing western history is to relate past to present in a meaningful way, the mythic approach has much to offer. It accounts for continuity *and* change. Custer is dead, his Last Stand long over. Why then do people continue to refight it? Why can they still envision it? And why are passions still aroused by the man? We may dismiss Custer as a minor figure historically. But he was once a national hero, a martyr to cause and country held up as a model for America's youth. His defenders still think him a paragon if not a saint, and he has been compared to Jesus, who died on *that* hill. His detractors regard him as a racist villain, fit symbol for America's mistreatment of its native peoples: "Custer died for your sins." In 1988 a Sioux activist likened him to Adolf Hitler and argued that the Custer Battlefield National Monument was as welcome in Indian country as a Hitler monument would be in Israel. In either guise, hero or villain, Custer continues to function as a vital presence in the public's imagination. Why?[24]

The study of western myth is closely allied to that of western literature, art, and film. Elliott West has rightly noted the disproportionate attention paid the western movie. After all, its plots were borrowed from stories, and the artists taught the filmmakers how to see. The 1986 PBS Television series "The West of the Imagination" and the companion volume of the same name by William Goetzmann and his son Will should go far in righting the balance and familiarizing a large audience with the mythic approach. Indeed, studies in western imagery— art, illustration, photography—frequently make connec-

tions between specific visual and general cultural perceptions. In similar fashion, western literature has been
mined for its symbolic content and examined for its role
in shaping popular ideas. Richard Slotkin's *Regeneration
through Violence* (1973) and *The Fatal Environment*
(1985), both grounded in literature, are the most ambitious attempts yet at tracing patterns of frontier mythology and their historical consequences. As well, his books
attest to the fact that far from glorifying old verities,
myth analysis can offer a searching perspective on American development. On the one hand, works like Slotkin's
assume something Turner labored to prove: American exceptionalism—that is, an American culture revealed in its
distinctive mythic patterns. On the other, they may best
facilitate a critical examination of those qualities that
were supposedly fostered by frontiering and that, according to Turner, combined to form the American character:
"Where are the women in this tradition?" asked Helen
Winter Stauffer and Susan Rosowski in *Women and Western American Literature* (1982), and it is a question that
cuts to the heart of a male myth steeped in escapist fantasies and as revealing for what it excludes as what it contains. In the western myth, Indians were simply part of
the savage nature the white pioneer was expected to subdue, a test of the sort that meets any quester after Elysium. The Indian *fact* offers its own rebuttal: The white
man's occupation of America was an armed invasion—
nothing more, nothing less—and the five-hundredth anniversary of Columbus's "discovery" of the New World is going to bring a response quite different from Turner's
celebration.[25]

When one moves from individuals and events and
omissions to the qualities or traits revered in western
myth, it is apparent that the myth generates its own critiques, its own counterimages—an anti-mythic literature.

Rugged individualists taming a raw wilderness? Roderick Nash's *Wilderness and the American Mind* (1982) and Lee Clark Mitchell's *Witnesses to a Vanishing America* (1981) show that frontiering and its apotheosis of ax and plow created a contrary reaction, a conservationist outlook that deplored the wastefulness inherent in pioneering and opened the way to resource management and federal controls. Buoyant optimism and the mastery of material things? The lunacy of such hopeful frontier slogans as "Rain follows the plow" was revealed in the 1930s when the interior of the continent turned into a dust bowl and precipitated an internal migration that exposed the hollow promise of western opportunity. The California dream? Ask the Okies. Cowboy freedom in a spacious land where all were equal? Ask the multitude of western wage earners who found the pay low, conditions hard, strife endemic, social structures rigid, and independence illusory. Or ask any racial minority struggling to get ahead in the West. Six-gun justice and self-reliance? The chilling rate of contemporary violence would seem rebuttal enough to such a cherished tradition. In fact, frontier violence was probably exaggerated—as Robert Dykstra demonstrated in *The Cattle Towns* (1968)—but the legitimation accorded violence by the frontier tradition may not be. Abundant natural resources ensuring all a chance to prosper? The anti-myth points to the depletion and spoliation of a rich heritage, a destructive "Myth of Superabundance," selfishness and resource monopolization, agribusiness, a boom-and-bust economy, a continuing reliance on the federal government. More colonialism and precious little individual opportunity. Myth, after all, is myth.[26]

For the historian, the western myth offers a skewed but revealing national portrait, a study not in what was, but what once seemed desirable. To the extent that it was always false, we have a measure of the distance between expectation and reality in western and American history. To the extent that it now seems unbecoming, we have a measure of the distance between the values of yesterday and today. The myth and the anti-myth are keys to the western past and the western present that can also unlock the American past and the American present. One can ask no more of a regional history.

But bromides will not cure a persistent malaise. Western historians remain convinced that their field is in crisis, the last roundup imminent. In the end, perhaps the clinching argument for the colonial model is this self-consciousness about their status within the historical profession. Nothing betokens the colonial more surely than a sense of inferiority. It has been a hard fall from the heady days when Turner held a chair at Harvard and frontiering defined national history to the reproaches of Pomeroy and Nichols. Told that their traditional concerns belong to the "cactus and sagebrush" school of history (literally the bush leagues), western historians are apologetic, defensive, uncertain of their legitimacy: Let us hang our heads that we are not what we are not. A little assertiveness might be more in order. Historians who spend a lifetime studying the varieties and vagaries of seventeenth-century Puritanism or putting a New England town under the microscope feel no compunction in dismissing western historians as parochial, their concerns as glorified antiquarianism. Cowboys and Indians.

Patricia Limerick put a brave face on her experiences at Harvard's Charles Warren Center. None of her colleagues there "found enormous significance in the American West," and this disinterest "only added to the value of their company" by stimulating spirited discussion. But other western historians are understandably discouraged by such encounters. Limerick's thesis could well have been honed in her exchanges with the other Harvard fellows—conquest takes many forms, as she well knows, and cultural imperialism is a potent one. Dismissiveness seems not a stimulant but part of a pattern: Easterners prefix everything western with the all-purpose pejorative "cowboy"—cowboy music, cowboy stories, cowboy art, cowboy history—the easier to ignore it. And they dismiss the yokels "out there" in "flyover country" with their cowboy hats, red necks and empty faces designed, as Leslie Fiedler reported years ago after escaping from the horrors of intellectual isolation in Montana back to the safety of New York, principally for squinting into the setting sun. Eastern superiority and condescension and western sensitivity, resentment, and powerful need for approval—these are the very definition of a colonial relationship. And this relationship still casts a long shadow over western history, which will remain in its perpetual state of crisis just so long as it feels it must take all its cues from others.[27]

PART III

THE GLOBAL WEST

10

BEYOND THE LAST FRONTIER
Toward a New Approach
to Western American History

MICHAEL P. MALONE

IN A RECENT address to the Western History Association, Howard Lamar of Yale University noted the remarkable progress made over the past quarter century in advancing the scholarship of western history. Traditional frontier topics have been treated with impressive new conceptualizations and methodologies, and long-neglected social, ethnic, female, and twentieth-century subjects are now being addressed fully and with greater sophistication. Indeed, there is, as Lamar put it, "much to celebrate."[1]

Yet most of us who labor in western studies still bear the onus, as heavy as it was twenty-five years ago, of working in a field that is deemed by many to be intellectually barren and cluttered with trivia. Our own Walter Prescott Webb said as much three decades ago, and a number of our colleagues say so today. Many historians still confuse the West as a defunct frontier process with the West as a geographical region of the United States, and this garbled terminology serves to hinder serious study of the region's modern past and to nudge western history toward antiquarianism. Several leading universities in the West have deemphasized the study of their own region, as if to say that it has no significant history, or at least that its history is less relevant than, say, that of old

Byzantium or Central Asia.[2] In demonstrating their cosmopolitanism, these universities default on their responsibility as cultural leaders of their own communities and
puzzle citizens who harbor the quaint notion that their
homeland has a significant history.

It is my contention in this chapter that western regional history is stigmatized because western historians
rely on the frontier thesis advanced by Frederick Jackson
Turner and modified by Walter Prescott Webb. Not only is
Turner's paradigm timeworn, it is also the fundamental
cause of the mischievous treatment of frontier and West—
as if the terms were synonymous. In the following pages, I
will reassess this paradigm and its influence and argue in
favor of a revised approach to interpreting the region and
its history. This is attempted, of course, not in the spirit of
having seen a burning bush but rather as one more step
forward in an ongoing historiographic journey.

The Turner Thesis, first articulated in 1893, is familiar enough to readers that there is little point in summa-
rizing it at length. But a look back at the frontier interpretation and its evolution over time is essential to set
the stage for suggesting some new directions. The key
point of the young University of Wisconsin historian that
captivated the discipline of American history for four decades was that the United States was no cultural appendage of Europe but rather a new and superior civilization.
The source of its liberation from the Old World was the
cycle of frontiering, which lasted from the early seventeenth to the late nineteenth centuries. The West was defined both as place—a zone of free land beyond the western edge of settlement—and as process—where social
atomization shattered mores. Turner's frontier was a sociocultural furnace that forged a new Americanism em-
bodying democracy, individualism, pragmatism, and a
healthy nationalism.[3]

Inevitably, such an overstated environmental determinism, neglecting the forces of cultural inheritance and other historical factors, provoked a reaction. Critics pointed out the imprecision of Turner's terminology and assertions, the fact that such American institutions as parliamentary democracy clearly derived from the European heritage, and the obvious inadequacy of a rurally focused frontier thesis to explain the rise of an industrial/urban-based economy and social order.[4] By midcentury, in the broad field of United States history, the Turner Thesis still counted heavily, but only as one among several interpretations.

In the subfield of western history, however, the frontier interpretation figured more largely, though potent criticisms surfaced. Among the most telling of these criticisms were Henry Nash Smith's *Virgin Land* (1950) and Earl Pomeroy's articles "Toward a Reorientation of Western History" (1955) and "The Changing West" (1962). Smith believed that Turner's hypothesis was part of a pastoral tradition of frontier mythology that obscured the complex reality of the American heritage. Pomeroy's work, more damaging and highly influential, argued that Turner's paradigm neglected the sociocultural imitativeness of pioneers and especially the critical importance of western cities that served more as conductors of tradition than as matrices of innovation.[5]

Yet the Turner Thesis has proven remarkably resilient. Foremost among the neo-Turnerians, Ray Allen Billington deserves much of the credit for the endurance of Turner's work. In a corpus of writings that includes a leading text (expertly revised by Martin Ridge), a definitive biography of Turner, and an impressive revision of the paradigm itself (*America's Frontier Heritage* [1966]), Billington refashioned the Turner Thesis, sheared its overstatements, and fleshed out nuances and subtleties that made it plausible to scholars no longer satisfied with monocausal explanations. Recently, a new generation of historians has found lasting merit in Turner's approach. These include Jackson K. Putnam, who has penned an excellent appraisal; Michael C. Steiner, who stresses Turner's sectional interpretations over his frontier thesis; and William Cronon, who imaginatively argues that the new environmental history actually arises naturally from the old frontier hypothesis.[6]

Texas historian Walter Prescott Webb set forth an interpretation that in one sense paralleled the Turner Thesis, yet actually served to amend and advance it. Webb insisted that he had intentionally not read Turner before articulating his thesis, but he did not hesitate to call himself a Turnerian. In his monumental work *The Great Plains* (1931), Webb advanced an interpretation of the region that seems at least as environmentally deterministic as Turner's. He depicted the aridity of the Great Plains as an overriding shaping force that compelled settlers to shed or modify their humid-lands institutions in order to cope with such a drastically new environment. These changes involved new technologies such as barbed wire and deep-reaching windmills and new laws governing land and water. In one of the most graphic images in western historiography, Webb viewed the ninety-eighth meridian as an "institutional" fault line beyond which old institutions and mores had to be refashioned to cope with aridity.[7]

Both lay and professional audiences welcomed *The Great Plains*, and Webb soon found himself heralded as a leading regionalist. Over the years, he broadened his focus. In *The Great Frontier* (1952), he again revealed the range of his imagination, applying the Turnerian approach to world history since 1500, which he viewed as governed by expanding frontiers and a burgeoning European "metropolis" in a "400-year boom." In his wry *Harper's* essay of 1957, "The American West: Perpetual Mirage," he expanded his arid-lands interpretation to the entire West.[8]

In the subdiscipline of western United States history, Webb's arid-lands interpretation has had a lasting impact that compares favorably with Turner's. Others pursued his environmental emphasis in new directions, the most formidable being the Kansan James C. Malin. A pioneer of interdisciplinary and quantitative methodologies that are now widely accepted, Malin resembled Marc Bloch and the French *Annales* historians in his emphasis upon "holistic" approaches to subregions and rural areas. In his studies of the Central Plains "grasslands," he was truly a prophetic forerunner of today's historians of human-ecological relationships. The distinguished historical geographer D. W. Meinig also presented distinctive environmental interpretations, in more sophisticated terms than did either Webb or Malin.[9] In the final analysis, however, neither Malin nor Meinig nor anyone else has ever rivaled Webb's achievement in raising up a truly regional paradigm that both juxtaposed with and complemented Turner's frontier emphasis.

Arguably, we should consider the Turner and Webb theses entirely apart from each other. For, while Turner's environmental interpretation focused upon frontiering and a *to*-the-region approach, Webb's focused upon social evolution *within* the region itself, after first settlement. In this sense, Webb was a genuine western regionalist, whereas Turner was not. However, Webb was, after all, a Turnerian, and it seems clear that rather than contrasting with one another, these two models of western history commingled in a homogeneous blend. Both men wrote institutional history and focused upon frontiers and pioneering. Both were preoccupied with the frontier's closing and were pessimistic about what the frontier's end portended for American institutions. And both were skeptical of "new frontiers," which is ironic in that Webb lived long enough to witness President Kennedy's use of that term for his administration's program.

So, to what extent has this historiographic legacy confined us? Substantially and in several ways, it would seem. It has led us to focus too much of our attention upon frontiering and, concomitantly, to neglect the study of the modern West. As scholars like William Cronon and Patricia Nelson Limerick note, it has led us to conceptualize the West rigidly in the context of "closing" frontiers; and as Michael Steiner argues, its pastoral focus has tended to avoid cities and the industries and societies they house as somehow un-American. For a long time, Turner's heroic frontier seemed devoid of females and his emphasis upon assimilation and Americanization worked against serious consideration of the region's ethnic diversity.[10] In these and other ways, the historiographic legacy of the West, more so than that of the United States at large, has been confining, in some ways truly antiquarian.

Of course, conceding these weaknesses, it should be countered that western regional history has certain strengths that contrast favorably with serious shortcomings in general United States historiography. At a time when many respected voices are calling for a return to good narrative history that appeals to a broad public, western historians can point to a long tradition of excellent frontier narratives that reaches from Francis Parkman to Bernard De Voto, David Lavender, and Robert Utley. Although the use of quantification and the application of the methodologies of the "new" social, economic, and political histories came slowly to western studies, they did come, and in commendable fashion, as the work

The wide open spaces of the American West exist in fact as well as in myth. As this photograph shows, a realistic picture of the West is not necessarily dreary and dull. Used on the first panel and on the poster for the Trails through Time exhibit, the image conveys a sense of the continuity of western American history: The twentieth century's Interstate 15 follows the route of the nineteenth century's Old Spanish Trail, through Cedar Valley, Utah. Courtesy Frank Jensen.

(Above) A strong sense of the long-term presence of Indian people in the region provides the foundation of the New Western History. The stairway at Acoma Pueblo, New Mexico, represents that long history; it illustrates, as well, the impact Indian people made on what some white Americans called "unsettled wilderness." Before the arrival of Europeans, Indian people had already had a major impact on the West; their trails, running south to north as well as east to west, add complexity and drama to the old model of white Americans sweeping westward into vacant space. Courtesy Jerry Jacka.

(Bottom opposite) Specializing in exposed rock, western landscapes offered abundant opportunities for travelers to register their presence. Inscription Rock, in El Morro National Monument, New Mexico, records the travels of Spanish explorers and colonizers in the seventeenth century. Two centuries later, Anglo-American explorers added their names, marking their comparatively late entry into an already complicated regional history. Courtesy Museum of New Mexico.

(Above) In the stereotyped world of mythmakers, Westerners came in two forms: Indians representing "savagery" and white people representing "civilization." In the real West, however, the cast of characters was immeasurably more complex. Westerners were often African Americans and Asian Americans as well as whites and Indians, and even the labels "white" and "Indian" hide the region's complexity. "Indian" meant many different tribes; "white people" included English, Cornish, Welsh, Irish, Portuguese, Italian, Greek, French, Flemish, German, Austrian, Polish, Slovenian, Czech, Danish, Swedish, Finnish, Norwegian, Russian, Serbian, Spanish, and Basque. The meeting of the Santa Fe Trail traders Bernard Seligman, Zadoc Staab, and Lehman Spiegelberg with two members of the Kiowa tribe embodies the American West's standing as one of the great meeting grounds of the world. Courtesy Colorado Endowment for the Humanities.

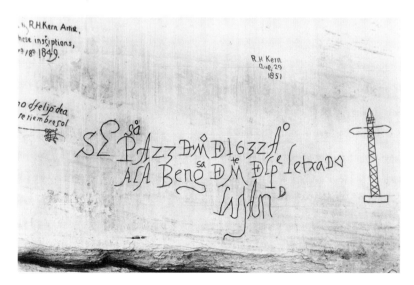

(Left) Not all relations between traders and Indians were friendly. Although many traders were well intentioned, they were nonetheless disruptive trespassers in Indian territory. They brought new diseases to which the Indians had no immunity, and they introduced the addictive drug alcohol. Many used liquor to lubricate transactions with Indians, as illustrated in this Indian hide drawing of a trader's use of alcohol to manipulate and disorient his customer. Courtesy Henry Holt & Company.

(Left) The harsh winter of 1886–87 was a terrible blow to the Plains cattle industry. The industry's sharp decline, combined with the strong currents of nostalgia in western thinking, led to a widespread image of the "disappearing cowboy," with that romantic occupation going the way of the lost frontier. In fact, the cattle business remained an important, if still unstable, part of the western economy, and cowboys—sometimes driving pickup trucks, but cowboys nonetheless—continued to work the cattle. Cattle drives, like this one through a Wyoming town, still go on in the twentieth century. Courtesy Denver Public Library Western History Collection.

(Right) In spite of the old habit of calling the migration into the western United States "westering," many of the emigrants were in fact "eastering." People originating in the Pacific Basin—immigrants from China, Japan, Korea, the Philippines, Southeast Asia, Polynesia, and Micronesia—provided essential labor for western industries, supplied miners and were miners themselves, and added considerably to the diversity of languages and customs in western America. Courtesy Sweetwater County Museum.

The tin can made an
early entrance into
western American his-
tory. Miners, especially,
did not have either the
opportunity or the incli-
nation to produce their
own food; imported sup-
plies tied them to the
economy of the eastern
United States. A land so
open and endless
seemed to provide the
happiest opportunities
for littering; a transient
population could dine
one night and leave the
trash behind the next
morning. The dream of
the West as an end-
lessly absorptive dump-
ing ground has had an
extraordinary power. In
the late twentieth cen-
tury, with nuclear
waste, pesticide pollu-
tion, and salinity
buildup in irrigated
soils, that dream has
lost its power to soothe.
Courtesy Colorado His-
torical Society.

(Top opposite) For traditional historians, the topic of the "military in the West" referred exclusively to the frontier army. If anything, the military played a larger
role in western economies in the twentieth century than in the nineteenth. In the
course of national expansion, Washington funded armies and forts to protect trade
and settlement, built roads, and subsidized railroads and towns. In the twentieth
century, with large expanses of western lands under federal control, the West has
been affected by federally funded land and water projects and military programs,
including western military bases and nuclear testing. These World War II–era air-
men load a bomber at Lowry Field, later Lowry Air Force Base, in Denver. Courtesy Colorado Historical Society.

(Bottom opposite) A clear favorite among the people working on the Trails exhibit,
this photograph of determined souls pushing a stalled car through mud on U.S. 550
in Colorado offers a fine illustration of the ongoing difficulties of western transportation. Moreover, in the summer of 1989, the picture seemed to symbolize the struggle to get the study of western American history free from its ruts; in the following
two years, the path toward the revitalization of western historiography proved a
great deal smoother than the muddy road that stretched before these Coloradoans
in 1930. Courtesy Colorado State Archives.

(Above) Not all western workers came, or come, to the West to stay. Often encouraged by the U.S. federal government, Hispanic laborers crossed the U.S.-Mexico border to harvest western produce. Although some intended to settle permanently in the United States, others hoped to return, financially improved, to their homes. Generally, migrant families lived in poor conditions at the mercy of their employers, but western migrant laborers often spoke out for better lives. This panel protested workers' housing conditions at Fort Lupton, Colorado; panel members are Shirley Sandage, Rudolph Dominguez, Jim Mason, Gregorio Salazar, and Leonel Sanchez. Courtesy Denver Public Library Western History Collection.

(Bottom opposite) The rivers of the arid West posed a particular challenge to the Anglo-American determination to master nature. Resolved to show that even the most trying rivers could be used for navigation, Lt. Joseph Christmas Ives tried to take a steamboat up the Colorado River in 1857, represented here in Mojave Canyon. He hoped the steamboat would carry a lesson to the Indians on the power of white Americans, but, as he wrote in his *Report upon the Colorado River of the West*, his "slow progress and the long detentions" proved "a source of intense satisfaction and fun" to the Indians. "They can foot it on the shore," he wrote, "or pole along a raft upon the river without interruption; and that we should spend days in doing what they can accomplish in half as many hours, strikes them as unaccountably stupid." Their "gleeful consciousness of superiority" kept the Indians, if not Ives, "in excellent humor." Courtesy Colorado Historical Society.

Far from dwindling after the "end of the frontier" in 1890, migration into the American West accelerated in the twentieth century and kept its international character. Recently the West has seen a large influx of Southeast Asian refugees, like Kim Cha Vang, a Hmong mother and refugee in Salt Lake City. The themes of the nineteenth century reappear in the twentieth: The West keeps its role as a refuge and as a place where diversity can provide the occasion for conflict, education, puzzlement, distress, or celebration. Courtesy Utah Arts Council (photo by Carol Edison).

The western army faced the unenviable task of mediating between settlers who wanted more land and safer trade routes and Indians who fought to protect their traditional lives and lands from emigrant incursions. Charged to protect whites from Indians and Indians from whites, this group of "Buffalo soldiers" had good reason to take advantage of this opportunity to unwind. Courtesy Colorado Endowment for the Humanities.

Source of many of the strongest and most persistent images of the West as a romantic realm of male adventure, the artist Frederic Remington did on occasion recognize the unevenness of the path of progress in the American West. His drawing *A Bit of a Rough Road* conveys the precariousness of western transportation, the intractability of western nature, and the vulnerability of western enterprises to sudden upsets. Courtesy Denver Public Library Western History Collection.

A BIT OF ROUGH ROAD.

With its mountains and deserts, vast distances and uncooperative rivers, the American West makes relatively few concessions to the human desire for easy travel. Letting nature determine the route on some occasions, humans have at other times refused to take nature's "no" for an answer. To men and women of a certain attitude, the deep, uncrossable canyon of the Colorado River became a challenge to design and construct a bridge, a tribute to the Anglo-American determination to cover the region with a transportational network of more or less straight lines. Courtesy Utah State Historical Society.

In the traditional version of western history, the frontier was a struggle between humans and nature, a struggle that concluded with victory for the humans. Reality carried a different message. Floods, blizzards, dust storms, droughts, avalanches, and landslides, like this one at Thistle, Utah, in 1983, made clear statements that the human attempt to master space is far from complete. Every trail from footpath to highway is an ongoing conversation between humanity and nature, a dialogue in which the two parties sometimes agree, sometimes argue, and sometimes explode in conflict. Courtesy Utah State Historical Society.

(Above) Sponsored by five state endowments for the humanities, the Trails exhibit covered Arizona, Colorado, New Mexico, Utah, and Wyoming. This map not only showed viewers the states under discussion, it also dramatized the difference in scale between the American Northeast and the American West. In conventional tellings of national history, the tiny state of Massachusetts dominates the story, while events in the Rocky Mountain states get only the briefest attention. By a powerful if unexamined assignment of significance, the small spaces of the northeastern United States provided the stage for a history that shook and shaped the world; in the western United States, vast spaces provided a setting for quaint, colorful, and ultimately inconsequential history. This map, the exhibit planners hoped, might ask viewers to consider a possible reapportionment of historical significance. Courtesy Viki Mann, Mann Communications.

(Above) The introduction of livestock into the West was certainly as consequential as the introduction of machines. Imported by the Spanish, horses changed the terms of native life on the Plains, while the introduction of sheep, cattle, and goats transformed the land. "Hooved locusts," the preservationist John Muir called sheep grazing on public lands, and this wave of sheep grazing in Colorado dramatically illustrates the impact of livestock on the western environment. Courtesy Denver Public Library Western History Collection.

(Bottom opposite) Far from being a remote backwater set apart from the major currents of national history, the nineteenth-century American West was often on the forefront of industrialization and urbanization. The importance of the railroad for territorial expansion and economic development represents the central role of machines in the transforming of the plains, deserts, and mountains of the West. At the "photo opportunity" at Promontory Point, Utah, celebrating the completion of the transcontinental railroad in 1869, the "builders" of the railroad—owners, financiers, managers—posed for pictures; the Chinese workers were not invited to participate. Courtesy Denver Public Library Western History Collection.

(Above) For decades, westerners have ridden the roller coaster of the boom/bust economy. Mining rushes did not end in the nineteenth century, nor were they limited to the search for the precious metals of gold and silver. In our own century, copper, coal, oil, uranium, and oil/shale developments have inspired the familiar rushes of population, with heavy use of trails and roads, as eager job seekers flooded into boomtowns. In the energy boom of the 1970s and early 1980s, the Rocky Mountain region was a particular target of large-scale, if temporary, industrial development, producing overnight communities like this trailer park off Interstate 80 outside Rock Springs, Wyoming. Courtesy Mike McClure.

(Bottom opposite) Four and a half centuries of the Euroamerican invasion and conquest of the West have produced a remarkably varied, and often wildly improbable, set of results. Responding to the record of the past, the western historian has occasion to draw on the full range of emotion—amusement as well as regret, hilarity as well as sorrow. At the third annual Arizona Accordion Club picnic, April 16, 1939, the improbability of the legacy of conquest reached one of its frequent peaks as accordions and eager musicians assembled in the desert framed by saguaros. Courtesy Arizona Humanities Council.

(Above) Change, adaptation, and human complexity ruled the story of the American West. Contrary to the fantasies of some easterners, the West and its people could not, and would not, stay "pristine." The traditional and the modern coexisted; horses and autobuses traveled the same trails; Indian people and Euroamericans not only appeared in the same pictures, they were part of shared, reciprocally shaped stories. In the 1920s, this Albuquerque Stage Bus occupied common ground with a Navaho hogan and a Navaho man on horseback. Courtesy Museum of New Mexico.

In the months since the Trails symposium, press coverage of the New Western History has concentrated on its supposed negativity in painting a bleak and desolate picture of a devastated region. Contrary to media images, our main hope has been to move the field's center of gravity westward. Instead of a frontier process floating, dirigible-like, across the continent, the New Western History looks at a region where people of diverse origins have had actual, measurable effects on real places. The sign for the Jackrabbit Trading Post on Route 66, in Joseph City, Arizona, sums up the message of the New Western History: "Here It Is!" Courtesy University of Oklahoma Press, © Quinta Scott.

of such scholars as Walter Nugent and Paul Kleppner attests.[11] Western historians can claim that they have maintained a better balance of social-scientific rigor and accessible writing style than have most of their peers in the profession.

It is easy to demonstrate the growing sophistication of western scholarship. The annual conference programs of the Western History Association demonstrate a much heavier emphasis upon serious social, economic, and political topics than they do upon the "Old West." So do the issues of the organization's journal, the *Western Historical Quarterly*. The remarkable upsurge in the study of western women, of ethnic and nationality groups, and of urban areas in recent years contrasts with anything that preceded it. And, it should be noted, historians of "traditional" frontier topics have, in recent years, produced many books of indisputable merit. Although it is true that most twentieth-century topics still cry out for consideration, it is also true that path-breaking volumes such as Richard Lowitt's on the New Deal and Gerald Nash's on World War II are at last appearing.[12]

Yet it is not enough to answer critics of the field simply by pointing to the many instances of first-rate scholarship. Scholarship alone does not address the need for a new or revised interpretative model to replace the old Turner Thesis. William Cronon is correct in arguing that "we have not yet figured out a way to escape him. His work remains the foundation not only for the history of the West, but also for much of the rest of American history as well. . . . [N]o new synthetic paradigm for Western history has yet emerged to replace Turner's."[13]

At this point, a rather obvious question emerges. Is such a paradigm essential for regional study? Is it not best simply to apply the most effective models and examples of national historiography to this particular part of the United States? Or to emulate such widely heralded practitioners of the craft as the historians of the French *Annales* school? Of course, both are commendable aims. The broader field of United States history is the general context in which western regionalism lies, and the best American generalists naturally direct the field. Similarly, the *Annales* historians, particularly Fernand Braudel and Emmanuel Le Roy Ladurie, set a high standard by their efforts to construct a "total history," employing quantitative methods and a wide variety of sources to comprehend human-ecological systems, the rhythms of "everyday life," and the "mentalities" of peoples and places.[14]

Neither of these approaches, however, can offer a true basis for regional study. Sadly, the entire discipline of history in the United States is in a state of crisis, according to critics like Bernard Bailyn, Oscar Handlin, and Theodore Hamerow. Ever more specialized and guided by "new" social science methodologies that are unconvincing and unappealing to many, American historians have lost many of their audiences and bases of support. Thomas Bender and other thoughtful historians search, seemingly in vain, for some form of synthesis, some hoop for the barrel. As for the *Annalistes*, they have not yet managed to achieve their heralded "holistic" history, and their tendency to avoid political and other "event-oriented" history and to downplay the role of the individual in human affairs probably will not endear them to western regionalists.[15]

Western historians, in sum, must learn from the best work in national and international scholarship. But only those working in the subdiscipline itself are truly situated to direct the proper reorientation of western history, and until western regionalists achieve such a reorientation, they will be forced either to continue following the old trails or to take up the unrewarding task of tracing national trends and events in western settings.

Aside from the classical interpretations of Turner and Webb, are there other established models that might hold the key to a new regional approach? Some might argue for another look at Herbert Eugene Bolton's influential works, both those that stressed the significance of the borderlands of the Spanish-Mexican Southwest and those that spoke of a broader unity in hemispheric history.[16] But neither of these approaches, however meritorious in its own right, seems to offer a fruitful rendering of the West as an expansive region.

Another approach that clearly does have some lasting relevance is the "colonial," or "plundered province," interpretation that grew up during the 1930s and 1940s. This persuasion, championed by Webb, De Voto, and lesser lights, resembled the southern regionalism articulated in 1930 by Robert Penn Warren, John Crowe Ransom, and their colleagues in *I'll Take My Stand*. It saw the West, as well as the South, as the victim of northeastern capitalistic exploitation of resources and population. This sort of political-polemical argument lives on—for instance, in Governor Richard Lamm's coauthored *The Angry West* (1982) or in the more appealing environmentalism of Wallace Stegner. But the plundered province school now seems more of a period piece than contemporary realism, given that most of the region has long since outgrown any real "colonial" relationship to the rest of the country.[17]

In the final analysis, it seems most logical to seek out the appropriate interpretative model for regional history by first identifying which factors do indeed make the West a region. General studies of American regions, such as those by Joel Garreau and Raymond Gastil, are of considerable help; but it is essential to look directly into this unique region itself.[18] For purposes of discussion, I would suggest four fundamental bonds of regional identity: (1) the abiding aridity of the West, (2) its exceptional reliance upon the federal government, (3) the recency and residual aura of its frontier experience, and (4) its still heavy dependency upon extractive industries. These intertwined strands of regionalism seem to me to suggest the most convincing determinants of true western identity and behavior.

The strongest of all bonds of western regionalism, the bond that most defines it as *place*, is the simple and overriding fact that except for the rain-drenched mountains of the northwestern rim and the humid plains along its eastern reaches, the West is dry. Water is its key resource, and water capture and delivery systems the cardiovascular complex of its socioeconomic life process. It is the most urban part of America, a fact made seemingly incongruous by the stark isolation of great cities surrounded by endless desert expanses, urban oases in a fragile environment.

The West as "desert" is, of course, the essence of the Webb arid-lands interpretation. However much it was overstated and couched in polemical and poetic language, this paradigm has great enduring persuasiveness. The most influential recent articulation of the arid-lands interpretation is that of Donald Worster, particularly in his *Rivers of Empire* (1985). Placing perhaps an overemphasis upon California and the arid and irrigated Southwest, Worster depicted the region as a "hydraulic society," dangerously overdependent upon a wasteful and environmentally doomed nexus of federal dams and water systems. Even if Webb and Worster, along with other regional spokesmen like Marc Reisner, overstated their case, there is no disputing that their emphasis upon western aridity

148

and water development pierces the heart of regional identity.[19]

No close observer of the region can miss the exceptionally heavy reliance of the West upon the federal government, a reliance that is as old as its life in the Union. Although all of the United States has experienced the burgeoning of federal activism, the West (in this case including Alaska) has experienced it in a truly revolutionary manner. The roots of dependency date to territorial days and earlier and especially to the great land sequestrations of 1891–1935. The New Deal–World War II era brought vast changes to the West, drastically enlarging the role of Uncle Sam as financier, regulator, and caretaker, beginning the demise of economic colonialism, and laying the federally subsidized hydroelectric-military-scientific foundations upon which would arise the giant "high-tech" systems of the postwar era.[20]

Historians have recently been making impressive progress in defining the modern West's relationship with Washington, most notably in the areas of reclamation, conservation, and Indian policies. But key aspects of that relationship remain largely unexplored—for instance, the post-1940 funding of military bases and defense industries, the sponsorship of science, agricultural and trade policies, and internal improvements like highways, airports, and harbors. Surely one of the greatest of all facts of life about this vast region is that no state of the Far West (the Montana–New Mexico tier westward) is less than 29 percent federally owned—Nevada is 87 percent, Alaska an incredible 96 percent—whereas no state to the east is more than 12 percent federal land. At one and the same time, this situation produces an enormous federal dependency and the shrill bleating of the "Sagebrush Rebellion." Yet, anyone who doubts that this heavy federal presence is a regionally centripetal force need only glance at the behavior of western congressmen and governors, who spend much of their time lobbying for federal water projects, farm subsidies, military bucks, and for or against new wilderness areas.[21]

And then one returns once again to the frontier as a factor in western regionalism, a third bond of identity. In this era of anti-Turnerian reaction, there is a tendency to discount the lasting influence of this three-century phenomenon that ended here. The most recent and provocative theorizing along this line is surely Patricia Nelson Limerick's *The Legacy of Conquest* (1987). One may or may not accept this book's main contention, that the West is the American region most marked by a legacy of human and environmental conquest. I do not. But its presentist approach, along with its argument that the Turnerian emphasis upon the frontier and its closing has led western historiography into a cul-de-sac, is a fruitful one.[22]

I should like to return to this later, for Limerick, Cronon, and other scholars who have emerged from the distinguished Yale doctoral program are persuasive in this argument. But the point to be made here is that, in revising Turner, one must take care not to throw the frontier baby out with the bathwater, regardless of whether frontier is defined as the settlement process itself or as the entire legacy and mystique that this process has left behind.

Accepting Limerick's admonition about our preoccupation with closing frontiers, it still seems self-evident that a major part of the region's shared cultural heritage lies in the drama and recency of the frontier's passing—as late as the post–World War I years in some parts of the arid West—and in the very fact of the region's preoccupation with it. One encounters this "Old West" syndrome everywhere west of Kansas City and Dallas, particularly in the rural interior: cowboy clothes, music, art, food, and jargon; pickups with rifles in the rear window; barbecues on the patio; a "Mint," "Longbranch," or "Stockman's" bar in every gulch; round Skoal cans in the backpockets of ragged jeans. For good or bad, it *is* what most westerners think is their heritage. It is what they mean by "West." The problem with the frontier focus of western historiography is not that it is based on unreality but rather that the Frontier school tilted toward Filiopietism, exclusivity, and insularity and away from cosmopolitanism and multicausal contexts.

Fortunately, some of this country's foremost historians have presented admirable models for conceptualizing the frontier phenomenon in better regional and global focus. In *The Peopling of British North America* (1986), Bernard Bailyn depicted the first, Atlantic frontier of America not as an innovating protocivilization but rather as "a periphery, a ragged outer margin of a central world, a regressive, backward-looking diminishment of metropolitan accomplishment . . . [a] far distant outback of late seventeenth-century Britain." Bailyn's frontier looks more like the outskirts than the birthplace of a civilization. In *The Great Frontier* (1983), a little book that every western historian should read, the accomplished world historian William H. McNeill noted how a close and comparative study demonstrates that labor-short frontiers could in fact produce the libertarian-egalitarian societies that Turner depicted in America. More often, however, global frontiers created hierarchical, even slavery-based systems. It all depended on local conditions and upon the cultural baggage the frontier folk brought with them.[23]

McNeill actually took about the same approach that Webb did in his *The Great Frontier* nearly four decades ago, conceptualizing the global imperialism of Europe after Columbus. But McNeill brought to this formidable task a far greater historical expertise than Webb could. Another distinguished world historian, L. S. Stavrianos, took the same tack, also with impressive results, in *Global Rift* (1981). In his lengthy and well-informed book, Stavrianos depicted wave after wave of capitalistic expansionism radiating out of the core metropolis of northwestern Europe, reducing first eastern Europe to "third world" or economically colonial status, then the Americas, finally the long-established civilizations of India, Russia, and China, and the nearly impenetrable heartland of Central Africa. The key fact of modern history, according to Stavrianos, has been this European conquest of the earth and since 1914, the successful struggle of one third world after another to break the bonds of colonialism.[24]

A number of other well-known scholars, such as Theodore von Laue, have similarly pursued this global theme. Among the more renowned is Immanuel Wallerstein, who has in many writings fashioned a complex paradigm for modern world history. In Wallerstein's interpretation, a capitalist "world-economy" arose out of the crisis of feudalism in Europe during 1300–1450, dominated in turn by the Dutch, the British, and the Americans. The world system has come to encompass the earth, dividing it into "core" and "periphery" zones of commodity linkages that cross national boundaries and through which various states in turn have prospered at the expense of others.[25]

Many historians of the West will not warm to Wallerstein's socioeconomic jargon; but his essential argument, which is similar to that of Stavrianos and Webb, has much to offer. In one sense, these world historians simply provide the proper context and cosmopolitan perspective. So, of course, do those western-oriented historians who are studying comparative frontiers and regions. Focusing upon such epic movements as those of the Cossacks eastward in Russia, the Boers northward in South Africa, or the Paulistas westward into the Amazon Basin, these historians offer a larger and better perspective to see beyond the introspectiveness of Turner's America.

Such comparative studies need not focus only on narrowly defined frontiers. Witness Earl Pomeroy's insightful and balanced "The West and New Nations in Other Continents," Walter Nugent's revealing depiction of Type I (stable-agricultural) and Type II (unstable-extractive) frontiers, or Howard Lamar's recent juxtaposition of Canadian and American plains experiences during the 1930s.[26] Viewed in this manner, the westering frontier of the United States looks only in part like the forge of a unique nationality. It looks more like one major part of a worldwide process of global integration that is continuing to remake this and other regions.

These broader perspectives have more to offer, however, than just broadened perspectives. By guiding western regionalists beyond their long-term preoccupation with the American frontier and its closing, they help facilitate the fundamental reconceptualization of the field that so many of its scholars have been seeking. In order to explore this larger dimension, though, it is necessary first to consider the fourth bond of regionalism identified earlier—one that is closely related to frontiering itself: the central importance of extractive industries.

Of course, extractive industries are important to all American regions. The humid Southeast is, in fact, now stealing away large shares of two of the West's greatest industries: livestock and wood products. But, both historically and contemporarily, the West has relied upon its extractive industries more than other regions and has paid the price in a long succession of boom-and-bust cycles.

This was patently obvious back in pioneering times.

Witness the collapse of placer mining in the early 1870s, of open-range cattle ranching in the 1880s, of silver mining in the 1890s, and of homesteading in the 1890s and the years following World War I. It was equally obvious in more recent times, with the huge gluts of natural products in the 1920s that brought on the calamity of the Great Depression and with the wrenching economic downturns of the past several years. A few years ago, prophets like John Naisbitt saw the West breaking out of this natural products reliance with its proliferation of high-tech and high-service industries. But the hard truth is that the West still relies heavily upon the same extractive industries it has relied upon for a century and more: agriculture, mining, wood products, fisheries, and fossil fuels.[27] Today, this reliance is the West's greatest vulnerability.

Western historians have done relatively little to address the evolution of these key modern industries, although William Robbins is pointing the way with his thoughtful treatments of regional lumbering.[28] There is no comprehensive history of modern western agriculture, or of a petroleum industry that has transformed the Southwest, or of a modern mining industry that became based upon copper rather than precious metals and upon open pits rather than deep mines.

Why have scholars failed to write these studies? Surely, two reasons are the persistence of a frontier interpretation that for decades has shunted historians away from post-1890s developments and a failure to see that old-time frontiers and continuing exploitations of resource bounties are really two aspects of the same process. One of America's greatest historians, David M. Potter, offered this insight many years ago in his influential *People of Plenty* (1954). Potter argued that Turner had focused too narrowly upon the frontier, that the frontier was but one, albeit the greatest, manifestation of what really was the fundamental shaping force of American civilization: material abundance.[29] From the days of the fur trade and gold rush to those of uranium and oil shale, the West has been America's leading source of resources and its playing field of reckless exploitation.

Stepping back to assess the picture fully, we may now see that these four forces are at the same time individually discrete and components of a larger whole. Patricia Nelson Limerick was correct in arguing that "no simple, unitary model" can ever replace the old frontier interpretation and that western historians, like modern physicists, "have had to learn to live with relativism."[30] True enough, but that relativism is far from total. The four forces of regionalism described here, along perhaps with others such as the remarkable new cosmopolitanism resulting from the upsurge in Asian and Latin American immigration, constitute a new, multifaceted model for regional study. This model is not singular as were those of Turner and Webb, but is an amalgam of interrelated factors, like the combined field theory with which theoretical physicists met the relativity of Einstein, which had replaced the earlier positivism of Newton.

Two of these bonds of regionalism serve primarily to define the West as *place*. Both the Webb-Worster aridlands interpretation and the prevalence of the federal government stress the individuality of the region as a part of the United States, a part that is different ecologically, socially, politically, and culturally from other parts. On the other hand, the combined factors of booming and busting frontiers and extractive industries keyed to world markets and trends have more to do with ongoing *processes*, processes that have shaped and continue to shape the region in a global context.

The very word "frontier" is perversely mischievous,

blurring such disparate concepts as long-ago settlement with current and future resource exploitation and an aura of mythology. As a source of regional identity in the American West, "frontier" might well be replaced by the term "globalization"—the ongoing integration of this long-remote place into the human community.[31] From the age of the first Paleo-Indian migrations to that of the microchip, the West as region has been defined by the dialectical tension of those historical factors that defined it as place with those that dictated its changing role in the world order.

When viewed through the stereopticon of American-place and global-process, the evolution of the West since Turner's enunciation of his thesis in 1893 is intriguing. Even in summary, it becomes readily apparent that the closing of the frontier that Turner saw as cataclysmic in his census maps was overstated, oversimplified, and insular.

For example, frontiering in the form of homesteading continued long into the twentieth century, often with dire consequences to people and places. Ironically, even as the mythmakers of Hollywood and pulp fiction were forging their stereotypes of the vanishing frontier, the reality of frontiering defined as the conquest of bounties of natural products was entering a new and more complex phase. Early in the century, revolutionary technologies were applied to low-grade cuprous ores and petroleum deposits in the Southwest, to lumber in the Northwest, and to mechanized agricultural units throughout the region. The American West became a world leader in these harvests, exporting new technologies and sending sophisticated petroleum geologists, mining engineers, and agricultural scientists to the ends of the earth. But soon the West fell victim to the global gluts and falling prices that resulted during the 1920s and 1930s. Thus the West, in a sense the economically "colonial" portion of the United States, set the pace in productivity for the truly colonial regions of the world.

These sweeping frontier-closing and postfrontier developments took place in the context of what McNeill aptly described as the close of the great frontier. This closure did not come with the "last stands" of Sam Peckinpah's aging heroes but rather with World War I and the global quota systems of the 1920s. These systems curtailed the great migrations that had girdled the planet since 1500. The Great Depression and World War II wrought revolutionary changes upon this region, as it did on the world at large. Just as the new American federalism of 1933–1945 began the demise of economic colonialism in the West, the two world wars instigated the collapse of imperialism in the Southern Hemisphere and Asia.

The explosion of European influence and migration became an implosion. European cities, inundated by "guest workers," came to seem as polyethnic and diverse as those of the western American borderlands and of other, formerly colonial areas.[32] During the peak years of United States global hegemony, 1945–1970, the western resource economy generally prospered, and federal and private investments in reclamation and water development, as well as in defense/aerospace/high-tech industries, worked a revolution in regional growth.

After 1971, American global economic hegemony began to ebb; and as it did, both the nation at large and, even more startlingly, the western region passed through convolutions that resulted from an accelerated integration into a global economy. At first, during the 1970s, the upsurge in high-technology industries, spawned by federal investments in defense-related research, coincided with booming fossil fuel and agricultural markets to pro-

157

pel the West forward in relation to other American regions. To observers like Paul Johnson and Kirkpatrick
Sale, it seemed that the resource- and technology-rich
"Sunbelt" of the West would displace the old "Rustbelt"
of the East.[33] This would have seemed sweet irony, if be-
lievable at all, to the Populists of yesteryear.

But the boom of the 1970s skidded into the regional
depression of the 1980s. As Peter Drucker noted in a truly
remarkable *Foreign Affairs* essay, the world economy has
changed fundamentally during the past two decades. The
third world is coming of age; demographic patterns are
changing; and the new technologies of America, Europe,
and Japan are spreading around the earth. Suddenly the
world is different. The established industrial nations no
longer control the resources and markets of Asia and the
Southern Hemisphere as they once did. And with the dramatic rise in global applications of biotechnology and
computerized and automated production, transportation,
and communications systems, the planet is awash in natural products. As the American region most involved in
the production and export of natural products, the West,
especially the rural West, is hardest hit.[34]

Thus the West is experiencing a wrenching cycle of
change comparable to that of the 1890s, which Turner
mistakenly took to be a singular frontier's closing. A
world oil glut saps western energy industries; imports of
old-growth lumber from British Columbia undercut a
western industry already losing out to the perennial forests and nonunion labor of the American Southeast; Chil-
ean imports and international wage differentials devas-
tate a copper industry already losing its markets to fiber
optics. Farmers and ranchers face the hard fact that very
soon among the great nations only Japan and the Soviet
Union may not be food *exporters*. And those twin pillars of
wasteful federal support of western agriculture, crop sub-

sidies and water systems, may both collapse in a parsimonious future. Nor do the West's vaunted high-tech industries provide any panacea. Silicon Valley, Orange County, North Dallas, Phoenix, and other centers of the computer industry are suffering pressure from foreign producers, particularly those of Japan and East Asia.[35]

So the western past is still very much with us, and like the past of any other place, it is filled with subtleties and complexities rich with meaning. Clearly, the regional bonding forces presented above have continued to mold the evolving West throughout the century since Turner's manifesto. Indeed, the struggle against aridity, the federally bankrolled strategy to develop American institutions in a vast semiarid region—that is the essence of western history. So, perhaps, is that sense of western exceptionalism and that frontier preoccupation that are the most burdensome legacies of Turner and his disciples. But so, more subtly, are the processes that we have imprecisely called frontiering but that are really the ever more complex methods by which we harvest the region's vast resources and attempt to trade them in an ever more closely knit world economy. This was true in the ages of Astor and Hill. It is equally true in today's era of soaring Japanese banks in Los Angeles, foreigners mass-purchasing western farmlands, and the increasingly complex flows of workers and products across the border with Mexico.

A number of scholars in the western history field are pursuing various aspects of the themes suggested here. For instance, the many who, like Howard Lamar and Walter Nugent, are conducting comparative regional studies; the attempts of Spencer Olin and his associates to conceptualize Orange County, California, in a national and multinational economy; and William Robbins's sophisticated approach to modern regionalism and economic interdependency.[36]

Were Turner and Webb, the two founders of this scholarly subdiscipline of American history, still alive today, one would like to believe that such a broadening synthesis would be their orientation to the field. After all, Turner once declared that "local history must be read as a part of world history"; and Webb not only pioneered the Great Frontier approach, which explained how the West was shaped by broad historical processes; he also pioneered the arid-lands interpretation, which best explains this region as part of the United States.[37] Both were, after all, true scholars who read widely and avoided overspecialization.

In the end, it is the greatest of all challenges to western historians, and to other regionalists as well, to work out the contours of the new synthesis that must surely replace the older interpretations. Although earlier interpretations continue to bear considerable truth and relevance, they cannot begin to explain the complexities of this diverse and changing region. The developing new synthesis is simultaneously less appealing to romantic appetites and far more challenging to comprehend. But what it has to offer is a fuller and richer understanding of what makes the West the truly fascinating place that it is.

11

FRONTIERS AND EMPIRES IN THE LATE NINETEENTH CENTURY

WALTER NUGENT

IN THE LATE nineteenth century, Europeans and their colonial descendants around the world pushed into new regions on a scale they had never before managed and with an assuredness they would never again possess after 1914. Sometimes they expanded into frontiers and sometimes into empires. The purpose of this chapter is to suggest ways in which frontier building and empire building were similar and ways in which they were different.[1]

Europeans began sailing around southern Africa to South and East Asia, and westward to the Americas, just before 1500. They established the Spanish and Portuguese seaborne empires in the sixteenth century and the French, Dutch, and English in the seventeenth. From the European standpoint, the eighteenth century became a "second age of discovery," with the exploration of the Pacific. There were new varieties of European expansion: demographic, with the rise of population in modern Britain, Europe, and North America; economic, with the beginning of industrialization; political, with the independence of the United States in 1776 and Latin America during and just after the Napoleonic wars (1810–1822); and diplomatic-imperial, in the form of contacts and conquests involving North Africa, the Middle East, China (1839–1842), and Japan (1853). Up to this point the "rise of the

West," or "expansion of Europe," is a familiar story. It principally involved political or military elites.

But during the nineteenth century, Europe's population began to move across borders and even across the Atlantic. The population of the United States, without much help from Europe and without significant Malthusian checks, multiplied by one-third every decade up to 1860. The arrival of steam-powered industry and transportation in the third quarter of the century transformed European expansionism into a mass movement. Advances in technology also created a North Atlantic nexus of political and economic energy that drove much of the world until 1914, and in some places until after 1945. In the four hundred years since Vasco da Gama and Columbus, Europe's expansive power and self-confidence were never greater than in the forty-odd years before 1914, and in the 1880s it was probably greatest of all.

The thesis here is that in the 1870–1914 period, the frontier impulse and the imperial impulse were related in source and performance; that frontiers may be distinguished and a typology of frontiers developed; and that empire building (imperialism), in context, appears to be a special type of frontier. The key to the typology, though not its only ingredient, is demography. Demographic stability, or the lack of it, provided firmness or transiency for frontiers and empires. In general, empires proved transient and frontiers evolved into permanent societies.

A few more words, however, should be said about why the late nineteenth century—especially the 1880s—was special. Why might Europeans and Americans of that time have thought their achievements unique and their ballooning self-confidence justified? In the 1880s several factors—economic, technological, cultural-nationalistic, and political—converged to produce an exuberant proliferation of expansionist episodes. The slightly longer period of 1873 to 1896 was once regarded, especially in Britain, as a "Great Depression" largely because British growth lost ground compared with earlier Victorian times and because the long-term trend in money supply was deflationary. But "Great Depression" does not fit the larger transatlantic context.[2] Even a neoclassical historical economist who retains the term and rightly points to the severity of the 1873–1878 and 1893–1897 depressions in the United States properly calls the 1880s "a decade of buoyant growth" in the United States as well as in Britain.[3] From the economic standpoint, in fact, expansion lasted in the United States from the recovery in late 1878 until the panic of mid-1893, and in Britain, France, and Germany from late 1879 to 1891. Industrial production rose 20 to 25 percent in France and Britain in those years and about 50 percent in Germany.[4] This robust material climate was a necessary part of the expansionism of the period.

Economic growth and technological innovation were legion during the 1880s. Steel output doubled in France, tripled in Britain, and quintupled in Germany and the United States.[5] Not so different in population size at that time, Germany and the United States led Europe and the Americas in demographic and industrial expansion. The basic railway networks of Europe and North America were mostly in place by the early 1890s. In the 1880s alone, four new transcontinental lines were added to the Union Pacific/Central Pacific line of 1869, while John A. Macdonald's National Policy bore fruit (if often bitter for prairie farmers in the 1880s and 1890s) in the completion of the Canadian Pacific in 1885. Elsewhere, the trans-Siberian railroad began in 1891, while other railroad building—less dramatic than those immense efforts yet critical for their regions—flung lines across the Argentine pampas and the São Paulo plateau, as well as throughout eastern Germany, divided Poland, Austria-Hungary, and Romania.

Sudden, effective improvements in public health and sanitation lowered mortality and disease rates after 1880—dramatically in European and American cities.[6] Public authorities and physicians began to accept the germ theory and the grim costs of bad sanitation. *Scientific American* advised its readers that "of the cases of disease now current in civilized communities, about *one-third* could have been prevented by intelligent sanitation, personal or general." Microorganisms were everywhere, people learned.[7] Sanitation regulations also improved the safety of migrant embarkation and debarkation ports such as Hamburg, New York, Santos, and Buenos Aires, as well as the steamships cruising between them.

The period saw not only great economic and technological change but also an unprecedented churning of people. Eight million Europeans migrated between 1880 and 1890 alone, across provincial and national boundaries within Europe and among New World countries. They used the newly built networks of railroads within Europe, steamships to cross the Atlantic, and railroads again to travel to inland cities, coffee plantations, mines, or wheat fields.[8] Millions ventured out of Hamburg, Bremen, Antwerp, Naples, Trieste, and Odessa to journey to North and South America—and, often, back again. As late as the 1920s, Ukrainians and other East Europeans completed the settlement of the Canadian prairie frontier. They also ended a farm-seeking migration process that, in its basic shape, began around 1720 when Germans from the Rheinland-Pfalz and Scots-Irish from Ulster started migrating to farmsteads in eastern Pennsylvania and northern Virginia. In the early nineteenth century Germans and Italians similarly colonized Brazil's Rio Grande do Sul. From about 1850 through the

1880s British, German, and Scandinavian farm families peopled the upper Mississippi Valley and Great Plains while other Europeans migrated to newly available farmland in New Zealand, Australia, and South Africa. In this traditional transatlantic migration, a family traded in, so to speak, a small, no longer competitive farm in northern Europe for a larger, efficient, potentially productive one in the United States, Canada, or southern Brazil. Repatriation was uncommon in this farm-seeking family migration.

Increasingly after 1880, however, transatlantic steamships carried temporary migrants, sometimes called *golondrinas* or birds of passage. Most of them were young men seeking marginal wage advantages somewhere in the Americas, putting aside cash or sending it home, returning to Europe after a season or two, and migrating again when opportunity appeared. Labor-seeking temporary migration within Europe was an old practice; examples can be found in the seventeenth century or even earlier without stretching definitions of "labor-seeking" too far. With steam-powered transportation in place, the range of opportunities expanded from trans-Alpine or trans-Elbian to transatlantic, creating a migrant labor pool involving hundreds of thousands of people every year traveling thousands instead of hundreds of miles out of Europe, mainly to Canada, the United States, Brazil, and Argentina and often back again.

Nearly two and a half times as many people left Europe in the 1880s than in the 1870s. After a dip in the 1890s, the number of migrants reached 11.4 million from 1901 to 1910, the all-time high for one decade.[9] The new element in the 1880s was the labor-seeking temporary migration, adding to the continuing farm-family migration. Most of the eight hundred thousand people who went to Argentina in the 1880s were labor seekers, and so, with certain differences, were the five hundred thousand who went to Brazil, the nine hundred thousand who went to Canada, and the nearly five million who went to the United States, the destination of half to two-thirds of all European emigrants throughout the whole period of mass emigration from the 1840s to World War I. Borders were more open at that time than they were before or after, government policies generally encouraged migration rather than restricted it, and the means of travel were more accessible. The Atlantic became a two-way boulevard, and the demographic character of both Europe and the Americas changed irrevocably.

So did their frontiers, the lands within the New World countries previously unoccupied by people of European stock. Elsewhere in the world, the migration of Europeans could also mean farm settlement or wage seeking, as it did in Australia and New Zealand. It could also represent empire building. The availability of "free" land in the United States and Canada (both with attractive homestead policies), the tenant contracts on the Argentine pampas and São Paulo's coffee plantations (both areas opened to development and settlement at about the same rate as the North American Great Plains), as well as the wages to be earned in factories and mines in the United States and elsewhere, attracted Europeans irresistibly to the New World's many frontiers. The newly founded African and Asian colonies of the Great Powers were far less enticing. Unless one counts Canada, Australia, and perhaps North Africa as empires—and they were very different from Rhodesia, India, Indochina, and the Philippines—it becomes clear that empire builders were not in the same demographic class as frontier settlers or labor seekers.

An important similarity between frontiers and empires lies in the fact that no "new" (to Europeans) region was truly empty. No region of the world, tropical or temperate, to which people of European stock migrated in the 1870–1914 period lacked an indigenous people. The permanence or transience of the European approach depended greatly on what those indigenous people were like and how successfully they could resist or absorb the Europeans. Some of the indigenes were militarily weak, loosely organized socially, or technologically simple. Others were strong, old, highly developed civilizations that did not share the European and Euro-American sense of racial superiority toward them. Some indigenes lived in areas recognized in international law to be within the limits of the sovereign territory of a European-stock nation, as was true of Native Americans from Patagonia to the Arctic or aboriginal Australians. Others lived in places sometimes far distant from the intruding European-stock nation, as was the case with Africans or Indians. Frontiers, in other words, were within territorial boundaries; empires were outside them. This difference bore consequences, to be sure, but it should not obscure the fact that both were targets of European-stock migration.

In the frontier group were the largest of the New World nations, territorially and in population (except Mexico): Canada, the United States, Brazil, and Argentina.[10] All four confronted relatively weak native peoples and therefore contained extensive "free" lands within their own borders. The second group included the most powerful European states: Germany, France, and Britain. Creating or adding to far-flung empires, they superimposed themselves upon peoples and civilizations older than their own (as in South and East Asia) or at least radically different from their own (as in Africa and Oceania). The frontierspeople and the empire builders—all Europeans or Euro-Americans sharing the same transatlantic economy, technology, and migration pool, all migrants, all in some way expanders—differed less in who they themselves were than in whom they met.[11]

Between the New World frontier societies and the Old World empire builders, as well as within each group, national peculiarities strongly nuanced the expansionist drive. In the case of the four Euro-American countries, the task was to colonize the interior: the Great Plains of Canada and the United States, the potentially coffee-bearing plateau of São Paulo and adjacent areas, and the pampas of central and northern Argentina. The three European imperial powers, on the other hand, thrust into the African interior from all points of the compass, into Indonesia and other Pacific islands, into Malaysia and Indochina, and to the limited degree possible, into the Chinese empire.

Sometimes the Europeans made permanent inroads, sometimes not. In places where political control was already consolidated in Western-style, formally liberal political systems, the frontier area was assimilated in every functional way. Familiar cases are the United States and Canada: Despite lingering western-state or prairie-province resentment toward Washington or Ottawa, no one could possibly argue that today the American and Canadian Wests are anything but secure parts of those countries. But in places where political control was newly imposed from Europe and kept in place by an authority more military than moral and more physical than cultural, such control seldom survived long after 1945. In the German case (though for intra-European, not intrinsically colonial, reasons), it endured only until 1918.

These different results can be explained by dissimilarities in culture, technology, and military strength or in other ways. I would like to point out demographic considerations (among them the relative sizes of the indigenous populations) that, together with social and cultural factors, help explain their success or failure vis-à-vis the Europeans. In North America, native peoples offered fierce but sporadic and ineffective resistance. The Comanche and Apache of Texas and the desert Southwest brought the Spanish to a stalemate for two centuries on the thinly populated northern border of New Spain but gave way to the overwhelming mass of incoming Americans in the 1870s and 1880s.[12] A high cultural level was of no help. The civilized tribes of the southeastern United States were removed with ease (not to themselves) in the 1830s to a place hundreds of miles westward. In Brazil, the indigenes consisted chiefly of jungle peoples pushed out of the central plateaus in the eighteenth century.[13] In Argentina, the army drove the Araucanians off the pampas and largely exterminated them by 1880 in the "Conquest of the Desert," an effort "even more effective than the Indian wars of the [U.S.] Mid-west."[14] Several writers have pointed out that European-stock frontierspeople defeated the Sioux, the Araucanians, and the Zulus, all in or about 1879, and the *métis* and their Indian allies in western Canada in 1885.[15] No conveniently coincidental date marks native-white contact in Australia and New Zealand, because the Europeans had already taken over.[16]

The native peoples of the Western Hemisphere, though at times formidable, did not present to Europeans the intractable resistance of the Hindus, the Annamese, the Thai, or the Javanese. Nor were the Zulus, Abyssinians, or Sudanese easy marks. Thus, in the Western Hemisphere, the willingness of the Americans and Canadians to settle and not simply exploit their hinterlands and the relative powerlessness of the native peoples to prevent it meant firm and permanent control over the frontier. Their control was inhibited only by lack of caution in dealing with unfamiliar and delicate environments such as the High Plains and Great Basin of the United States or the northern prairies of Canada. In late-nineteenth-century Brazil, the unoccupied area was so utterly vast that even the headlong thrusts of coffee culture 300 to 500 miles inland got the Europeans less than halfway to the Andes. Fortunately for Brazil, no powerful enemy with expansionist designs lurked on the Pacific coast, threatening to cross the mountains into the Brazilian Far West. (None threatened the United States either.) The New World frontier countries did not compete with each other, having enough to do within their own boundaries.

In Africa, however, competition among the European powers weakened the grip of all of them, though they did not seem weak to the native peoples. Occasionally the European transplant took root, at least for a time, as was the case with the Danish coffee farmer (and writer) Isak Dinesen in Kenya.[17] The French in West Africa mingled well enough to leave more than just a residue of language, culture, and even genes, more than did the British. But then the French had also enjoyed much better relations with native peoples in North America in the seventeenth and eighteenth centuries than the British did in nineteenth-century Africa. Since 1945, however, the European presence everywhere in Africa, though often dogged, has been retreating. The sole remaining European-stock regime, South Africa, holds itself in control of a large indigenous majority by force, so far preventing a takeover by native peoples, such as happened in Zimbabwe in 1979.

Frontiers differed from each other, not just geographically but also demographically and culturally. Within the United States, many frontiers appeared and disappeared over time and space. They have been classified in various ways. One simple typology, resting on gross demographic contrasts, separates frontiers within the United States. It may also assist in comparing them with frontiers in other New World countries and with empire building in Africa and Asia. This typology includes two categories, which may be (neutrally) labeled I and II. Type I consists of farming frontiers. They appeared in the Virginia Piedmont and western New England early in the eighteenth century. They kept reappearing across the Appalachians, Mississippi, and Missouri until all the land that was truly cheap and arable had been occupied on the High Plains and the Canadian prairies early in the twentieth century. The people of the farming frontiers were the colorless many. Type II includes mining camps, cattle towns, and the tobacco plantations of the seventeenth-century Chesapeake Bay area before its population became self-sustaining. Type II's people were the colorful few: cowboys, forty-niners, prostitutes, gunfighters, and mountain men. They were transients on the make, most of them male. Type I frontiers included women and children; Type II frontiers rarely did. The myths and symbols of frontiers and the West in American culture derive largely from events that happened on Type II frontiers. Farm frontierspeople were too busy trying to raise families and eke out a living to become legendary. Yet the settlement of the interior of the United States (and Ontario and western Canada)—that is, the transformation of millions of acres from wilderness to farmland—resulted from the Type I frontier repeating itself for several generations in new settings. The major differences between the two frontiers can be seen in Table 11.1.

The Overland Trail provided passage for both frontier types. In the 1840s and 1850s, over three hundred thousand people trekked from settled areas and closing frontiers east of the Mississippi to points on the Missouri River, at or beyond the edge of farm settlement, and fol-

Table 11.1 Characteristics of Type I and Type II Frontiers

Type I	Type II
Farming, farm building	Mining, cattle, other extraction industries
Families, usually nuclear	Individuals
Balanced sex distribution	80–90 percent (or more) male
Many children	No children
A few over 45 years old	Almost none over 45 years old
High birthrate	Low birthrate
Relatively permanent	Transient
Peaceful	Violent
Colonizing	Imperialist, exploitative

lowed the Overland Trail across future Nebraska and Wyoming toward destinations to the west. Until the late 1840s, virtually all overlanders headed for Oregon's Willamette Valley. But beginning in 1847, Mormons followed the trail for much of its length until crossing the Continental Divide. Then, instead of proceeding northwest toward Oregon, they turned southwest until they reached the land between the Great Salt Lake and the western slope of the Wasatch Range. A third group of overlanders, quite distinct from either the Oregon settlers or the Mormons and much larger than either, followed the trail in the four summers from 1849 through 1852, passing through Mormon country and on west to the Sierras and the goldfields of California. Thus by 1850 the Overland Trail could lead to Oregon, Utah, or California—three very different frontiers.

The United States Census counted heads in all three areas for the first time in 1850. The age and sex structures of the areas were not the same (see Table 11.2). Oregon shows sex and age distributions normal for farming (Type I) frontiers in their early stages. In the later stages, the proportion of men in the population declines, gradually reaching parity with the proportion of women, first

Table 11.2 Age and Gender in Oregon, Utah, and California in 1850

Area/Type	Population	Male (%)	Age (%)		
			0–14	15–44	Over 44
Oregon (I)	13,000	62	38	54	8
Utah (I)	11,000	55	45	55	neglig.
California (II)	93,000	92	6	91	3

Source: U.S. Bureau of the Census, Historical Statistics of the United States, Colonial Times to 1970 (Washington, D.C.: Government Printing Office, 1975), Series A195–209, 1:25–36.

after young single men had established themselves and sent for brides and later as children and grandchildren replaced the pioneers. Utah exhibits an unusually balanced sex ratio for a frontier and more children than usual—evidence that the Mormons emigrated as families and that they continued their procreative duty. California, in contrast to both Oregon and Utah, was a classic Type II frontier.

A similar contrast appeared in the 1860 census in two neighboring territories farther east (see Table 11.3). By 1860 the western line of agricultural settlement, the "frontier line" (really the "Type I frontier line"), had penetrated eastern Kansas. At the same time, the Front Range of the Rockies from Pikes Peak to Denver was the

Table 11.3 Age and Gender in Kansas and Colorado in 1860

Area/Type	Population	Male (%)	Age (%)		
			0–14	15–44	Over 44
Kansas (I)	107,000	55	42	57	1
Colorado (II)	34,000	97	3	94	3

Source: U.S. Bureau of the Census, Historical Statistics of the United States, Colonial Times to 1970 (Washington, D.C.: Government Printing Office, 1975), Series A195–209, 1:25–36.

target of a gold rush, with the usual Type II characteristics. In the Type I cases (Oregon and Utah in 1850, Kansas in 1860), the males were in the majority, but only slightly, and children accounted for a large part of the population. Most of the rest were women and men in their twenties and thirties. The Type I frontier, in short, was a land of young people forming families simultaneously with farms—the demographic and economic sides of the same coin. The Type II frontiers of 1850 California and 1860 Colorado were very different—areas of young men in their late teens, twenties, and thirties. Women were absent and, therefore, so were children.

The social consequences of these demographic differences have never been quantified, but they seem incontestable. Vigilantism, shoot-outs, homicides, rapes, fights over mining claims and grazing rights, prostitution, and other social ills for which the early American West is so famous (overly so) were the products of the relatively few, the young males, who populated Type II frontiers. The Type I majority of frontierspeople were occupied more productively, and the female component made substantive contributions to community building and stability. One final difference needs to be noted. Type II frontiers were notoriously unstable; they could disappear as quickly as they formed. If the silver or gold played out or if a closer railhead opened for shipping the cattle east, the young men moved on. Type I frontiers were by no means perfectly stable. People climbing the agricultural ladder moved fairly often. But landowning, once achieved, usually meant roots.

This simple typology is about frontiers—that is, areas in their initial years of white settlement. It has much less to offer about most of the twentieth-century West, where farm-family frontiers have disappeared or never existed, yet where sex ratios have become normal and the age distribution much broader. Furthermore, some agricultural frontiers in the United States and Latin America, do not fit Type I easily and fit Type II only with difficulty. For the period before 1920, however, Types I and II appear to encompass most of the frontier activity, farm and otherwise, within the United States.

So too with Canada.[18] From the 1830s until cheap land was gone in the 1860s, Ontario was a Type I frontier quite similar to the area of the United States from Lake Ontario west to the Mississippi. But the Canadian search for farmland was diverted to the United States for the next thirty years by the Canadian Shield, that vast unplowable land of granite and muskeg between central Ontario and Winnipeg. Because of that barrier, Canada lost more people than it gained from migration between 1870 and 1900. After 1901, however, thanks to the Canadian Pacific Railroad, active recruitment of farm families by the railroad and by the Dominion government, an enlightened homestead policy, and favorable grain prices, the prairie provinces joined adjacent parts of the United States in becoming the last great Type I frontier. Canadian development, in other words, included expansive Type I frontier activity for about a century before the 1920s, except for 1870–1900. Canada also had Type II frontiers—in fact, predominantly so if one classifies the fur trade as such. Certainly the Fraser River gold rush of 1859 and the Yukon rush of the 1890s qualify. Because of the early presence of governmental authority (especially the Mounted Police), Canadian frontiers escaped the violence that marred some of the American ones. The Canadian experience shows that the social pathologies of the Type II frontiers in the United States were not an inevitable consequence of the demography.[19]

In Brazil and Argentina, the typology has to be revised considerably. In both countries, the lines of settlement moved rapidly west or northwest from the 1870s and 1880s to 1914 and beyond. European immigrants arrived in large numbers. Both countries earned prominent places in world agricultural markets—Brazil with coffee, Argentina with beef and wheat. Vast areas were opened to productive settlement, indeed settlement (by Europeans) of any kind, prodded by railroad building. Brazil's frontier tradition, however, had included sugar plantations in the northeast and, in the mid-nineteenth century, coffee plantations in the southeast, together with mining for gold and precious metals in Minas Gerais. Sugar and coffee production depended on the labor of African slaves until slavery was finally abolished in 1888. At that point the coffee planters, backed by the state of São Paulo, which they controlled politically, recruited families of immigrants (chiefly northern Italians) as a new labor force. Evaluations of the situation of these *colonos* vary. Some say their lot was miserable, others that it was "enviable" compared with that of slaves or Mexican peons. Nearly all scholars agree, however, that unless the family of *colonos* arrived with some wherewithal, they were not likely to become landowners in their own generation. Although it was possible to climb the agricultural ladder, it was very difficult. The distinctive feature of most migration from southern Europe to Brazil was its family character. Yet those families able to step into independent landholding were a small minority, with the rest functioning in some kind of sharecropping or tenant contract.[20]

In Argentina new arrivals on the pampas after 1880 were also likely to be northern Italians, but in the early years at least, they were usually single men who migrated back and forth seasonally rather than families. From farm laborers they rose in many cases—with families by that point—to tenants, owning their implements but not their land. The Argentine ladder to independent family-farm ownership was easier to climb than the Brazilian but harder than the North American. From the standpoint of the small farmer, neither Argentina nor Brazil had much of a Type I frontier. Neither country enacted effective homestead legislation or conducted a land survey to provide secure title. Independent landowning, though possible, was the exception. The moving frontier line of large young families so common in the United States and Canada was just not there. Land was available in Argentina and Brazil, indeed an almost endless supply—but not "free" land.[21]

In the *bandeirante*, Brazil had a frontier tradition. As the Brazilian writer Clodomir Vianna Moog describes him, the original *bandeirante* of colonial Brazil was an "emigrant . . . [who] came to Brazil without his wife, without his children, without his possessions, in search of wealth and adventure" and with "the intention of getting rich quickly and returning even more quickly." The *bandeirantes* "were initially conquistadors, not colonizers." Clearly Type II men. The North American archetype, Moog says, contrasted greatly. He was the "pioneer," the "colonizer, not conqueror," the man who with wife and children built a farm out of virgin soil.[22] Clearly a Type I man. The large coffee planters in Brazil resemble antebellum southern planters more than they do the Type I or Type II frontierspeople, and the *estancieros* of the pampas, with their horses, cattle, and thousands of hectares of land, resemble the great ranchers of Texas and the northern plains. Overlooking many qualifications and local variants, then, it can be said that the opening of the pampas and the coffee region after 1870 did not involve smallholders as in the Type I frontiers of the United States and Canada. Instead, one finds large landowners using a heavily immigrant labor force under various tenancy contracts. One could wedge some of these immigrants under the umbrella of Type I, since some did achieve the equivalent of homesteads. But not many did.

The landowner-tenant arrangement so common in Brazil and Argentina does have a parallel in the United States. Although not exact, it is suggestive. Large-scale irrigated agriculture, typical of California's Central Valley in the twentieth century and also present in Washington, Arizona, Colorado, and other western states, involves ownership of substantial acreage by a family or corporation using migrant wage laborers to work it. This is not Type I homesteading, although it could be considered Type II entrepreneuring. The migrant farm workers of the late nineteenth and early twentieth centuries in California (Chinese, Japanese, Filipino, Punjabi) exhibited the skewed age and sex distributions of Type II frontiers, whereas later migrants (Okie-Arkie, black, Mexican) did not. Large-scale agriculture using migrant labor goes on today. Either the frontier gave way to modern capitalism (as applied to agriculture) at some unspecified point or the frontier continues.[23] More likely, the Type I frontier concluded with the end of cheap arable land, while the Type II frontier continues without the demographic distinctiveness it once had. In the transatlantic context, among the four major frontier nations of 1870–1914, the Type I homesteading frontier became the anomaly—a great attraction as long as it lasted. Without it—and it never was really present in Argentina or Brazil—migrant wage labor became the norm in Pan-American agriculture as it had been for centuries in European. To simplify even further: In Type I frontiers, the farmer owned the land, the means of production; in Type II frontiers, some tenants (in Argentina, occasionally Brazil) owned implements, which were also means of production, while others (for example, migrant wage laborers today and in the past) owned essentially no means of production. This last group includes not only farm workers but also hard-rock miners, lumber workers, and other migrants, single or not.

What, finally, of empires? In an extended sense they too are Type II frontiers. They combined the demographic weaknesses and economic exploitativeness of older Type II frontiers, as well as the landlord-tenant/capitalist-worker relationships, which are continuing versions of socioeconomic relationships. Demographic examples include the British raj, Rhodesia, South Africa, the Belgian Congo, Francophone West Africa, and Indochina. In these important Asian and African cases a small European population, disproportionately male (partly because much of it was military), superimposed itself on an indigenous population that had existed for centuries or longer and had possessed every quality of a self-replenishing population, including normal sex and age distributions.[24]

Europeans had been colonists earlier, of course, creating the nations of the New World during the nearly four hundred years since Columbus. In fact, the apparent success of frontier making, especially by the United States, encouraged European empire building.[25] With obvious exceptions, such as the Puritans and Mennonites, the initial motives for that earlier colonization—by the Spanish in Mexico and Peru, the Portuguese in Brazil, and the British in Virginia—had been largely economic. In the 1870s and 1880s, with few exceptions (for example, the German colonies in East and West Africa, which were more the result of nationalistic policy than any population pressure), European empire building was exploitative.[26]

It was also frequent. When the 1880s opened, as indigenes were suppressed on the pampas and the Great Plains and as railroads and settlers quickly appropriated the land they vacated, the British were at war in Afghanistan, France annexed Tahiti, and the Boers defeated a

British force at Majuba Hill. In 1882 the British defeated the Arabs at Tel-el-Kebir and occupied Egypt and the Sudan. In 1883 the French began "protecting" Annam and Tonkin. Germany occupied Southwest Africa, Togo, and Kamerun in 1884, while Britain established protectorates in Basutoland, the Somali Coast, Nigeria, and New Guinea. In 1885 the Mahdi overran "Chinese" Gordon at Khartoum, but Germany annexed Tanganyika and Zanzibar, while Leopold II of Belgium became proprietor of the Congo. From then until 1890, Burma, Zululand, Baluchistan, much of Borneo, Uganda, and Sikkim went to the British. During that same period, Germany occupied parts of Oceania, including the Bismarck Archipelago, reaffirmed its treaty rights in Samoa, and stepped toward a base at Kiaochow in northern China. In 1892 France began ruling Dahomey. From a late-twentieth-century standpoint the outward thrust of Europe is astonishing for its reach as well as its rapidity—and the completeness of its reversal. Of all these places, only Tahiti remains politically connected to Europe.

New World frontier making, in contrast, involved many more people and, consequently, remained a reality. The Type I frontier ended, often painfully, with the overfarming of the High Plains in the Dakotas, the Front Range states, Oregon, Saskatchewan, and Alberta. Tens of thousands of homesteaders poured into those areas from 1901 to about 1915 (and into northwestern Alberta and Saskatchewan into the 1920s), and tens of thousands withdrew from many parts of the Great Plains and Great Basin after 1920, defeated by low crop prices, drought, and other problems. The cultural momentum of two hundred years of Type I frontiering, it seems, carried many would-be settlers farther than they should have gone. Miserable and tragic as homestead failures were, however, they pale in comparison with the carnage involved in the creation of the European empires and in their later collapse.

They also pale in comparison with the permanent harm done to indigenous peoples, as all such cross-cultural contact had done since 1492. If the cultures coming into contact with each other were different in substance but about equally complex, as was true of the British-Hindu or French-Annamese contacts, and if they shared the same diseases and immunities, then the European incursion did not last beyond about 1950. If the Europeans carried more diseases and the indigenous culture lacked immunities, then the indigenes were usually destroyed or, at best, made permanently dependent. According to William H. McNeill, land was "free" or "open" because culture combined with biology to the great disadvantage of the indigenes: "The 'empty' frontier Turner spoke of arose from the destruction of Amerindian populations by infections imported from the Old World, sporadically reinforced by resort to armed force," as well as by superior skills in agriculture, warfare, and administration or other factors.[27] In South and North America, much of this destruction took place on Type II frontiers.

The years from 1870 to 1914 were especially marked by the expansion of European empires and European-stock frontiers. Except for the numbers of Europeans involved—few with the empires, many with the frontiers—the lines between the two thrusts cannot be drawn sharply. Both resulted from similar impulses that included economic gain, self-improvement, conquest, greed, *missions civilisatrices*, and others—and without much consideration for the indigenous people and culture, primitive or advanced. Such was the world of a century ago. Perhaps one of its lessons is that enduring conquests (or defenses) are demographic.

12

LAYING SIEGE
TO WESTERN HISTORY

The Emergence of New Paradigms

WILLIAM G. ROBBINS

HERBERT HOOVER, a graduate of Stanford University and the first true westerner to become president of the United States, provides an appropriate symbol for the American West at the turn of the century. The story of the youthful mining engineer who went off to Australia in 1898 in the employ of the British firm Bewick, Moreing, and Company sharply challenges the notion that the American West functioned as an isolated frontier backwater of an emerging world power. The young Quaker's education itself suggests the influence of the region's major industry on university training—in his case, mining. Hoover's professional engineering experiences, first in Australia and later in China, also point to the revolutionary effects of capital in simultaneously reshaping landscapes and economies in various parts of the globe.[1] And the concomitant mass immigrations and the disruption of indigenous populations worldwide reflect the totality of the modernizing forces that must properly be called global capitalism.

That the area many easterners refer to as "out West" should be the focal point for American relations with the Pacific Rim should come as no surprise. From the beginning of the sea otter trade along the northern Pacific Coast at the close of the eighteenth century through the years of the California gold rush, the Pacific slope had been tied to oceanic routes for travel, for trade, and to a significant degree—particularly in the case of San Francisco—for sources of investment capital.[2] The transcontinental rail links that spanned North America during the last thirty years of the century firmed and further integrated easterly ties to what could truly be termed an increasingly international web of cultures, economies, and regions.[3] It is appropriate, then, that Herbert Hoover, who was educated in the West (including the public schools in Newberg, Oregon) and whose early career took him to the western edge of the Pacific Rim, should be acclaimed as modern America's first international citizen.[4]

The historic connectedness of the West to wider geographical and cultural phenomena, to reciprocal continental and transoceanic economic relations, has never been central to scholarly discussions about the region until recently. But the publication of two important books— Donald Worster's *Rivers of Empire* (1985) and Patricia Nelson Limerick's *Legacy of Conquest* (1987)—and the emergence of what has been dubbed the New Western History have served to refashion and redefine discourse about the place we call the West.[5] This reassessment of the position of the West in the national mythology has centered in part on one of the most powerful intellectual paradigms in American history: Frederick Jackson Turner's frontier thesis.

At one time Turner's ideas commanded our attention and gave scholars the social underpinnings for the task of understanding the frontier, especially in its westernmost form. For several decades his work served as the most influential set of legitimizing ideas for historical inquiry into the condition of western development. Turner also established the intellectual basis for a global concept of the frontier, one that appeared in more mature form in Walter Prescott Webb's *The Great Frontier* (1952).⁶ Now, nearly a century removed from the crafting of Turner's grand thesis, the old verities seem quaint and mythical, outdated reminders of a different national mood.

And if we are to believe recent press releases, newspaper articles, and journal essays, there are subversives loose in the halls of the academy these days, scholars prowling in search of some of western America's most hallowed icons, many of them shrouded in Turnerian metaphors. Although both the challengers and the defenders of the old conventions have indulged in considerable exaggeration and overstatement, I would argue that the present swirl of scholarly discussion centering on the field is the most exciting series of intellectual exchanges since the early assaults on the Turner Thesis in the 1930s.

The American West, perhaps more than any other major region, has always been important for its international connections and significance. Although the West has enjoyed oceanic links to distant places, peoples, and cultures and borderland ties to Mexico and Canada, historians—with few exceptions—have placed little emphasis on that fact. Henry Nash Smith observed that the agrarian tradition, so evident in Turner's writing, "made it difficult for Americans to think of themselves as members of a world community because it has affirmed that the destiny of this country leads her away from Europe toward the agricultural interior of the continent." Few historians, according to Donald Worster, have pursued Smith's criticism of the "isolation of western writing."⁷ This chapter will emphasize, albeit not exclusively, the more recent scholarship on the northern and southern borders of the American West to illustrate that the region has always been part of continental and worldwide human and economic networks, especially those associated with the global influence of modern capitalism.

ONE CONSEQUENCE of the recent debates over western history, discussions that embrace both empirical and theoretical formulations, is that historians of the American West are beginning to vie with those from other regions in framing discourse about our national culture and its relationship to larger global phenomena. Richard White, who has raised some of the more fundamental questions, believes that the dialogue has reinvigorated and will continue to stimulate the study of western history. The present acknowledgment of the importance of the Pacific Rim, he argues, has placed the West at the physical center of events in the larger realm of national affairs.[8] The heyday of southern history, once the preeminent field for the most progressive and exciting endeavors in American historiography, has passed. If the impressive vitality of the current literature on the West is any indication, the new geographical setting for the most challenging scholarly discourse is America beyond the Mississippi. As the long "American Century" draws to a close, the West would appear to be the most appropriate regional forum for that discussion.

And the stakes are high! If law represents the power to order the contemporary world, then broadly interpretative and widely accepted historical explanation represents the power to define a national culture. Certainly that is true of the Turner Thesis, which, at least until the onset of the Great Depression, provided a seemingly convincing approach to understanding the growth and development of the United States. In truth, it was an argument that fit the prevailing *mentalité* of the patriarchal, Anglo-Saxon-dominated world of the early twentieth century. It also posited the thesis that the American frontier was a unique and independent agent, little influenced by outside forces, and therefore a powerful environmental determinant in shaping human inhabitants to accord with its own requirements. With its strident emphasis on positivism and the exceptionalism of the American condition, Turner's Thesis offered an explanatory model that was largely unchallenged until the spiraling unemployment and economic crisis of the Great Depression.[9]

But the Turner myth, spurred by American global hegemony immediately following World War II, lived on in lecture halls and public forums, despite the early admonishments of Frederick Shannon, Henry Nash Smith, Earl Pomeroy, and a host of other critics.[10] Even though historical scholarship on the American West was little affected at the time, the exceptionalist theme began to erode in the wake of events both distant and domestic—the Vietnam war and the civil strife of the 1960s—when scholars began to take a less optimistic, more tragic view of the American past.[11] William Howarth put the case well in a recent review: "After Dallas and Vietnam it was hard to admire gunfighters or new frontiers. . . . [T]he old landscape of hope has faded: Today the western news is of dying farms and toxic dumps, the latest detonation at Ground Zero." Or as Peter Schrag of the *Sacramento Bee* observed: Long before the October 1989 earthquake and the collapse of the Nimitz Freeway, the story of the once Golden West had "turned toward the dark side of things."[12] It seems accurate to say that the "true" West, or the interpretations that are emerging in the New Western History, had its origins in the graduate academies of the late 1960s and the 1970s. European scholarship—especially that associated with social history, world-systems, and dependency modeling—and other academic disciplines have infused the new history with fresh insights and novel formulations and methodologies.

A sizable number of western historians whose ranks span generational boundaries have scoffed and grumbled at professional meetings and in book reviews about this hydra-headed attack. The packed session at the 1989 meeting of the Western History Association in Tacoma, Washington—"What's Wrong and Right with Western History"—is a case in point. The panelists, among them William Cronon, White, and Worster, engaged the audience in a sometimes sharply worded debate over the accomplishments and achievements of the old and new in western history. Later, in the hotel elevator following the session, a senior scholar expressed his resentment at what he called "Turner bashing" by the panelists.[13] References to the "Gang of Four"—Limerick, Worster, White, and Cronon—have also circulated in recent months. Still other critics refer to the "promotional tour" carried out by the scholars in question.

Much of that seems spiteful, with the customary accusations directed at revisionist scholarship—charges of misreading texts and quoting out of context. According to Martin Ridge, a considerable volume of the new work is an angry story that emphasizes resource exploitation and the retelling of efforts by underclass groups in the West to regain control of their own destiny. "It is a history," he charges, "where ideology is too often substituted for evidence."[14] But critics like Ridge ignore the fact that, to this writing, Frederick Jackson Turner still provides the most powerful *ideological* argument for interpreting the American past.

Beyond its Turnerian critique, the new scholarship also points to a pervasive anti-intellectualism in the writing of western history, a distrust of any work grounded in a larger theoretical framework. Some of that unease is

187

also directed at interpretations that invoke the dreaded "C" word—capitalism—in discussing the West and its larger world in the nineteenth and twentieth centuries. Collectively, those currents of disagreement with the revisionism of the last few years suggest that the field is literally under siege.

Richard White, one of the more innovative among the revisionists, praises the "conflict and controversy" that has contributed such vitality to the field: "There is more that is right with western history than is wrong with it." The great potential for the field, he notes, rests with younger scholars, some of whom do not even consider themselves western historians. It was White who phrased several of the more quotable verbal weapons in the arsenal of the New Western Historians at a conference in Santa Fe, New Mexico, in October 1989. He told a reporter that there was "a lot of vigor in our field. But let's face it, none of us will ever be as influential as Turner." Surveying the fray among his colleagues from his sanctuary at Montana State University, Michael Malone agrees that no "other single, overarching interpretation will ever hold sway the way Turner's frontier hypothesis once did." Malone, who has one scholarly foot in the camp of the revisionists, urges historians to examine larger sets of relationships, especially ones associated with political economy.[15]

But it is Patricia Limerick who has attracted the most attention. Her spirited book *Legacy of Conquest*, and her advocacy of the new history, has stirred sometimes less than polite discussion. In a December 1989 article in the *New York Times*, Richard Bernstein wrote a petulant and censorious essay on the New Western History in which he singled Limerick out for special criticism. Citing *Legacy* as the "fullest expression of the new history," Bernstein placed its author in the category of the "extreme critics" of Turner, scholars who were "throwing verbal caution to the winds." After personal interviews with Limerick and White—persuaded perhaps by Limerick's sardonic sense of humor and White's wry smile—Bernstein appeared to come full circle, indeed, to have become a convert himself. Writing in the *New York Times Magazine* in March 1990 he praised the intellectual breadth and depth of the new history.[16] But critics who resent Limerick's debunking of the Turnerian school (and who appear even more offended by her sharp wit at professional meetings) exaggerate her attacks on Turner.

Although *Legacy* is more anecdotal than theoretical, its author has a firm grasp of the larger arena of historical interpretation. The keepers of the Turnerian flame who find *Legacy* pretentious ignore the author's tribute to the grand master of western history as "a scholar with intellectual courage, an innovative spirit, and a forceful writing style." But like others who practice the art of historical interpretation, Turner viewed the past within the context of his own generation. And like Turner, Limerick also takes her "cues from the present." Sometime in the future, she points out, her argument "will be overtaken by unplanned obsolescence."[17]

Given the vibrant intellectual activity of recent years, it seems unlikely that a single thesis will ever again dominate western history. If, as Donald Worster claims, Turner once presided "over western history like a Holy Ghost," the articles and books now coming into print strongly hint that the Ghost itself has been laid to rest. In the 1960s and 1970s, as part of the growing influence of the new social history, some scholars began putting aside the Turnerian approach to study "particular western places, people, and events." That intellectual ferment, part of the broader current of change in historical scholarship and centered first in minority and ethnic studies, laid the groundwork for the present revolution in western history. And that is the special irony in Limerick's point! Because scholars who define themselves as urban, ethnic, labor, or environmental historians are doing some of the most exciting research in the field, their work has not been deemed *Western* history.[18]

The great variety of "new" histories that have emerged in the last two decades (social, labor, ethnic, and political) suggest that intellectual anarchy may be afoot in the land—that is, unless scholars are able to agree on some common moorings to anchor their arguments. David Kennedy raised the question in the May 1990 *OAH Newsletter*: Have the new histories "been fruit or flower, substance or decoration?" They have been harmful, he concluded, to the degree that they have "fragmented the picture of the past" and to the extent that they have "deflected our collective attention from questions of power." The net influence of this spate of revisionism, Brian Dippie argues, "has been new topics rather than a consistent new direction." As it has for the broader arena of American history, the recent focus on class, ethnic, and gender factors has vastly expanded the conceptual framework for discourse on western history. Yet there is, in what appears an excessive fractionalizing of scholarly work, a need to look to some larger reckoning points.[19] Multiple viewpoints, even paradigms, may be healthy for the field, but we should still strive toward interpretations that are firmly grounded in the material structure that is history.

But that is the beauty of the debates that are swirling about the New Western History. Tempered in part by a far less optimistic vision of American culture, the new scholarship self-consciously focuses on the darker side, the tragic elements to western history. Donald Worster, for example, sees the West as a study of "willful injustice," a search for the messy truths behind the veil of innocence.

Much of the evil about America, he notes, is associated with western symbols and themes; hence, scholars of the region should also be first-rate social and cultural critics and face up to the tragedy in their midst. Turner's West was born to a theory, Worster argues in *Rivers of Empire*, "that has no water, no aridity, no technical dominance in it, that indeed has very little of the West as geographically defined today."[20] Worster's West is not one purely of the imagination; rather, it is a region where real people have struggled for survival under a variety of circumstances. That West is worthy of our greater attention.

The recent outpouring of monographs and interpretative essays suggests that scholars are doing their work well. The more-prominent published literature features research that places conquest, domination, ethnic and racial strife, questions of class and gender, and environmental disruption at the center of scholarly study. What has emerged, in the few efforts at synthesis currently in print, is a view of the West that is cast in a larger geographical framework and one that is decidedly more apocalyptic than utopian. There have been a number of disclaimers, including Larry McMurtry's argument that the tragic vision has already been told and "by abler historians than most of the revisionists." In balance, though, the new interpretations cling more closely to what Richard Etulain calls the "flawed and decaying Eden" of Joan Didion's modern California.[21]

ALTHOUGH THE writing of United States history has long suffered from a paucity of theoretical argument,[22] that has begun to change in the last two decades. And the most recent work on the American West is contributing its part to an expanding literature that is firmly and empirically grounded within a larger theoretical construct.

That effort should help scholars to think differently about basic facts, from a broader perspective, and to be more critical in context. William Cronon and Richard White, among others, have suggested theoretical routes that might prove productive in raising new questions for the field. In his study of dependency among the Choctaws, Pawnees, and Navajos, White posits the examination of an interrelated set of phenomena as the most fruitful approach to understanding relationships of power: "the extent to which economic activities within a region . . . reflect factors essentially controlled outside the area; the lack of economic diversification and choice; and domestic distortions—social and political, as well as economic—within affected societies."[23]

In truth, both White and Cronon seek a broader context to explain change in the American West—sets of relationships that transcend the region and link it with larger networks of power in other parts of the world. Cronon, who confided on one occasion that he sometimes feels like the hired gun for the neo-Turnerians, argues for a "frontier as process" *and* a "West as region" approach. But he is at one with White, Malone, and others in insisting that the issues be set out on "a broad continental canvas" that allows for the study of race, class, capitalism, and related themes. North America, Cronon points out, "developed within a larger system of political and economic relationships which have been affected by such things as changing international resource bases, the rise of the corporation, and the growth of the modern state."[24] Turner's ghost notwithstanding, scholars of the American West have actually been examining those issues for some time.

One might begin with the work of Josiah Royce, whose book on Gold Rush California was published in 1886. Royce wrote about American California, what he called the "exciting formative years, from 1846 to 1856." The great bonanza phenomenon may have been "exciting," but Royce's story was decidedly pessimistic, dwelling in part on violence, racial prejudice, and social irresponsibility. Although Royce purposefully neglected the Hispanic/Mexican influence, he discussed in detail the inhumane and ruthless conquest of the native population. Earl Pomeroy made the modern argument for the value of Royce's work in a 1970 essay: "Royce's concern with war, the tension of individual and community, and attitudes toward foreigners and members of racial minorities makes the history of pioneer California seem close to the moral and political issues of the 1970s."[25] But for their time, a heady sense of imperial, Anglo-centered nationalism emerged in the late nineteenth century and Turner's more positive thesis subsumed Royce's view.

In his provocative and informative book *Beyond the Frontier* (1989), Harold Simonson provides convincing evidence that the tragic vision associated with frontier metaphysics is present in all of the great American writers of the mid-nineteenth century: Emerson, Thoreau, Whitman, and especially Melville. Simonson finds that tempered and sober refrain even more apparent among writers nurtured in the late nineteenth century and early twentieth century (including Turner!). *Beyond the Frontier*, therefore, cautions proponents of the New Western History from staking too loudly their claims to having discovered the tragic element in frontier and western history. That theme, treated in Simonson's earlier book *The Closed Frontier* (1970), is addressed even more forcefully in *Beyond the Frontier*, principally through the works of Melville, Mark Twain, Ole Rölvaag, and Nathanael West.[26]

But my intention here is not to provide a detailed historiographical lineage to what is "old" in the New Western History, a task that necessarily would embrace, among many others, Melvyn Dubovsky's work in labor history and Roger Daniels's efforts in ethnic history.[27] That undertaking would require another essay in itself. Rather, my purpose is to discuss some of the recent monographic building blocks—centering on studies of the borderland/Southwest and the northern West—that provide the intellectual and ideological foundation for the New Western History. That is an impressive and rapidly expanding volume of literature, with special strengths in borderlands, Native American, ethnic, gender, and environmental studies, narratives that lend themselves to contradiction, irony, and tragedy, the dark underbelly of conquest and exploitation in the American West. The empirical basis for much of the new work is also solidly framed in theoretical argument.

BENEFITING IN part from historical circumstances that include the shattering and building of empires, the economic colonization of one nation by another, and the complex dynamics of race and class, researchers in borderlands studies and the American Southwest have led the field in pioneering new models of investigation. David Weber, the foremost borderlands scholar of the moment, points to one of the ironies of comparing Mexican and United States history: In Mexico "there has been no counterpart to the American idealization of frontier life. No myth about the salubrious impact of the frontier exists on which a Mexican Turner might construct a credible intellectual edifice."[28] The metaphor was a poor fit: In Mexico and the United States, expansion carried nearly opposite meanings. In contrast, its imperial neighbor to the north experienced a persistently advancing frontier that brought ever greater riches to the nation-state.

Scholars seeking alternative models for approaching frontier or borderlands studies would also do well to read the ongoing work of Donald Meinig, who is in the midst of writing a magisterial, three-volume historical geography of North America. Meinig grounds his thesis "on the elementary fact that the United States has neighbors. It shares the continent and adjacent seas with other states, nations, and peoples." For the conventional Hispanic borderland, Meinig sees a need for more precise description and careful analysis of the area's ever changing demography. The conquest of 1848, he contends, marked "the drawing of a line through what has become one of the world's great cultural borderlands."[29] Scholars would be wise to recognize the historically dynamic character of the borderlands human geography.

To further stake their claim to independence, borderlands scholars have shown little interest in the grand national mythologies associated with a "westward movement." Freed from those mental constraints, revisionist students of southwestern history and culture have more readily adopted the newer methodologies and theoretical models in their work. In that broader context, Mexico looms large in any analytical equation concerning the region; still relatively underdeveloped, it has been for most of its existence a peripheral nation in the world capitalist system. And perhaps its most striking feature—as many scholars have pointed out—is that America's southwestern borderland has been linked to systems of exploitation, to traditions of violence, and cultural and racial oppression, circumstances that have persisted to this writing.[30] Those combined forces provide the material structure for some of the more provocative scholarship of our time.

Begin with David Montejano's award-winning *Anglos and Mexicans in the Making of Texas, 1836–1986* (1987), a complex study of what are essentially political questions involving race, class, and the distinctions and inequalities between Anglos and Mexicans. Montejano's work, especially its theoretical argument, is thoroughly revisionist; his frontier, stripped of its legendary aspects, is one where cowboys are wage workers and indebted servants, where the coming of barbed wire represented a kind of enclosure movement that displaced landless people, and where the great cattle trails were instruments that linked the region to national and international markets. For Mexicans in Texas, the nineteenth century was characterized by the loss of their land base and the twentieth century by the "organization of Mexican wage labor." The lives of most Mexican people in Texas, Montejano concludes, had been reduced by the 1920s "to the status of landless and dependent wage laborers."[31] *Anglos and Mexicans* and other studies of its kind go far to reclaim voices left out of the conventional western story. Or, at least, they indicate that there is more than one version of the story to tell.

What Montejano and the revisionists have portrayed is a version of southwestern history that is considerably less than a triumphal narrative. Although Montejano's story is not one of total and unmitigated tragedy and failure, it is a sobering account of a struggle *for* space and *against* cultural and economic oppression, a thoroughly researched work that provides new terms and categories for analyzing western history. Montejano effectively uses the ever integrating forces of the market mechanism and the complexities of international relations to place this study of southern Texas in the larger context of continental and world affairs. The conquest of 1848, therefore, reflected new political realities; it did not mean a permanent separation of cultures, economies, and peoples.

The transborder character of revisionist scholarship on the Southwest is reflected in a series of excellent urban studies. Especially significant is the work of Oscar Martinez whose first book, *Border Boom Town* (1978), examines the historical development of Ciudad Juarez and its dependency upon El Paso and the United States business sector. The story of Juarez, the author points out, is closely linked to that of El Paso: "One city is an outpost of a developing country while the other is at the outer edge of a modern industrial power."[32] The modern history of the region involved the gradual penetration of the market system in the nineteenth century and the eventual integration of the area into multinational global financial strategies in the twentieth century. The forcible imposition of capitalist legal relations and contests over land ownership accompanied the transition from subsistence living to the integration of indigenous people as dependent wage laborers. Hence, for the forces of a modernizing capitalist system, the political boundary separating the United States and Mexico did not present an impenetrable barrier in the nineteenth century—nor does it in the late twentieth century.

The classic history of a community on the United States side of the border is Mario García's *Desert Immigrants* (1981), a study that details the racial and political discrimination, the second-class citizenship, and the cultural erosion that Mexican Americans in El Paso have experienced in the nearly one hundred fifty years since the conquest. The movement of Mexicans northward, García argues, should be placed in the larger context of geopolitics: the influx of external capital to the Southwest; the entrance of Mexicans into the wage-labor force in large numbers; the socioeconomic dislocations in Mexico because of foreign investments during the rule of Porfirio Díaz; and the persistence in the region of a mostly extractive and agricultural economy. More than a century after the conquest, García concludes, Mexicans "still suffer economic, political, and social disparities in contrast to Americans in El Paso."[33]

Central to the argument of many borderlands/southwestern scholars is the distinction between the developed and industrialized economy to the north and the developing economy to the south. In *The United States–Mexico Border* (1977), Raul Fernandez examines the unique juxtaposition of rich and poor countries, "between 'developed' and 'underdeveloped' nations," on the two sides of the border. Fernandez argues convincingly that scholarship on the Southwest must reckon with two important developments: imperial America's conquest of a large part of Mexican territory and the persistence of Mexican emigration northward, especially in the twentieth century. The latter fact, Fernandez concludes, is closely linked to "two vastly different socio-economic fabrics, a material representation of the ties that one can find elsewhere between advanced and backward nations."[34] Suffice it to say that much of the argument in revisionist work on the Southwest suggests that labor and class issues along the borderland are not an anomaly in the modern world.

To a large degree, methodology also is a distinguishing feature of borderlands and southwestern historiography. It is significant, I believe, that the work of many in this group emphasizes the importance of historical materialism. "Meaningful research and analysis," Fernandez insists, "must be grounded on the material forces and social relations of production which ultimately define the historical course of any group of people." It is sheer folly to concentrate one's research on blaming one group for committing atrocities against another—an approach, Fernandez points out, that "meets the requirements for moral indignation but goes no further."[35] In that sense, the methodology of historical materialism avoids existential posturing over social evils, permits the study of production and its contradictions, and explains the material circumstances of life and its emerging ideology.

There are several studies of the Southwest that deserve praise for their innovative and fresh methodological approaches. Thomas D. Hall's *Social Change in the Southwest, 1350–1880* (1989) examines the social transformation of the region and its progressive integration into wider global economic and cultural worlds. His work, which covers the period just before the coming of the Spaniards to the arrival of the railroad, presents a convincing empirically based argument that uses dependency theory as a general model for explaining change.

The significance of *Social Change in the Southwest* is its contention that alterations in the role and function of the frontier must be seen in the context of events elsewhere, that the West is a place with international connections and significance. Using dependency theory (the expansion of the developed world into undeveloped regions), Hall argues that the extraction of resources from one area and the appropriation of wealth by another block development and may even retard the internal dynamics of the affected society. In that sense, the American conquest of the Southwest vastly accelerated the internal expansion of the market mechanism and introduced a set of factors that simultaneously linked the peripheral Southwest with the trading network of the more-advanced states.[36]

Hall's methodological (and theoretical) approach is important in other respects. Although he has adopted dependency theory as a *general* model, he is cognizant of the more-problematic issues associated with its application. World-systems theory, he contends, is more a "paradigm" (in Thomas Kuhn's sense) than it is a "theory." The world-systems approach, in Hall's view, "is a model for applying analysis; the importance of a paradigm in that sense is in posing questions that can be answered via a known strategy." As such they cannot be tested or proved "but are more or less useful."[37]

Although removed in time and place, John Thompson's *Closing the Frontier* (1986) invokes a similar model to explain, albeit a bit more crudely, the incorporation of Oklahoma into the larger network of appropriation and exchange relations that shaped its politics into the twentieth century. Oklahoma, according to Thompson, was a peripheral, resource-rich area in a greater "expansionist economic system based in the Northeast and in Europe." As a frontier enclave, the state was both a source of inexpensive raw materials *and* "an outlet for excess population." The successes of corporate capitalism in appropriating the wealth of Oklahoma was merely one element of a larger picture—the expansion and development of a world capitalist system.[38] In the distribution of benefits from those reciprocal relationships, centers of capital far removed from the region reaped most of the wealth.

Perhaps the most complex and impressive of the recently published research on the Southwest is Sarah Deutsch's *No Separate Refuge* (1987), a study of a regional community of Hispanics in northern New Mexico and southern Colorado. The thrust of her inquiry is the gradual erosion of the community's autonomy as its residents are drawn into the network of market and wage relations. Deutsch offers a persuasive argument that employs gender as a category of analysis but that fully integrates corresponding issues of culture, class, and market and wage relations on the Anglo-Hispanic frontier. As Hispanic women increasingly entered the Anglo-dominated wage-earning work force in the twentieth century, they found themselves "isolated and peripheral for the first time."[39] *No Separate Refuge* is unique in that it illustrates the increasing marginalization of its constituents over time, a view that counters the positivist version that would have those communities progressively integrated and assimilated into the Anglo world as the twentieth century advanced.

THERE IS A marked difference in the emphasis of recent scholarly literature when one looks north to the United States–Canadian border. At least for the United States side, historians have been more conventional, less innovative, and slower to adopt the analytical and theoretical models that one finds in the current work on the Hispanic borderland and the Southwest. And yet, Donald Meinig reminds us, Canada, sprawled across the continent from the Atlantic to the Pacific, "is one of the great facts of American life." If Mexicans have been fearful of their proximity to the United States—a point recognized in borderlands studies—then it is not surprising that Canadians should attach special meaning to "continentalism," the persisting fear that the infinitely more powerful United States would devour its northern neighbor. Grasping that special reality, Meinig suggests, can help us understand the American impact on modern-day Canada.[40] And it might offer some inviting ideas for cross-border historical analysis and comparisons.

There are fundamental historical and cultural differences that characterize the political boundaries that separate the United States from its northern and southern neighbors. The northern boundary, despite the aggressive designs of the United States, was established through negotiation, not naked conquest. The differences between Canada and the United States, however, are still considerable: "The frontiersman," Seymour Martin Lipset contends, "has never been a figure for special glorification in Canadian literature." But the differences between the

United States and Mexico, centering on issues of race and class, are even greater. Population centers along the Unites States–Canadian border, Raul Fernandez points out, do not share the same historic conditions that prevailed among their southern counterparts. Even the references themselves carry different meanings: The "boundary" divides the United States and Canada, whereas the "border" separates the United States and Mexico. The larger meaning of "border" and its corollary "border town," according to Fernandez, "has negative connotations which imply conditions of unsettlement and hostility."[41] Those conditions have never existed, in that special sense, along the United States–Canadian boundary. Might not, then, that general perception influence the kind of scholarship that the northern West produces? I suggest that it does.

To begin with, the disparities in class are infinitely greater between the United States and Mexico than they are between the United States and Canada. And when one looks at entire national populations, the demarcation among cultures and societies is much sharper between the United States and Mexico. But on the American side of the former Mexican empire, the picture is less distinct. The great numbers of Spanish-speaking people (and increasingly people of other cultural and language groups) in California and the Southwest confuse the clear delineation of race and class, of cultures and societies. Historically, those conditions have never prevailed along the United States border with Canada. Perhaps one reason for the more conventional scholarship centering along the United States–Canadian border is that the cross-border characteristics of race and class are roughly similar.

In addition, there has been no historic mass movement of Canadians in the northern West to the United States on a scale that compares with the Southwest; indeed, if there has been a population exodus, it has been from the western United States northward. Those common demographic features between Canada and the United States would tend to mute the attendant tensions and contradictions. One Canadian scholar, who has underscored the common historical features that accompanied the expansion of the two nation-states north of the Rio Grande, finds the parallels between Canadian and American economic expansion westward significant, even striking.[42] If it is true, therefore, that historical scholarship tends to seek out points of greater social tension, it follows that the southern borderland may simply provide a more attractive arena of research for many.

In comparison with their American counterparts, Canadian scholars have been more adventurous and bold in seeking out larger paradigms for analysis and in producing innovative works that fit some of the components of the New Western History. Moreover, there are elements unique to Canadian historical literature (as there are to Mexican) that distinguish it from United States scholarship: (1) a persistent strain of anti-Americanism, one that can be traced to the movement of Loyalists northward during and after the American Revolution; (2) a continuing "healthy fear of being smothered by Manifest Destiny"; and (3) except for an occasional roundtable discussion, a general lack of interest among Canadian historians over the Turner myth. The absence of a counterpart to the Turner paradigm in Canada, according to Lipset, may be because the latter never developed a "universalistic ideology."[43]

Class conflict and industrial warfare have also influenced the work of Canadian scholars of the Canadian West to a greater degree than they have the work of their cross-border counterparts. Martin Robin, Patricia Marchak, and David Jay Bercuson, among others, have centered their research on hinterland extractive industries in western Canada. Their focus on closed and polarized communities, the effects of cyclical and seasonal employment, and the strength and militancy of the union movement has had a profound influence in shaping politics in and popular perceptions about the region.[44] At least to this date, American scholars have not enjoyed a comparable impact on popular thinking about *their* West.

Students of Canadian economic development have pointed to the domination of the western provinces by a chain of city-states, each controling a vast hinterland. Foremost among those using dependency theory as a general model for analysis is Patricia Marchak, whose several books and articles have detailed the historic vulnerability of single-industry economies within the larger framework of modern capitalism. Those backcountry communities, she points out, remain "underdeveloped" in the late twentieth century and have found it impossible to reverse the process of exploitation.[45] Although a kind of mutual intellectual exclusiveness exists among Canadian and American scholars, Marchak has influenced the work of some of her American counterparts.

But the concern of this chapter is innovative American scholarship, or the lack thereof, not Canadian. And there is ample evidence of a progressive "greening" of scholarly work on the northern West, although it is different from that of the Southwest. One of the early signs of the move away from the triumphal narrative was the publication in 1970 of Norman Clark's now classic study of Everett, Washington. *Mill Town* was not a celebratory account of the state's major industry—logging and lumbering—during its territorial and early statehood years. With graceful prose, Clark portrayed a less than flattering story of those years of burgeoning economic growth. Although the state experienced a dramatic increase in population between 1890 and 1920 and an equally impressive and expanding productive output, for Everett those achievements rested on "competitive plunder," a system, according to Clark, "constantly at war with rationality and order."[46]

Still the most innovative study of its kind on the northern West is Richard White's *Land Use, Environment, and Social Change* (1980), a broad-ranging application of the new environmental history to Island County in Washington's Puget Sound. White traces the impact of Indian and later "intruding peoples" on a common land base. He argues forcefully that the environmental history of Island County is applicable to a much wider area (indeed, I would suggest, it fits much of the Douglas fir bioregion).[47] To this day, White's study remains one of a kind.

My own *Hard Times in Paradise* (1988) examines the relationship between the outside capitalists who invested in the lush timber resource in southwestern Oregon and the set of communities dependent upon its exploitation for their survival. The study finds little autonomy among those communities. Rather, they prospered and suffered in accord with decisions made in distant corporate boardrooms, with the relative health of the American economy (especially its building-construction sector) and with the ever diminishing acreages of the once magnificent forests. *Hard Times* describes a population similar to the one portrayed in Marchak's *Green Gold*—single-industry communities with few economic prospects in the late twentieth century other than to provide inexpensive, low-tax homesites for California retirees.[48]

Some of the more exciting research on the northern West has centered on the state of Montana where scholars have crafted a widely respected historical literature, most of it anti-Turnerian. Among the best is Michael Malone's

The Battle for Butte (1981), an account of that high-mountain community's early and turbulent history. Butte's story to the present, Malone concludes, is one of "booms, busts, strikes, and severe dislocations." But the struggles in Butte were much larger: The entrepreneurial jousting for control of the area's rich copper veins "corrupted" the political culture of Montana and "left behind a bitter heritage." Elsewhere Malone has placed western mining into an international perspective. Full integration into the global economy by the 1970s, he observes, has placed mining and similar communities in the West increasingly at risk.[49]

Two other studies centering on Butte should be included among the recent and innovative literature on Montana: David Emmons's *The Butte Irish* (1989) and Jerry Calvert's *The Gibraltar* (1988). Emmons's study emphasizes that immigration and ethnicity, class consciousness, and industrialism are vital components to understanding the West. Other western states had towns like Butte and Anaconda, he argues, "places whose history is only now being told—and by non-western historians." The authors of the new scholarship, according to Emmons, "take pleasure in confounding the old historical calculus," because those stories of the agrarian frontier West were "self-indulgent and self-deceptive." Emmons places himself with Patricia Limerick and others who believe it is "time to tell the story of everyone who lived in the West."[50]

The world of agriculture in the northern West is the subject of two revisionist studies that examine homesteadinq efforts between 1900 and 1920: Paula Nelson's *After the West Was Won* (1986) examines homesteading in western South Dakota, while Barbara Allen's *Homesteading the High Desert* (1987) tells the story of similar efforts in south-central Oregon's high-desert country. Both of their arguments counter the Turner myth in at least three fundamental ways: (1) the era of open land did not end in 1890; (2) the frontier was not a place of economic opportunity; and (3) women were an equal and vital part, along with men, of the homesteading experience. Using oral histories as well as more conventional sources, Nelson and Allen trace the hardships and difficulties associated with dry-farming efforts in the first decades of this century. Allen concludes that settlement came to south-central Oregon "like a flood tide and receded almost as rapidly, leaving the inevitable debris in its ebb."[51]

Carlos Schwantes, who has written extensively on the northern West, has suggested in a more general way new approaches to the study of the West. His ideas about labor protest, disinheritance, and a "wageworkers' frontier," though reflecting Turnerian literary devices, nevertheless offer potentially fruitful alternatives for studying the hinterland West. His first book, *Radical Heritage* (1979), provides a cross-border analysis of radical labor and socialist activities in Washington and British Columbia. In *Coxey's Army* (1985), a more mature expression of his thinking, Schwantes tells a compelling story of "disinherited" wage-earning laborers responding to the first large-scale industrial depression in the United States.[52]

Even more significant, because it has attracted a wide readership, is Schwantes's *The Pacific Northwest*, a book that incorporates some of the revisionist ideas associated with the New Western History. Describing the region as a hinterland and, for much of its past, a tributary to more powerful cities and regions of the country, Schwantes—striving to avoid a triumphalist approach—enlists the lives of common people, including women, in his story. But it is the hinterland metaphor, argued consistently and persuasively throughout, that is most compelling: "The region's role as a supplier of raw materials gave economic life in the Pacific Northwest its special contours." In the end, however, Schwantes departs from this interpretation. Influenced in part by John Naisbitt's *Megatrends: Ten New Directions Transforming Our Lives* (New York: Warner Books, 1982), he suggests that the Northwest is beginning to shed its hinterland status,[53] a point that seems dubious, given the region's continued and heavy reliance on agriculture and natural resources and the fact that *Megatrends* has already proved faulty as a barometer for the future. Stable community living based on high-tech economic enterprise may prove as ephemeral for the northern West as its former dependence on mining and lumbering.

STUDIES THAT ADDRESS various elements of the New Western History, so apparent in the recent work on the southern and northern West, are also obvious in scholarship on the Great Plains, the urban environment, issues of resource dependency, the proliferation of gender-based inquiries, California as a phenomenon in itself, and the West as one component in a global constellation of an ever changing capitalist system. Some of these approaches deserve mention because they suggest new ways and fresh perspectives for thinking about the West.

Among the vital points of inquiry in the field are the crosscurrents between the increasingly sophisticated work on women's history and its intersection with the New Western History. Sarah Deutsch's *No Separate Refuge* deserves mention again for its elaboration of gender (and class) relations among Hispanic communities. Carrying the discourse on women in the West in a different and equally sophisticated direction is Peggy Pascoe's *Relations of Rescue* (1990), a book that traces the lives of western Protestant women and their search for female authority. Pascoe's account suggests once again how the study of gender can enhance our understanding of western history.[54] One suspects that future work in the field will contribute to the further integration of the gender issue as part of the larger mosaic that is western history.

For the Great Plains region, both Donald Worster and Frederick Luebke have pioneered new models for analyzing human occupation of the Great Plains. Although Worster's award-winning study of the Dust Bowl is the better known, Luebke has contributed a series of provocative essays that trace the influence of various human populations as they swept into and occupied the corridor adjacent to the Platte River. To the Platte Valley came Americans from the more eastern states and sizable numbers of European immigrants: Irish, English, Swedes, Germans, Danes, Poles, and Czechs. Nebraska, a state shaped by railroads, was but a unit in a larger world of change that linked the revolutionary forces of technology, increased agricultural production on the Great Plains, and the disruption of the agricultural economies of Europe into a web of reciprocal and interrelated effects and consequences. Primarily an agricultural people, according to Luebke, Nebraskans "have tended to see themselves as victims of distant and oppressive economic forces."[55]

In that sense the Great Plains of the nineteenth century were at one with changes that have occurred in coastal California in the second half of the twentieth century, where silicon-based production has led to the fuller integration of the region into an international capitalist system. The two best examples of the emergence of these new forms of postindustrial production systems are the Silicon Valley complex to the south and east of San Francisco and the once-thriving center of fruit growing, Orange County. For the latter, Spencer Olin and an interdisciplinary team of scholars have completed an important, broad study of the transformation of the county from an agricultural to a postindustrial, high-tech base. In recent years the region's bankers, financiers, and corporate executives, according to Olin, have entered into foreign investment and global economic ventures that have "completely reshaped not only the economic and suburban landscapes, but . . . the political landscapes as well."[56] By the 1980s Orange County had emerged as part of an international trade and capital-flow network that involved a functional production system within a global territorial structure.

World wars, international intrigues and boycotts, and the manipulations in the 1970s and 1980s of the energy cartels have had far-reaching influences on some of the more isolated parts of the West. Andrew Gulliford's *Boomtown Blues* (1989), a history of the boom-and-bust cycles associated with oil shale extraction on Colorado's Western Slope, shows clearly that those economic gyrations are not exclusive to the late twentieth century. When Exxon stopped work on its Colony Oil Shale Project in western Colorado on May 2, 1982, the subsequent "bust" was only the most recent in a cycle of economic downturns that have occurred throughout the West during the last century. Citizens on Colorado's Western Slope, Gulliford argues, once again "found themselves powerless to control the external economic forces dictating development."[57]

Among the more significant contributions of recent years is the ongoing work of Walter Nugent, a senior scholar whose impressive play with census data has led to inquiries that fit the West into a larger global network involving the movement of people and capital. Coupling national demographic statistics with the worldwide expansion of the industrial nations, Nugent traces European migrations in the late nineteenth and early twentieth centuries to manufacturing centers in the United States, to the mines and grain-producing regions in North and South America and Australia, and to coffee plantations in Brazil. Although the oceanic exodus from Europe was truly global in scope, Nugent reminds us that nearly two-thirds of the emigrants who left Europe between 1840 and World War I went to the United States. One might quarrel with the *Annales* typologies Nugent uses to describe his categories of frontier characteristics, but his wide-ranging analysis points to the fundamental impulses and consequences of that vast movement of peoples, cultures, and economies: "gain, self-improvement, conquest, greed, *missions civilisatrices*, and others—and without much consideration for the indigenous people and culture, primitive or advanced."[58]

Finally, the American West has provided the setting for some of the more innovative conceptual modeling for the new urban history. And to the degree that those studies treat their urban units as part of the greater West with reciprocal influences that extend beyond national borders and ocean barriers, they fit the prescription for the New Western History. Carl Abbott, who has presented the best synthesis of urban scholarship on the West, points out that the dramatic population growth of World War II introduced fundamental changes in "the economic functions of western cities." Moreover, that metropolitan explosion reflected larger structural alterations in the American economy. Cities in the region, Abbott observes, "have led and benefited from the increasing internationalization of the United States during the 1960s and 1970s." The most powerful metropolitan enclaves in the West—San Francisco, Los Angeles, Houston, Dallas–Fort Worth—vastly expanded and intensified their regional influences. Much of the hinterland West, Abbott notes, found itself increasingly dependent upon the money and markets of California's metropolitan empires.[59] In other words, as conduits between local hinterlands and continental and world financial networks, major western cities reaped great advantages. And the more they prospered, the more their respective outbacks suffered.

THE CLOSING YEARS of the twentieth century may prove auspicious ones for the field of western history. First came the publication in 1989 of state-of-the-art essays edited by Gerald Nash and Richard Etulain intended to "delineate major trends and approaches" to the twentieth-century West. Later that year, D. C. Heath published a collection of documents and essays designed for courses in western and frontier history. Edited by Clyde Milner, this volume included important primary sources and essays published during the last twenty years that bear on important issues in western history.[60]

And then, as the capstone to the renewed efforts at synthesis in western history, the University of Nebraska Press in 1989 released the first survey of the twentieth-century West since the publication in 1978 of Gerald Nash's well-known *The American West in the Twentieth Century*. Authored by Michael Malone and Richard Etulain and chosen as one of the History Book Club selections, *The American West* clearly shows the influence of the new research. In seven chapters, the authors address most of the conventional textual themes: economics, politics, social patterns, culture, gender, war, and depression. The volume also includes an excellent bibliography.

Although Malone and Etulain do not portray the modern West as an unalloyed success story, they do indicate modest progress in what can best be described as a pluralist world: in the election of conservatives and lib-

erals, minorities, and women to public office; in the movement of people of color into the mainstream of public life;
and in the forward thrust of all groups in the region on
"the road to modernity." In the end, however, the authors
resort to a timeworn and positivist argument: "The old
political order of western 'colonial' subservience to the
East, and of confrontational politics between exploitative
corporations and their allies on the one side and down-
trodden farmers and workers on the other, now seemed
quaintly historical."[61] In essence, the Malone-Etulain effort at synthesis is more conventional than innovative,
more inclined to straddle historical controversy than to
take a stand, more prone to follow standard interpretation than to seek "life-out-on-a-limb"—to invoke Patricia
Limerick's phrase.

There are hints and suggestions of other works in progress. Perhaps the most keenly awaited is Richard
White's *It's Your Misfortune and None of My Own*, to be
released in late 1991 by the University of Oklahoma
Press. According to White, the "text doesn't mention the
frontier," because the term is ethnocentric and derived
from a Euro-American perspective. In lieu of the customary moving-frontier approach, White treats the West as a
region and centers on competition among differing
peoples over a common land base: "The whites moving
into the West represented one of a series of migrations
but not the only one," he insists. White does not focus exclusively on disaster and sorrow, but he is fully aware
that expansion had its costs.[62]

What, then, can we say about the new revisionist approach to western history? Has it—with its multifaceted
agenda that raises issues of gender, class, ethnicity, the
capitalist world-system, and environmental costs—prevailed over the more conventional Turnerian-influenced
model? In truth, that is the wrong question, because since

the earlier publications of Earl Pomeroy and Gerald Nash, the field has been in need of fresh perspective, of greater cross-disciplinary analysis, of scholars who would think about the region as part of a larger global order. That university presses everywhere are now churning out such work is an indication of the vitality and innovative capacity of western history.

Although we may admire Larry McMurtry's play with words, he is dead wrong when he describes the recent revisionist tendencies in western history as a Herfalo, a "wretched animal" that proved a disappointment to everyone, including its creator, who had experimented by crossing a buffalo with a Hereford. But if we define a revisionist as "someone who sees basic facts in a different way,"[63] I would argue that we need more interpretations of that kind. There is virtue to rethinking the past unencumbered by Turnerian or frontier apronstrings. With the wealth of exciting and creative work under way in western history, we can take heart from Rabbit's advice to Pooh Bear: "In every tree there's honey."

NOTES

PREFACE

1. Richard Maxwell Brown of the University of Oregon, Albert Camarillo of Stanford University, and Alfonso Ortiz of the University of New Mexico also made major presentations in Santa Fe, but limits of time prevented them from preparing the papers for publication. Richard Etulain of the University of New Mexico, Howard Lamar of Yale University, and John Mack Faragher of Mount Holyoke College served as respondents and commentators.

CHAPTER 1. BEYOND THE AGRARIAN MYTH

1. Originally, this essay was given as the opening address at the "Trails: Toward a New Western History" conference, Santa Fe, New Mexico, September 1989.

2. Josiah Gregg, *The Commerce of the Prairies* (Lincoln: University of Nebraska Press, 1926), 31.

3. Paul Horgan, *Josiah Gregg and His Vision of the Early West* (New York: Farrar, Straus, Giroux, 1972), esp. 110.

4. Ian Frazier, *Great Plains* (New York: Farrar, Straus, Giroux, 1989), 1, 209–210, 214.

5. Robert G. Athearn, *The Mythic West in Twentieth-*

Century America (Lawrence: University Press of Kansas, 1986), 273.

6. Henry Nash Smith, *Virgin Land: The American West as Symbol and Myth* (Cambridge, Mass.: Harvard University Press, 1950), 187.

7. Ibid.

8. Ibid., 251.

9. Richard Hofstadter, *The Progressive Historians: Turner, Beard, Parrington* (New York: Alfred A. Knopf, 1968), 103–104.

10. Ibid., 106.

11. As one of my predecessors at the University of Kansas, George Anderson, once put it, the history of the West was about growth in "banks, rails, and mails." See his essay of that title in John G. Clark, ed. *The Frontier Challenge: Responses to the Trans-Mississippi West* (Lawrence: University Press of Kansas, 1971), 275–307.

12. Gerald D. Nash, *The American West Transformed: The Impact of the Second World War* (Bloomington: Indiana University Press, 1985), 215–216.

CHAPTER 2. TRASHING THE TRAILS

1. Lorenzo Sawyer, *Way Sketches: Containing Incidents of Travel across the Plains* (New York: Edward Eberstadt, 1926), 32–33.

2. Donald Worster, *Dust Bowl: The Southern Plains in the 1930s* (New York: Oxford University Press, 1979), and *Rivers of Empire: Water, Aridity, and the Growth of the American West* (New York: Pantheon Books, 1985).

3. William deBuys, *Enchantment and Exploitation: The Life and Hard Times of a New Mexico Mountain Range* (Albuquerque: University of New Mexico Press, 1985).

4. Walter Crockett to Dr. Black, October 15, 1853, University of Washington Library. Cited in Richard White, *Land Use, Environment, and Social Change: The Shaping of Island County, Washington* (Seattle: University of Washington Press, 1980), 35.

CHAPTER 3. WESTERN WOMEN AT THE CULTURAL CROSSROADS

1. A slightly different version of this essay was presented at the "Trails: Toward a New Western History" conference in Santa Fe, New Mexico, in September 1989. I would like to thank Patty Limerick for her invitation to speak at that conference and Valerie Matsumoto and John Faragher for their insightful comments on my presentation there.

2. Christine Stansell, "Women on the Great Plains, 1865–1890," *Women's Studies* 4 (1976): 87–98; John Mack Faragher, *Women and Men on the Overland Trail* (New Haven, Conn.: Yale University Press, 1979); Julie Roy Jeffrey, *Frontier Women: The Trans-Mississippi West, 1840–1880* (New York: Hill and Wang, 1979); Lillian Schlissel, *Women's Diaries of the Westward Journey* (New York: Schocken Books, 1982). A vocal critic of this interpretation is Sandra L. Myres, *Westering Women and the Frontier Experience, 1800–1915* (Albuquerque: University of New Mexico Press, 1982).

3. See Beverly Stoeltje, "A Helpmate for Man Indeed: The Image of the Frontier Woman," *Journal of American Folklore* 88 (January-March 1975): 25–41; Susan Armitage, "Through Women's Eyes: A New View of the West," in Armitage and Elizabeth Jameson, eds., *The Women's West* (Norman: University of Oklahoma Press, 1987), 9–18; Corlann Gee Bush, "The Way We Weren't: Images of Women and Men in Cowboy Art," in *Women's West*, 19–

34; Sandra Myres, "Women in the West," in Michael Malone, ed., *Historians and the American West* (Lincoln: University of Nebraska Press, 1983), 369–386; and Glenda Riley, "Frontier Women," in Roger L. Nichols, ed., *American Frontier and Western Issues: A Historiographical Review* (Westport, Conn.: Greenwood Press, 1986), 179–198.

4. Review essays include Joan Jensen and Darlis Miller, "The Gentle Tamers Revisited: New Approaches to the History of Women in the American West," *Pacific Historical Review* 49 (May 1980): 173–214; Paula Petrik, "The Gentle Tamers in Transition: Women in the Trans-Mississippi West," *Feminist Studies* 11 (Fall 1985): 678–694; Elizabeth Jameson, "Toward a Multicultural History of Women in the Western United States," *Signs* 13 (Summer 1988): 761–791; Antonia Castañeda, "Gender, Race, and Culture: Spanish-Mexican Women in the Historiography of Frontier California," *Frontiers* 11, no. 1 (1990): 8–20; Myres, "Women in the West"; and Riley, "Frontier Women." Anthologies include Armitage and Jameson, eds., *Women's West*; Lillian Schlissel, Vicki Ruiz, and Janice Monk, eds., *Western Women: Their Land, Their Lives* (Albuquerque: University of New Mexico Press, 1988); Joan Jensen and Darlis Miller, eds., *New Mexico Women: Intercultural Perspectives* (Albuquerque: University of New Mexico Press, 1986); and Karen Blair, ed., *Women in Pacific Northwest History: An Anthology* (Seattle: University of Washington Press, 1988).

5. Jeffrey, *Frontier Women*; Myres, *Westering Women*; Glenda Riley, *Frontierswomen: The Iowa Experience* (Ames: Iowa State University Press, 1981); Glenda Riley, *The Female Frontier: A Comparative View of Women on the Prairie and the Plains* (Lawrence: University Press of Kansas, 1988).

6. Myres, *Westering Women*.

7. Two notable attempts to do this are Antonia Cas-

tañeda, "Comparative Frontiers: The Migration of Women to Alta California and New Zealand," in Schlissel et al., eds., *Western Women*, 283–300, and Sarah Deutsch, *No Separate Refuge: Culture, Class, and Gender on an Anglo-Hispanic Frontier in the American Southwest, 1880–1940* (New York: Oxford University Press, 1987).

8. On this point, see Richard White, "Race Relations in the American West," *American Quarterly* 38, no. 3 (1986): 396–416.

9. Jensen and Miller, "Gentle Tamers Revisited"; Jameson, "Multicultural History"; Castañeda, "Gender, Race, and Culture"; Lillian Schlissel, Vicki Ruiz, and Janice Monk, "Introduction" to *Western Women*, 1–9; Rosalinda Méndez Gonzáles, "Distinctions in Western Women's Experience: Ethnicity, Class, and Social Change," in Armitage and Jameson, eds., *Women's West*, 237–251; Joy Harjo, "Western Women's History: A Challenge for the Future," in *Women's West*, 305–309.

10. Ramón Gutiérrez, *When Jesus Came, the Corn Mothers Went Away: Power and Sexuality in New Mexico, 1580–1846* (Stanford, Calif.: Stanford University Press, 1991); Deutsch, *No Separate Refuge*; Vicki Ruiz, *Cannery Women, Cannery Lives: Mexican Women, Unionization, and the California Food Processing Industry, 1930–1950* (Albuquerque: University of New Mexico Press, 1987); Patricia Zavella, *Women's Work and Chicano Families: Cannery Workers of the Santa Clara Valley* (Ithaca, N.Y.: Cornell University Press, 1987); Julia Kirk Blackwelder, *Women of the Depression: Caste and Culture in San Antonio, 1929–1939* (College Station: Texas A&M University Press, 1984); Antonia Castañeda, "Presidarias y Pobladores: Spanish-Speaking Women in Monterey, California, 1770–1821," Ph.D. diss., Stanford University, 1990; Deena Gonzalez, "The Spanish-Mexican Women of Santa Fe: Patterns of Their Resistance and Accommodation,

1820–1890," Ph.D. diss., University of California, Berkeley, 1985. For articles, see Adelaida del Castillo, ed., *Between Borders: Essays on Mexicana/Chicana History* (Encino, Calif.: Floricanto Press, 1990); Ellen DuBois and Vicki Ruiz, eds., *Unequal Sisters: A Multicultural Reader in U.S. Women's History* (New York: Routledge, 1990); and Vicki Ruiz and Susan Tiano, eds., *Women on the United States–Mexico Border: Responses to Change* (Westminster, Mass.: Allen and Unwin, 1987).

11. The major book-length study is Evelyn Nakano Glenn, *Issei, Nisei, War Bride: Three Generations of Japanese American Women in Domestic Service* (Philadelphia: Temple University Press, 1986). Collections of articles include Asian Women United of California, *Making Waves: An Anthology of Writings by and about Asian American Women* (Boston: Beacon, 1989); DuBois and Ruiz, eds., *Unequal Sisters*; Genny Lim, ed., *The Chinese American Experience: Papers from the Second National Conference on Chinese American Studies* (San Francisco: Chinese Historical Society of America and the Chinese Culture Foundation of San Francisco, 1984); and Nobuya Tsuchida, ed., *Asian and Pacific American Experiences: Women's Perspectives* (Minneapolis: Asian American/Pacific American Learning Resource Center and General College, University of Minnesota, 1982). Recent articles not available in these collections include Nazli Kibria, "Power, Patriarchy, and Gender Conflict in the Vietnamese Immigrant Community," *Gender and Society* 4 (March 1990): 9–24; Jill Ker Chay, "Freed from the Elders but Locked into Labor: Korean Immigrant Women in Hawaii," *Women's Studies* 13, no. 3 (1987): 223–234; George Anthony Peffer, "Forbidden Families: Immigration Experiences of Chinese Women under the Page Law, 1875–1882," *Journal of American Ethnic History* 6 (Fall 1986): 28–46; Eun Sik Yang, "Korean Women of America: From

Subordination to Partnership, 1903–1930," *Amerasia* 11 (Fall/Winter 1984): 1–28; and Evelyn Nakano Glenn, "Split Household, Small Producer, and Dual Wage Earner: An Analysis of Chinese American Family Strategies," *Journal of Marriage and the Family* 45 (February 1983): 35–46. Work in progress includes Judy Yung, "Unbinding the Feet, Unbinding Their Lives: Social Change for Chinese Women in San Francisco, 1902–1945," Ph.D. diss., University of California, Berkeley, 1990; Sucheng Chan, "Chinese Women in California, 1860–1910: A Demographic Overview" and "The Exclusion of Chinese Women, 1874–1943," both in Chan, ed., *Living under Exclusion: The Chinese in the United States, 1882–1943* (forthcoming); and Valerie Matsumoto, "From Aunt Miya to Fem-A-Lites: Japanese American Acculturation and Ethnic Identity, 1930–45" and "Desperately Seeking 'Deirdre': Gender Roles, Multicultural Relations, and the Nisei Literati of the 1930s," papers presented at the seventh and eighth Berkshire Conferences on the History of Women, 1987 and 1990.

12. Two excellent bibliographic guides to this literature are Patricia Albers, "From Illusion to Illumination: Anthropological Studies of American Indian Women," in Sandra Morgen, ed., *Gender and Anthropology: Critical Reviews for Research and Teaching* (Washington, D.C.: American Anthropological Association, 1989), 132–170, and Rayna Green, *Native American Women: A Contextual Bibliography* (Bloomington: Indiana University Press, 1983).

13. Susan Armitage and Deborah Gallaci Wilbert, "Black Women in the Pacific Northwest: A Survey and Research Prospectus," in Blair, ed., *Women in Pacific Northwest History*, 136–151; Anne Butler, "Still in Chains: Black Women in Western Prisons, 1865–1910," *Western Historical Quarterly* 20 (February 1989): 19–36;

Lawrence de Graaf, "Race, Sex, and Region: Black Women in the American West, 1850–1920," *Pacific Historical Review* 49 (May 1980): 285–314.

14. See Jameson, "Multicultural History."

15. Glenda Riley, *Women and Indians on the Frontier* (Albuquerque: University of New Mexico Press, 1984).

16. Ruiz, *Cannery Women, Cannery Lives.*

17. Deutsch, *No Separate Refuge*; Gonzales, "Spanish-Mexican Women of Santa Fe."

18. Henry Nash Smith, *Virgin Land: The American West as Symbol and Myth* (Cambridge, Mass.: Harvard University Press, 1950).

19. Patricia Nelson Limerick, *The Legacy of Conquest: The Unbroken Past of the American West* (New York: W. W. Norton, 1987), esp. 26–28.

20. Riley, *Women and Indians*; Susan Armitage, "Everyday Encounters: Indians and the White Woman in the Palouse," *Pacific Northwest Forum* 7 (Summer/Fall 1982): 27–30.

21. Sherry Smith, "Beyond Princess and Squaw: Army Officers' Perceptions of Indian Women," in Armitage and Jameson, eds., *Women's West*, 63–75.

22. Sylvia Van Kirk, *"Many Tender Ties": Women in Fur Trade Society in Western Canada, 1670–1870* (Norman: University of Oklahoma Press, 1983); Jennifer S. H. Brown, *Strangers in Blood: Fur Trade Company Families in Indian Country* (Vancouver: University of British Columbia Press, 1980); Jacqueline Peterson, "The People Between: Indian-White Marriage and the Generation of Metis Society and Culture in the Great Lakes Region, 1680–1830," Ph.D. diss., University of Illinois, Chicago, 1981, and "Women Dreaming: The Religiopsychology of Indian-White Marriage and the Rise of Metis Culture," in Schlissel et al., eds., *Western Women*, 49–68; John Mack Faragher, "The Custom of the Country: Cross-Cultural

Marriage in the Far Western Fur Trade," in *Western Women*, 199–226; Albert Hurtado, *Indian Survival on the California Frontier* (New Haven, Conn.: Yale University Press, 1988); Darlis Miller, "Cross-Cultural Marriages in the Southwest: The New Mexico Experience, 1846–1900," *New Mexico Historical Review* 57 (October 1982): 335–359; Rebecca McDowell Craver, *The Impact of Intimacy: Mexican-Anglo Intermarriage in New Mexico, 1821–1836*, Southwestern Studies No. 66 (El Paso: Texas Western Press, 1982).

23. Historians of Hispanic women have taken the lead in this kind of work. See especially Deena Gonzalez, "The Widowed Women of Santa Fe: Assessments on the Lives of an Unmarried Population, 1850–1880," in DuBois and Ruiz, eds., *Unequal Sisters*, 34–50; Sarah Deutsch, "Women and Intercultural Relations: The Case of Hispanic New Mexico and Colorado," *Signs* 12 (Summer 1987): 719–739; Ramón Gutiérrez, "Honor Ideology, Marriage Negotiation, and Class-Gender Domination in New Mexico, 1690–1846," *Latin American Perspectives* 12 (Winter 1985): 81–104; and Castañeda, "Gender, Race, and Culture" and "Comparative Frontiers."

24. Peggy Pascoe, *Relations of Rescue: The Search for Female Moral Authority in the American West, 1874–1939* (New York: Oxford University Press, 1990); Lisa Emmerich, " 'To Respect and Love and Seek the Ways of White Women': Field Matrons, the Office of Indian Affairs, and Civilization Policy, 1890–1938," Ph.D. diss., University of Maryland, College Park, 1987; Robert Trennert, "Victorian Morality and the Supervision of Indian Women Working in Phoenix, 1906–1930," *Journal of Social History* 22 (Fall 1988): 113–128; Helen Bannan, "Newcomers to Navajoland: Transculturation in the Memoirs of Anglo Women, 1900–1945," *New Mexico Historical Review* 59 (April 1984): 165–185.

25. "Ford Foundation Awards SIROW New Curriculum Grant," *SIROW Newsletter* 34 (January 1989): 1; "Regional Scholarship Features Research on Women of Color," *SIROW Newsletter* 35 (April 1989): 1.

CHAPTER 4. THE TRAIL TO SANTA FE:
THE UNLEASHING OF THE WESTERN PUBLIC INTELLECTUAL

1. Frederick Jackson Turner, *The Frontier in American History*, ed. Wilbur Jacobs (Tucson: University of Arizona Press, 1986), 298, 323.

2. Ray Allen Billington and Martin Ridge, *Westward Expansion: A History of the American Frontier*, 5th ed. (New York: Macmillan, 1982), and Robert E. Riegel and Robert G. Athearn, *America Moves West*, 5th ed. (New York: Holt, Rinehart, Winston, 1971).

3. Attempting to go beyond the liberal use of conjunctions, the Restored Old Western History ran into even greater trouble. In the 5th edition of *Westward Expansion*, the entire index entry on the Chinese reads, "Chinese, build the railroad, p. 583." Devoted to the building of the western railroad, page 583 also has these sentences on the Chinese: "The construction gangs were in the mountains then, battering their way over steep grades and around precipices of living rock, but the promoters had solved their worst problem—how to obtain labor in a frontier community—by importing gangs of Chinese coolies. Seven thousand pig-tailed workers hacked out the right-of-way, their broad straw hats and flapping trousers forming a picturesque sight as they trundled wheelbarrows of dirt or scampered away from charges of blasting powder."

4. As a recent example of the use of the undefined term

"post-frontier," see Richard Etulain and Michael Malone, *The American West: A Twentieth-Century History* (Lincoln: University of Nebraska Press, 1989).

5. See Thomas Kuhn, *The Structure of Scientific Revolutions*, 2d ed. (Chicago: University of Chicago Press, 1970), and Gene Wise, *American Historical Explanations: A Strategy for Grounded Inquiry*, 2d ed. (Minneapolis: University of Minnesota Press, 1980). Reading Peter L. Berger and Thomas Luckmann, *The Social Construction of Reality: A Treatise in the Sociology of Knowledge* (Garden City, N.Y.: Anchor Books, 1967), changed everything in these matters for me.

6. The works of Carey McWilliams, who was originally from Steamboat Springs, Colorado, are to my mind the most impressive in this category. At the very time that the Restored Old Western History was rebuilding the frontier empire, McWilliams was writing of Mexican-American history, agribusiness, western racial discrimination, Japanese-American relocation, water politics, and the unsettling society and culture of California. See *Factories in the Field: The Story of Migratory Farm Labor in California* (Boston: Little, Brown, 1940); *Ill Fares the Land: Migrants and Migratory Labor in the United States* (Boston: Little, Brown, 1942); *Brothers under the Skin* (Boston: Little, Brown, 1943); *Prejudice: Japanese-Americans; Symbol of Racial Intolerance* (Boston: Little, Brown, 1944); *Southern California Country: An Island on the Land* (New York: Duell, Sloane, and Pearce, 1946); *North from Mexico: The Spanish-Speaking People of the United States* (Philadelphia: J. B. Lippincott, 1949); *California, the Great Exception* (New York: Current Books, 1949).

7. My apologies to Kai T. Erikson if I have mangled his story.

8. Howard Lamar, quoted in Richard Bernstein, "Un-

settling the Old West," *New York Times Magazine*, March 18, 1990, 34, 56–57, 59.

9. I first presented this list in Donald Worster et al., "*The Legacy of Conquest*, by Patricia Nelson Limerick: A Panel of Appraisal," *Western Historical Quarterly* 20 (August 1989): 320–321.

10. Western Governors' Association, *Beyond the Mythic West* (Salt Lake City: Gibbs-Smith, 1990).

11. Joseph Wood Krutch, *The Modern Temper: A Study and a Confession* (New York: Harcourt, Brace, 1929), and *More Lives than One* (New York: William Sloane Associates, 1962), 211.

12. Quotations from Robert Utley, "Foreword," in Editors of Time-Life Books, *The Old West* (New York: Prentice Hall Press, 1990), 7, and Gerald Nash, "The West as Utopia and Myth," *Montana The Magazine of Western History* 41 (Winter 1991): 70.

CHAPTER 6. ANOTHER LOOK AT
FRONTIER/WESTERN HISTORIOGRAPHY

1. Patricia Nelson Limerick, *The Legacy of Conquest: The Unbroken Past of the American West* (New York: W. W. Norton, 1987), 17–32; Donald Worster, "New West, True West: Interpreting the Region's History," *Western Historical Quarterly* 18 (April 1987): 141–156. For criticism of Limerick, see Donald Worster et al., "*The Legacy of Conquest*, by Patricia Nelson Limerick: A Panel of Appraisal," *Western Historical Quarterly* 20 (August 1989): 303–322; and Vernon Carstensen, "A New Perspective on the West? A Review of *The Legacy of Conquest*," *Montana The Magazine of Western History* 38 (Spring 1988): 84–85. Worster's arid West definition is criticized for being too

narrow by a number of scholars, including Martin Ridge, "The American West: From Frontier to Region," *New Mexico Historical Review* 64 (April 1989): 138.

2. Gerald D. Nash, "Where's the West?" *The Historian* 49 (November 1986): 1–9. See also Walter Nugent, "Western History: Stocktakings and New Crops," *Reviews in American History* 13 (September 1985): 319–329; and Sandra L. Myres, "What Kind of Animal Be This?" *Western Historical Quarterly* 20 (February 1989): 5–17.

3. Charles S. Peterson, "The Look of the Elephant: On Seeing Western History," *Montana The Magazine of Western History* 39 (Spring 1989): 69–73.

4. Roger L. Nichols, ed., *American Frontier and Western Issues: A Historiographical Review* (Westport, Conn.: Greenwood Press, 1986), 4–6.

5. Ibid., 1–2; Gerald Thompson, "Frontier West, Process or Place?" *Journal of the Southwest* 29 (Winter 1987): 366–367.

6. Ridge, "Frontier to Region," 140.

7. Frederick Jackson Turner, *The Frontier in American History* (New York: Holt, Rinehart, and Winston, 1947), 269.

8. Ray Allen Billington, *Land of Savagery, Land of Promise: The European Image of the American Frontier in the Nineteenth Century* (New York: W. W. Norton, 1981). Anthologies of world myths that include the United States draw the majority of American examples from the frontier and the West. Of course, see Henry Nash Smith, *Virgin Land: The American West as Symbol and Myth* (Cambridge, Mass.: Harvard University Press, 1950). See also American studies scholarly journals, such as *American Quarterly*, which contain countless articles on the ingredients of America's myths. Historians might well consider applying the techniques of Joseph W. Campbell to American mythology.

9. See Robert F. Berkhofer, Jr., "Space, Time, Culture, and the New Frontier," *Agricultural History* 38 (January 1964): 21–30.

CHAPTER 8. A LONGER, GRIMMER, BUT MORE INTERESTING STORY

1. William G. Robbins, "Western History: A Dialectic on the Modern Condition," *Western Historical Quarterly* 20 (November 1989): 429–449.

2. For a few examples of books on these themes, see Richard White, *The Roots of Dependency: Subsistence, Environment, and Social Change among the Choctaws, Pawnees, and Navajos* (Lincoln: University of Nebraska Press, 1983); Edward Spicer, *Cycles of Conquest: The Impact of Spain, Mexico, and the United States on the Indians of the Southwest, 1533–1960* (Tucson: University of Arizona Press, 1962); Sarah Deutsch, *No Separate Refuge: Culture, Class, and Gender on an Anglo-Hispanic Frontier in the American Southwest, 1880–1940* (New York: Oxford University Press, 1987); David Montejano, *Anglos and Mexicans in the Making of Texas, 1836–1986* (Austin: University of Texas Press, 1987); Albert L. Hurtado, *Indian Survival on the California Frontier* (New Haven, Conn.: Yale University Press, 1988).

3. Elizabeth Johns, *Storms Brewed in Other Men's Worlds: The Confrontation of Indians, Spanish, and French in the Southwest, 1540–1795* (College Station: Texas A&M University Press, 1975); Penny Petrone, *First People, First Voices* (Toronto: University of Toronto Press, 1983); George Sabo III, "Reordering Their World: A Caddoan Ethnohistory," in Sabo and William M. Schneider, eds., *Visions and Revisions: Ethnohistorical Perspectives on Southern Cultures* (Athens: University of Georgia

Press, 1989), 25-47. Work done on perceptions of Indians during the contact period of the eastern frontier suggests how useful this approach might be when applied to the Far West. See James Axtell, "Through Another Glass Darkly: Early Indian Views of Europeans," in his *After Columbus: Essays in the Ethnohistory of Colonial America* (New York: Oxford University Press, 1988), 125-143; Mary Helms, *Ulysses' Sail: The Ethnographic Odyssey of Power, Knowledge, and Geographical Distance* (Princeton, N.J.: Princeton University Press, 1988); James Merrell, *The Indians' New World: Catawbas and Their Neighbors from European Contact through the Era of Removal* (Chapel Hill: University of North Carolina Press, 1989); Christopher L. Miller and George R. Hamiell, "A New Perspective on Indian-White Contact: Cultural Symbols and Colonial Trade," *Journal of American History* 73 (September 1986): 311-328.

4. Lillian Schlissel, *Women's Diaries of the Westward Journey* (New York: Schocken Books, 1982); Andrew J. Rotter, " 'Matilda For Gods Sake Write': Women and Families on the Argonaut Mind," *California History* 58 (Summer 1979): 128-141; Elliott West, *Growing Up with the Country: Childhood on the Far Western Frontier* (Albuquerque: University of New Mexico Press, 1989).

5. Robert G. Athearn, *The Mythic West in Twentieth-Century America* (Lawrence: University Press of Kansas, 1986); Patricia Nelson Limerick, *The Legacy of Conquest: The Unbroken Past of the American West* (New York: W. W. Norton, 1987).

6. Patricia Nelson Limerick, *Desert Passages: Encounters with the American Deserts* (Albuquerque: University of New Mexico Press, 1985); Stephen Fender, *Plotting the Golden West: American Literature and the Rhetoric of the California Trail* (Cambridge: Cambridge University Press, 1981); Robert Thacker, *The Great Prairie Fact and*

the Literary Imagination (Albuquerque: University of New Mexico Press, 1989); Howard Roberts Lamar, "Seeing More than Earth and Sky: The Rise of a Great Plains Aesthetic," *Great Plains Quarterly* 9 (Spring 1989): 69–77; Becky Duvall Reese, *Texas Images and Visions* (Austin: University of Texas Press, 1983); Vera Norwood and Janice Monk, eds., *The Desert Is No Lady: Southwestern Landscapes in Women's Writing and Art* (New Haven, Conn.: Yale University Press, 1987).

7. Douglas Unger, *Leaving the Land* (New York: Harper and Row, 1984); James Welch, *Winter in the Blood* (New York: Harper and Row, 1974); Patricia Henley, *Friday Night at Silver Star* (St. Paul: Graywolf Press, 1986); Craig Lesley, *Winterkill* (Boston: Houghton Mifflin, 1984); Kent Haruf, *The Tie That Binds* (New York: Penguin Books, 1986); William Kittredge, *We Are Not in This Together* (St. Paul: Graywolf Press, 1984); Louise Erdrich, *Love Medicine* (New York: Holt, Rinehart, and Winston, 1984); David Quammen, *Blood Line: Stories of Fathers and Sons* (St. Paul: Graywolf Press, 1988).

8. Robert Utley, *Cavalier in Buckskin: George Armstrong Custer and the Western Military Frontier* (Norman: University of Oklahoma Press, 1988), and *Billy the Kid: A Short and Violent Life* (Lincoln: University of Nebraska Press, 1989).

CHAPTER 9. AMERICAN WESTS:
HISTORIOGRAPHICAL PERSPECTIVES

1. Frederick J. Turner, "The Significance of the Frontier in American History," *Annual Report, American Historical Association, 1893* (Washington, D.C.: Government Printing Office, 1894), 199. Turner's ideas have inspired a literature of their own—biographical, analytical, critical.

For examples of all three approaches, see Ray Allen Bil-
lington, *Frederick Jackson Turner: Historian, Scholar,
Teacher* (New York: Oxford University Press, 1973), *The
Genesis of the Frontier Thesis: A Study in Historical Crea-
tivity* (San Marino, Calif.: Huntington Library, 1971), and
America's Frontier Heritage (New York: Holt, Rinehart,
Winston, 1966).

Turner did not characterize the frontiersman as notable
for introspection and reflection, but western historians
have been given to both. Comments on the state of the
field abound, along with up-to-date historiographical surveys. The annotated bibliographies in the various edi-
tions of Billington's *Westward Expansion: A History of the
American Frontier* (New York: Macmillan, 1949–1982
[5th ed. with Martin Ridge]) set the standard for the field.
For a topical listing of titles, see Rodman W. Paul and
Richard W. Etulain, comps., *The Frontier and the American West* (Arlington Heights, Ill.: AHM Publishing, 1977);
for extended historiographical discussions of selected
themes, see Michael P. Malone, ed., *Historians and the
American West* (Lincoln: University of Nebraska Press,
1983), and Roger L. Nichols, ed., *American Frontier and
Western Issues: A Historiographical Review* (Westport,
Conn.: Greenwood Press, 1986).

For the extensive periodical literature on the West, see
Oscar Osburn Winther, *A Classified Bibliography of the
Periodical Literature of the Trans-Mississippi West
(1811–1957)* (Bloomington: Indiana University Press,
1964), and Winther with Richard A. Van Orman, *A Sup-
plement (1957–67)* (Bloomington: Indiana University
Press, 1970). For the period since 1967, see the *Western
Historical Quarterly*'s topical lists of recent articles. Of
the many reflections on western history and its future, a
model of calm and lucid judgment is Howard R. Lamar,
"Much to Celebrate: The Western History Association's

Twenty-Fifth Birthday," *Western Historical Quarterly* 17 (October 1986): 397–416. In view of the many excellent guides to recent western history scholarship, I have limited myself to titles pertinent to the points I wish to make.

2. Frederic Remington, "Chicago under the Mob," *Harper's Weekly*, July 21, 1894, in Peggy Samuels and Harold Samuels, eds., *The Collected Writings of Frederic Remington* (Garden City, N.Y.: Doubleday, 1979), 152; Turner, "Significance," 227. For Remington's context, see G. Edward White, *The Eastern Establishment and the Western Experience: The West of Frederic Remington, Theodore Roosevelt, and Owen Wister* (New Haven, Conn.: Yale University Press, 1968).

3. Turner, "Significance," 227.

4. Robert G. Athearn, *The Mythic West in Twentieth-Century America* (Lawrence: University Press of Kansas, 1986); Earl Pomeroy, "Toward a Reorientation of Western History: Continuity and Environment," *Mississippi Valley Historical Review* 41 (March 1955): 579–600.

5. Leslie A. Fiedler and Arthur Zeiger, eds., *O Brave New World: American Literature from 1600 to 1840* (New York: Dell, 1968), 273; Loren Baritz, "The Idea of the West," *American Historical Review* 66 (April 1961): 618–640; Walter Prescott Webb, *The Great Frontier* (Boston: Houghton Mifflin, 1952) and *The Great Plains* (Boston: Ginn, 1931); Turner, "Significance," 201. For an extended treatment of the Fiedler-Zeiger-Baritz theme, see Howard Mumford Jones, *O Strange New World: American Culture, the Formative Years* (New York: Viking Press, 1967).

6. Pomeroy, "Reorientation," 600, 581–582, respectively.

7. Earl S. Pomeroy, *The Territories and the United States, 1861–1890: Studies in Colonial Administration* (Philadelphia: University of Pennsylvania Press, 1947);

Howard R. Lamar, *Dakota Territory, 1861–1889: A Study of Frontier Politics* (New Haven, Conn.: Yale University Press, 1956), and *The Far Southwest, 1846–1912: A Territorial History* (New Haven, Conn.: Yale University Press, 1966), 5; Paul F. Sharp, *Whoop-Up Country: The Canadian-American West, 1865–1885* (Minneapolis: University of Minnesota Press, 1955); Lewis L. Gould, *Wyoming: A Political History, 1868–1896* (New Haven, Conn.: Yale University Press, 1968), ix. Responses to Pomeroy's call for intensive investigation of frontier justice and territorial politics include John D. W. Guice, *The Rocky Mountain Bench: The Territorial Supreme Courts of Colorado, Montana, and Wyoming, 1861–1890* (New Haven, Conn.: Yale University Press, 1972), James E. Hendrickson, *Joe Lane of Oregon: Machine Politics and the Sectional Crisis, 1849–1861* (New Haven, Conn.: Yale University Press, 1967), and Ronald H. Limbaugh, *Rocky Mountain Carpetbaggers: Idaho's Territorial Governors, 1863–1890* (Moscow: University Press of Idaho, 1982). As the citations indicate, Yale's Western Americana Series, with Lamar on the advisory board, was a major outlet for territorial studies; Hendrickson's book began as a Ph.D. dissertation under Pomeroy's supervision.

The issue of radicalism in western politics remains an open one, and populism is a favorite focus. Recent scholarship supports its reform (and even radical) credentials: Lawrence Goodwyn, *Democratic Promise: The Populist Moment in America* (New York: Oxford University Press, 1976); and Robert W. Larson, *New Mexico Populism: A Study of Radical Protest in a Western Territory* (Boulder: Colorado Associated University Press, 1974) and *Populism in the Mountain West* (Albuquerque: University of New Mexico Press, 1986). John Thompson's *Closing the Frontier: Radical Response in Oklahoma, 1889–1923* (Norman: University of Oklahoma Press, 1986) argues for a radical reform tradition in Oklahoma cut short by the frontier's closure. Studies of the New Deal in the West emphasize the importance of federal aid and benefits and the conservative fears of statism, resulting in only a brief flirtation with the Democratic party: Michael P. Malone, *C. Ben Ross and the New Deal in Idaho* (Seattle: University of Washington Press, 1970), and Francis W. Schruben, *Kansas in Turmoil, 1930–1936* (Columbia: University of Missouri Press, 1969).

8. Pomeroy, "Reorientation," 588–589; William H. Goetzmann, "The Mountain Man as Jacksonian Man," *American Quarterly* 15 (1963): 402–415 (and see the exchange with Harvey Lewis Carter and Marcia Carpenter Spencer in the *Western Historical Quarterly* 6 [January 1975]: 17–32 and [July 1975]: 295–302); John E. Sunder, *Bill Sublette, Mountain Man* (Norman: University of Oklahoma Press, 1959); Lewis Atherton, *The Cattle Kings* (Bloomington: Indiana University Press, 1961); Gene M. Gressley, *Bankers and Cattlemen* (New York: Alfred A. Knopf, 1966). Gressley was particularly interested in the middlemen in the investment process: the western attorney or banker who represented the eastern investor, and the commission agent who brought borrower and lender together. For a case study of one western businessman's varied activities and particularly his role in securing eastern capital, see Robert C. Nesbit, *"He Built Seattle": A Biography of Judge Thomas Burke* (Seattle: University of Washington Press, 1961). Burke was deeply involved in railroad promotion, which has a substantial literature of its own. See, for example, Robert G. Athearn, *Rebel of the Rockies: A History of the Denver and Rio Grande Western Railroad* (New Haven, Conn.: Yale University Press, 1962), and Julius Grodinsky, *Transcontinental Railway Strategy, 1869–1893: A Study of Businessmen* (Philadelphia: University of Pennsylvania Press,

1962). The role of eastern investment in the fur trade, the cattle industry, and western transportation remains an important theme in western historical scholarship, as the bibliographies cited in note 1 above attest.

9. Richard C. Wade, *The Urban Frontier: The Rise of Western Cities, 1790–1830* (Cambridge, Mass.: Harvard University Press, 1959), 1; Duane A. Smith, *Rocky Mountain Mining Camps: The Urban Frontier* (Bloomington: Indiana University Press, 1967), 4; Earl Pomeroy, *The Pacific Slope: A History of California, Oregon, Washington, Idaho, Utah, and Nevada* (New York: Alfred A. Knopf, 1965); Arthur L. Throckmorton, *Oregon Argonauts: Merchant Adventurers of the Western Frontier* (Portland: Oregon Historical Society, 1961); Clark C. Spence, *British Investments and the American Mining Frontier, 1860–1901* (Ithaca, N.Y.: Cornell University Press, 1958). For a standard work on western mining that balances frontierism and colonialism, see Rodman Wilson Paul, *Mining Frontiers of the Far West, 1848–1880* (New York: Holt, Rinehart, Winston, 1963). John W. Reps, *Cities of the American West: A History of Frontier Urban Planning* (Princeton, N.J.: Princeton University Press, 1979), is a monumental work focused on traditional urban history concerns—town building, boosterism, growth. For the new urban history, focused on social issues (family, ethnicity, class) as well as economics and politics, see Ralph Mann, *After the Gold Rush: Society in Grass Valley and Nevada City, California, 1849–1870* (Stanford, Calif.: Stanford University Press, 1982), and Kathleen Underwood, *Town Building on the Colorado Frontier* (Albuquerque: University of New Mexico Press, 1987).

10. W. Turrentine Jackson, *Wagon Roads West: A Study of Federal Road Surveys and Construction in the Trans-Mississippi West, 1846–1869* (Berkeley: University of California Press, 1952); Forest G. Hill, *Roads, Rails,*

235

and Waterways: The Army Engineers and Early Transportation (Norman: University of Oklahoma Press, 1957); William H. Goetzmann, *Army Exploration in the American West, 1803-1863* (New Haven, Conn.: Yale University Press, 1959) and *Exploration and Empire: The Explorer and the Scientist in the Winning of the American West* (New York: Alfred A. Knopf, 1966). For a concise, balanced overview of the Indian wars, see Robert M. Utley, *The Indian Frontier of the American West, 1846-1890* (Albuquerque: University of New Mexico Press, 1984). The view from above can be gleaned from Robert G. Athearn, *William Tecumseh Sherman and the Settlement of the West* (Norman: University of Oklahoma Press, 1956), and Paul Andrew Hutton, *Phil Sheridan and His Army* (Lincoln: University of Nebraska Press, 1985). For the army's economic importance on the frontier, see William E. Lass, *A History of Steamboating on the Upper Missouri River* (Lincoln: University of Nebraska Press, 1962), and Robert W. Frazer, *Forts and Supplies: The Role of the Army in the Economy of the Southwest, 1846-1861* (Albuquerque: University of New Mexico Press, 1983); for its social role, Edward M. Coffman, *The Old Army: A Portrait of the American Army in Peacetime, 1784-1898* (New York: Oxford University Press, 1986).

11. Pomeroy, "Reorientation," 596; Irwin Unger, *These United States: The Questions of Our Past*, 4th ed. (Englewood Cliffs, N.J.: Prentice-Hall, 1989), chap. 19; C. Vann Woodward, *The Burden of Southern History* (Baton Rouge: Louisiana State University Press, 1960), 3-25.

12. Pomeroy, "Reorientation," 598; Gerald D. Nash, *The American West in the Twentieth Century: A Short History of an Urban Oasis* (Englewood Cliffs, N.J.: Prentice-Hall, 1973), 268, and *The American West Transformed: The Impact of the Second World War* (Bloomington: Indiana University Press, 1985), 216; William G.

Robbins, "The 'Plundered Province' Thesis and the Recent Historiography of the American West," *Pacific Historical Review* 55 (November 1986): 584.

13. Patricia Nelson Limerick, *The Legacy of Conquest: The Unbroken Past of the American West* (New York: W. W. Norton, 1987), 26–28.

14. Pomeroy, "Reorientation," 600; Michael P. Malone and Richard B. Roeder, eds., *The Montana Past: An Anthology* (Missoula: University of Montana Press, 1969), vi; Malone and Roeder, *Montana: A History of Two Centuries* (Seattle: University of Washington Press, 1976), vii.

15. Nichols, ed., *American Frontier and Western Issues*, 2. For an alarmist report on the decline of intellectual history, see John Higham and Paul K. Conkin, eds., *New Directions in American Intellectual History* (Baltimore: Johns Hopkins University Press, 1979); for an opposite reply, Arthur Schlesinger, Jr., "Intellectual History: A Time for Despair?" *Journal of American History* 66 (March 1980): 888–893. Peter N. Stearns, "The New Social History: An Overview," in James B. Gardner and George Rollie Adams, eds., *Ordinary People and Everyday Life: Perspectives on the New Social History* (Nashville: American Association for State and Local History, 1983), 3–21, is a salesman's pitch; William Palmer, "Lawrence Stone and the Revival of Narrative," *South Atlantic Quarterly* 85 (Spring 1986): 176–182, offers a sober assessment of social science/quantitative history's actual impact on the discipline.

16. Nichols, ed., *American Frontier and Western Issues*, 5; Spencer C. Olin, Jr., "Toward a Synthesis of the Political and Social History of the American West," *Pacific Historical Review* 55 (November 1986): 602. Olin echoes the case presented by Samuel P. Hays, "Politics and Social History: Toward a New Synthesis," in Gardner and Adams, eds., *Ordinary People and Everyday Life*, 161–179.

17. Pomeroy, "Reorientation," 590; Mario Barrera, *Race and Class in the Southwest: A Theory of Racial Inequality* (Notre Dame, Ind.: University of Notre Dame Press, 1979); Sarah Deutsch, *No Separate Refuge: Culture, Class, and Gender on an Anglo-Hispanic Frontier in the American Southwest, 1880–1940* (New York: Oxford University Press, 1987), 11. Similar themes dominate Hispanic history: Richard Griswold del Castillo, *La Familia: Chicano Families in the Urban Southwest, 1848 to the Present* (Notre Dame, Ind.: University of Notre Dame Press, 1984); Thomas E. Sheridan, *Los Tucsonenses: The Mexican Community in Tucson, 1854–1941* (Tucson: University of Arizona Press, 1986); and Vicki Ruiz, *Cannery Women, Cannery Lives: Mexican Women, Unionization, and the California Food Processing Industry, 1930–1950* (Albuquerque: University of New Mexico Press, 1987). This social-history focus, and a later time period, distinguish Chicano history from borderlands history and the towering figure of Herbert Eugene Bolton, though efforts toward integration are afoot: Gerald E. Poyo and Gilberto M. Hinojosa, "Spanish Texas and Borderlands Historiography in Transition: Implications for United States History," *Journal of American History* 75 (September 1988): 393–416.

18. The outstanding work on Indian-white relations is Francis Paul Prucha's *The Great Father: The United States Government and the American Indians* (Lincoln: University of Nebraska Press, 1984). Prucha has also prepared *A Bibliographical Guide to the History of Indian-White Relations in the United States* (Chicago: University of Chicago Press, 1977); it should be supplemented with the specialized volumes in the Newberry Library Center for the History of the American Indian Bibliographical Series, published by Indiana University Press, which provide guidance to the work of ethnohistorians as well.

For comparative colonial histories involving Indians, see James Gump, "The Subjugation of the Zulus and Sioux: A Comparative Study," *Western Historical Quarterly* 19 (January 1988): 21–36; for links to overseas colonial administration, see Walter L. Williams, "United States Indian Policy and the Debate over Philippine Annexation: Implications for the Origins of American Imperialism," *Journal of American History* 66 (March 1980): 810–831.

19. John Mack Faragher, *Women and Men on the Overland Trail* (New Haven, Conn.: Yale University Press, 1979), 187; Julie Roy Jeffrey, *Frontier Women: The Trans-Mississippi West, 1840–1880* (New York: Hill and Wang, 1979), 106. Also see Sylvia Van Kirk, *"Many Tender Ties": Women in Fur-Trade Society in Western Canada, 1670–1870* (Norman: University of Oklahoma Press, 1983); Jennifer S. H. Brown, *Strangers in Blood: Fur Trade Company Families in Indian Country* (Vancouver: University of British Columbia Press, 1980); Patricia Y. Stallard, *Glittering Misery: Dependents of the Indian Fighting Army* (San Rafael, Calif.: Presidio Press, with Old Army Press, Fort Collins, Colo., 1978); Anne M. Butler, *Daughters of Joy, Sisters of Misery: Prostitutes in the American West, 1865–90* (Urbana: University of Illinois Press, 1985); Jacqueline Baker Barnhart, *The Fair but Frail: Prostitution in San Francisco, 1849–1900* (Reno: University of Nevada Press, 1986); and Arlene Scadron, ed., *On Their Own: Widows and Widowhood in the American Southwest* (Urbana: University of Illinois Press, 1988).

20. Polly Welts Kaufman, *Women Teachers on the Frontier* (New Haven, Conn.: Yale University Press, 1984), xxii; Paula Petrik, *No Step Backward: Women and Family on the Rocky Mountain Mining Frontier, Helena, Montana, 1865–1900* (Helena: Montana Historical Society

Press, 1987); Kermit L. Hall, "The 'Magic Mirror' and the Promise of Western Legal History at the Bicentennial of the Constitution," *Western Historical Quarterly* 18 (October 1987): 431.

21. For approaches to the western myth, see the Institute of the American West, *Inventing the West* (Sun Valley, Ida.: Sun Valley Center for the Arts and Humanities, 1982), and Paul O'Neil, *The End and the Myth* (Alexandria, Va.: Time-Life Books, 1979); for its impact abroad, see Ray Allen Billington, *Land of Savagery, Land of Promise: The European Image of the American Frontier in the Nineteenth Century* (New York: W. W. Norton, 1981); for its possibilities in the classroom, see Elliott West, "Cowboys and Indians and Artists and Liars and Schoolmarms and Tom Mix: New Ways to Teach the American West," in Jacques Barzun et al., *Essays on Walter Prescott Webb and the Teaching of History* (College Station: Texas A&M University Press, for the University of Texas at Arlington, 1985), 36–60. The only textbook in western history to give the myth serious attention is Robert V. Hine, *The American West: An Interpretive History*, 2d ed. (Boston: Little, Brown, 1984).

22. Henry Nash Smith, *Virgin Land: The American West as Symbol and Myth* (Cambridge, Mass.: Harvard University Press, 1950); Webb, *Great Plains*, 491–496; Earl Pomeroy, *In Search of the Golden West: The Tourist in Western America* (New York: Alfred A. Knopf, 1957), 89.

23. Nichols, ed., *American Frontier and Western Issues*, 5; Ramon F. Adams, *Six Guns and Saddle Leather: A Bibliography of Books and Pamphlets on Western Outlaws and Gunmen*, rev. ed. (Norman: University of Oklahoma Press, 1969), *Burs under the Saddle: A Second Look at Books and Histories of the West* (Norman: University of Oklahoma Press, 1964), and *More Burs under the Saddle:*

Books and Histories of the West (Norman: University of Oklahoma Press, 1979); Don Russell, *The Lives and Legends of Buffalo Bill* (Norman: University of Oklahoma Press, 1960); Joseph G. Rosa, *They Called Him Wild Bill: The Life and Adventures of James Butler Hickok*, rev. ed. (Norman: University of Oklahoma Press, 1974); William A. Settle, Jr., *Jesse James Was His Name; or, Fact and Fiction Concerning the Careers of the Notorious James Brothers of Missouri* (Columbia: University of Missouri Press, 1966); Robert K. DeArment, *Bat Masterson: The Man and the Legend* (Norman: University of Oklahoma Press, 1979); Jack Burrows, *John Ringo: The Gunfighter Who Never Was* (Tucson: University of Arizona Press, 1987); Kent Ladd Steckmesser, *The Western Hero in History and Legend* (Norman: University of Oklahoma Press, 1965); Ramon F. Adams, *A Fitting Death for Billy the Kid* (Norman: University of Oklahoma Press, 1960); Robert M. Utley, "Billy the Kid and the Lincoln County War," *New Mexico Historical Review* 61 (April 1986): 93–120, "Who Was Billy the Kid," *Montana The Magazine of Western History* 37 (Summer 1987): 2–11, and *High Noon in Lincoln: Violence on the Western Frontier* (Albuquerque: University of New Mexico Press, 1987); Stephen Tatum, *Inventing Billy the Kid: Visions of the Outlaw in America* (Albuquerque: University of New Mexico Press, 1982). Because of western history's popular appeal, many of the specialized bibliographies in the field are geared to the collector rather than the academic historian: Custer and cowboys, gunfighters and overland trail narratives. For other studies of the myth rather than the man, see the exhibition catalog *Buffalo Bill and the Wild West* (New York: Brooklyn Museum, distributed by the University of Pittsburgh Press, 1981), and Michael Lofaro, ed., *Davy Crockett: The Man, the Legend, the Legacy, 1786–1986* (Knoxville: University of Tennessee Press, 1985).

24. See Bruce A. Rosenberg, *Custer and the Epic of Defeat* (University Park: Pennsylvania State University Press, 1974); Paul A. Hutton, "From Little Bighorn to Little Big Man: The Changing Image of a Western Hero in Popular Culture," *Western Historical Quarterly* 7 (January 1976): 19–45; and Brian W. Dippie, *Custer's Last Stand: The Anatomy of an American Myth* (Missoula: University of Montana Publications in History, 1976). Another event whose myth has received extensive attention is the Alamo; particularly useful is the exhibition catalog introduced by Paul Andrew Hutton and prepared by Susan Prendergast Schoelwer, *Alamo Images: Changing Perceptions of a Texas Experience* (Dallas: DeGolyer Library and Southern Methodist University Press, 1985). The Sioux spokesman was Russell Means in a ceremony at the Custer Battlefield on the anniversary of the Last Stand.

25. West, "Cowboys and Indians and Artists and Liars and Schoolmarms and Tom Mix," 51–52; "The West of the Imagination" (six videocassettes available from Films for the Humanities, Princeton, N.J.); William H. Goetzmann and William N. Goetzmann, *The West of the Imagination* (New York: W. W. Norton, 1986); Richard Slotkin, *Regeneration through Violence: The Mythology of the American Frontier, 1600–1860* (Middletown, Conn.: Wesleyan University Press, 1973) and *The Fatal Environment: The Myth of the Frontier in the Age of Industrialization, 1800–1890* (New York: Atheneum, 1985); Helen Winter Stauffer and Susan J. Rosowski, *Women and Western American Literature* (Troy, N.Y.: Whitstone, 1982), vi. For bibliographical guidance, see Brian W. Dippie, "Of Documents and Myths: Richard Kern and Western Art," *New Mexico Historical Review* 61 (April 1986): 147–158; James H. Maguire, "A Selected Bibliography of Western American Drama," *Western American Literature* 14 (August

1979): 149–163; and Richard W. Etulain, *A Bibliographical Guide to the Study of Western Literature* (Lincoln: University of Nebraska Press, 1982). There is a voluminous literature on western films; one of the best books from the viewpoint of the cultural historian interested in western myth was also one of the first: George N. Fenin and William K. Everson, *The Western from Silents to Cinerama* (New York: Orion Press, 1962). For images of the Indian in the nineteenth century, see Brian W. Dippie, *The Vanishing American: White Attitudes and U.S. Indian Policy* (Middletown, Conn.: Wesleyan University Press, 1982).

26. For the values celebrated in the western myth, see Brian W. Dippie, "The West That Was and the West That Is," *Gilcrease* 8 (July 1986): 1–15; for the environmentalist critique, see Roderick Nash, *Wilderness and the American Mind*, 3rd ed. (New Haven, Conn.: Yale University Press, 1982), and Lee Clark Mitchell, *Witnesses to a Vanishing America: The Nineteenth-Century Response* (Princeton, N.J.: Princeton University Press, 1981); for the entrenchment of bureaucratic expertise, see Samuel P. Hays, *Conservation and the Gospel of Efficiency: The Progressive Conservation Movement, 1890–1920* (Cambridge, Mass.: Harvard University Press, 1959); for an angry indictment of the pioneering heritage that created an ecological catastrophe, see Donald Worster, *Dust Bowl: The Southern Plains in the 1930s* (New York: Oxford University Press, 1979); for the California dream, see Kevin Starr, *Americans and the California Dream, 1850–1915* (New York: Oxford University Press, 1973) and *Inventing the Dream: California through the Progressive Era* (New York: Oxford University Press, 1985); for the plight of the Okies and the reception they met, see Walter J. Stein, *California and the Dust Bowl Migration* (Westport, Conn.: Greenwood Press, 1973); for the cowboy myth, there are several sources, none better illustrated than the exhibi-

tion catalog prepared by Lonn Taylor and Ingrid Maar, *The American Cowboy* (Washington, D.C.: American Folklife Center, Library of Congress, 1983); for the workingman's reality, see Carlos A. Schwantes, "The Concept of the Wageworkers' Frontier: A Framework for Future Research," *Western Historical Quarterly* 18 (January 1987): 39–55; for a balanced treatment that qualifies the extent of frontier violence while pointing out that it was often directed toward minority groups, see W. Eugene Hollon, *Frontier Violence: Another Look* (New York: Oxford University Press, 1974); for general qualifications on the violent tradition, see Robert Dykstra, *The Cattle Towns* (New York: Alfred A. Knopf, 1968), and Frank Richard Prassel, *The Western Peace Officer: A Legacy of Law and Order* (Norman: University of Oklahoma Press, 1972); for the argument that the tradition of frontier violence is potent and dangerous, see Joe B. Frantz, "The Frontier Tradition: An Invitation to Violence," in Hugh Davis Graham and Ted Robert Gurr, eds., *The History of Violence in America: A Report to the National Commission on the Causes and Prevention of Violence* (New York: Bantam Books, 1969), 127–154; for the monopolization and depletion of resources, see Donald J. Pisani, *From the Family Farm to Agribusiness: The Irrigation Crusade in California and the West* (Berkeley: University of California Press, 1984), Donald Worster, *Rivers of Empire: Water, Aridity, and the Growth of the American West* (New York: Pantheon, 1985), and Stewart L. Udall, *The Quiet Crisis* (New York: Holt, Rinehart, Winston, 1963), the latter for the "Myth of Superabundance."

27. Limerick, *Legacy of Conquest*, 10; Leslie Fiedler, "Montana; or The End of Jean-Jacques Rousseau," in his *An End to Innocence: Essays on Culture and Politics* (Boston: Beacon Press, 1955), 134–135. Fiedler, of course, professed to be perplexed that Montanans took exception

when he was only reporting the facts. A westerner might take a measure of comfort in Tom Wolfe's image of a New York intellectual hankering after Britsh acceptance, proving once again that old habits, especially colonial ones, die hard (*Mauve Gloves and Madmen, Clutter and Vine* [New York: Farrar, Straus, Giroux, 1976]; 118).

CHAPTER 10. BEYOND THE LAST FRONTIER: TOWARD A NEW
APPROACH TO WESTERN AMERICAN HISTORY

1. Howard R. Lamar, "Much to Celebrate: The Western History Association's Twenty-Fifth Birthday," *Western Historical Quarterly* 17 (October 1986), 397–416. See also Gene M. Gressley, "The West: Past, Present, and Future," *Western Historical Quarterly* 17 (January 1986): 5–23.

2. Walter P. Webb, "The American West: Perpetual Mirage," *Harper's* 214 (May 1957): 30–31. See also W. N. Davis, Jr., "Will the West Survive as a Field in American History?: A Survey Report," *Mississippi Valley Historical Review* 50 (March 1964): 672–685; for an instance of one American historian's condescension toward and apparent confusion of the West as frontier and as region, see James Henretta, quoted in Patricia Nelson Limerick, *The Legacy of Conquest: The Unbroken Past of the American West* (New York: W. W. Norton, 1987), 20.

3. Frederick Jackson Turner, "The Significance of the Frontier in American History," in *Frontier and Section: Selected Essays of Frederick Jackson Turner*, ed. Ray Allen Billington (Englewood Cliffs, N.J.: Prentice-Hall, 1961), 37–39, 61–62. For two especially useful explications, see Ray Allen Billington, *The Genesis of the Frontier Thesis: A Study in Historical Creativity* (San Marino, Calif.: Huntington Library, 1971); and Jackson K. Putnam, "The Turner Thesis and the Westward Movement:

A Reappraisal," *Western Historical Quarterly* 7 (October 1976): 377–404.

4. The best compendium of critiques and defenses is George Rogers Taylor, ed., *The Turner Thesis: Concerning the Role of the Frontier in American History*, 3d ed. (Lexington, Mass.: Heath, 1972). Also of enduring merit are Richard Hofstadter, *The Progressive Historians: Turner, Beard, Parrington* (New York: Alfred A. Knopf, 1968); Lee Benson, *Turner and Beard: American Historical Writing Reconsidered* (Glencoe, Ill.: Free Press, 1960); and David W. Noble, *The End of American History* (Minneapolis: University of Minnesota Press, 1985).

5. Henry Nash Smith, *Virgin Land: The American West as Symbol and Myth* (Cambridge, Mass.: Harvard University Press, 1950); Earl Pomeroy, "Toward a Reorientation of Western History: Continuity and Environment," *Mississippi Valley Historical Review* 41 (March 1955): 579–600; and Earl Pomeroy, "The Changing West," in John Higham, ed., *The Reconstruction of American History* (London: Hutchinson, 1962), chap. 4.

6. Ray Allen Billington and Martin Ridge, *Westward Expansion: A History of the American Frontier*, 5th ed. (New York: Macmillan, 1982); Ray Allen Billington, *Frederick Jackson Turner: Historian, Scholar, Teacher* (New York: Oxford University Press, 1973); Ray Allen Billington, *America's Frontier Heritage* (New York: Holt, Rinehart, Winston, 1966); Martin Ridge, "Frederick Jackson Turner, Ray Allen Billington, and American Frontier History," *Western Historical Quarterly* 19 (January 1988): 5–20; Putnam, "Turner Thesis and Westward Movement," 377–404; Michael C. Steiner, "The Significance of Turner's Sectional Thesis," *Western Historical Quarterly* 10 (October 1979): 437–466; and William Cronon, "Revisiting the Vanishing Frontier: The Legacy

of Frederick Jackson Turner," *Western Historical Quarterly* 18 (April 1987): 157–176.

7. Walter Prescott Webb, *The Great Plains* (Boston: Ginn, 1931), 8–9; Necah Stewart Furman, *Walter Prescott Webb: His Life and Impact* (Albuquerque: University of New Mexico Press, 1976), 12–14, 42–45; Gregory M. Tobin, *The Making of a History: Walter Prescott Webb and "The Great Plains"* (Austin: University of Texas Press, 1976), chaps. 8–10; one harsh reaction was Fred A. Shannon's *An Appraisal of Walter Prescott Webb's "The Great Plains": A Study in Institutions and Environment, by Fred A. Shannon, with Comments by Walter Prescott Webb, a Panel Discussion, and a Commentary by Read Bain*, Critiques of Research in the Social Sciences: III (New York: Social Science Research Council, 1940).

8. Walter Prescott Webb, *The Great Frontier* (Boston: Houghton Mifflin, 1952); and Webb, "American West: Perpetual Mirage."

9. James C. Malin, *History and Ecology: Studies of the Grassland*, ed. Robert P. Swierenga (Lincoln: University of Nebraska Press, 1984), xiii–xxvi; James C. Malin, *Winter Wheat in the Golden Belt of Kansas: A Study in Adaptation to Subhumid Geographical Environment* (Lawrence: Regents Press of Kansas, 1944); and James C. Malin, *The Grassland of North America: Prologema to Its History* (Lawrence: Regents Press of Kansas, 1947). The best examples of D. W. Meinig's conceptualization of western regionalism are "American Wests: Preface to a Geographical Interpretation," *Annals of the Association of American Geographers* 62 (June 1972); 159–184; *The Great Columbia Plain: A Historical Geography, 1805–1910* (Seattle: University of Washington Press, 1968); *Imperial Texas: An Interpretive Essay in Cultural Geography* (Austin: University of Texas Press, 1969); and

NOTES TO PAGES 144-145

Southwest: Three Peoples in Geographical Change,
1600–1970 (New York: Oxford University Press, 1972).
10. Cronon, "Revisiting the Vanishing Frontier," 172;
Limerick, *Legacy of Conquest,* 24–30; Sandra L. Myres,
"Women in the West," in Michael P. Malone, ed., *Histo-*
rians and the American West (Lincoln: University of Nebraska Press, 1983), chap. 16; Joan Jensen and Darlis
Miller, "The Gentle Tamers Revisited: New Approaches
to the History of Women in the American West," *Pacific*
Historical Review 49 (May 1980): 173, 213; and Frederick
C. Luebke, "Ethnic Minority Groups in the American
West," in *Historians and the American West,* chap. 17.
11. Among the best examples of the work of these narrative historians are Francis Parkman, *The Discovery of*
the Great West (Boston: Little, Brown, 1869), and Bernard
De Voto, *The Year of Decision: 1846* (Boston: Houghton
Mifflin, 1942); or David Lavender, *Bent's Fort* (New York:
Doubleday, 1954), and Robert M. Utley, *High Noon in Lin-*
coln: Violence on the Western Frontier (Albuquerque: University of New Mexico Press, 1987). Among many instances of the application of quantification to recent
western history, see Walter Nugent, "The People of the
West since 1890," in Gerald D. Nash and Richard W. Etulain, eds., *The Twentieth-Century West: Historical Inter-*
pretations (Albuquerque: University of New Mexico Press,
1989), chap. 1; and Paul Kleppner, "Politics without Parties: The Western States, 1900–1984," in *Twentieth-*
Century West, chap. 10.
12. Lamar, "Much to Celebrate," 401; Rodman W. Paul
and Michael P. Malone, "Tradition and Challenge in
Western Historiography," *Western Historical Quarterly* 16
(January 1985): 27–53; Walter Nugent, "Western History: Stocktakings and New Crops," *Reviews in American*
History 13 (September 1985): 319–329; Richard W. Etulain, "Visions and Revisions of the American West: Re-

cent Trends in Western Historiography," paper presented to the annual convention of the Organization of American Historians, St. Louis, April 9, 1989. See also the essays in Malone, ed., *Historians and the American West*; Roger L. Nichols, ed., *American Frontier and Western Issues: A Historiographical Review* (New York: Greenwood Press, 1986); Clyde A. Milner II, ed., *Major Problems in the History of the American West* (Lexington, Mass.: Heath, 1989); Richard Lowitt, *The New Deal and the West* (Bloomington: Indiana University Press, 1984); and Gerald D. Nash, *The American West Transformed: The Impact of the Second World War* (Bloomington: Indiana University Press, 1985).

13. Cronon, "Revisiting the Vanishing Frontier," 160.

14. Fernand Braudel, *The Structures of Everyday Life*, trans. Sian Reynolds (New York: Harper and Row, 1981); Braudel, *The Mediterranean and the Mediterranean World in the Age of Philip II*, vols. 1 and 2, trans. Sian Reynolds (New York: Harper and Row, 1972); Emmanuel Le Roy Ladurie, *The Territory of the Historian*, trans. Ben Reynolds and Sian Reynolds (Chicago: University of Chicago Press, 1979); Emmanuel Le Roy Ladurie, *The Mind and Method of the Historian*, trans. Ben Reynolds and Sian Reynolds (Chicago: University of Chicago Press, 1981); and Ernst Breisach, *Historiography: Ancient, Medieval, and Modern* (Chicago: University of Chicago Press, 1983), 370–378.

15. Bernard Bailyn, "The Challenge of Modern Historiography," *American Historical Review* 87 (February 1982): 6–8; Oscar Handlin, *Truth in History* (Cambridge, Mass.: Belknap Press, 1979), 22–23, 273–274; Theodore S. Hamerow, *Reflections on History and Historians* (Madison: University of Wisconsin Press, 1987), chaps. 3, 5; Thomas Bender, "Wholes and Parts: The Need for Synthesis in American History," *Journal of American His-*

tory 73 (June 1986): 120–136; Thomas Bender, "Wholes and Parts: Continuing the Conversation," *Journal of American History* 74 (June 1987): 123–30; and Thomas Bender, "Making History Whole Again," *New York Times Book Review*, October 6, 1985, 1, 42–43.

16. Among Herbert Eugene Bolton's many writings, the most relevant are *Wider Horizons of American History* (Notre Dame, Ind.: University of Notre Dame Press, 1967); *The Spanish Borderlands: A Chronicle of Old Florida and the Southwest* (New Haven, Conn.: Yale University Press, 1921); and "The Epic of Greater America," *American Historical Review* 38 (April 1933): 448–474. See also John F. Bannon, ed., *Bolton and the Spanish Borderlands* (Norman: University of Oklahoma Press, 1964).

17. Twelve Southerners, *I'll Take My Stand: The South and the Agrarian Tradition* (New York: Harper, 1930); Walter Prescott Webb, *Divided We Stand: The Crisis of a Frontierless Democracy*, rev. ed. (Austin: University of Texas Press, 1944); Bernard De Voto, "The West: Plundered Province," *Harper's* 169 (August 1934): 355–364; Bernard De Voto, "The West against Itself," *Harper's* 194 (January 1947): 1–13; Richard D. Lamm and Michael McCarthy, *The Angry West: A Vulnerable Land and Its Future* (Boston: Houghton Mifflin, 1982); Wallace Stegner and Page Stegner, "Rocky Mountain Country," *Atlantic Monthly* 241 (April 1978): 45–91; Wallace Stegner, *The American West as Living Space* (Ann Arbor: University of Michigan Press, 1987); William G. Robbins, "The 'Plundered Province' Thesis and the Recent Historiography of the American West," *Pacific Historical Review* 55 (November 1986): 577–597; Gene Gressley, "Colonialism: A Western Complaint," *Pacific Northwest Quarterly* 54 (January 1963): 1–8; and Gene Gressley, "Colonialism and the American West," in his *The Twentieth-Century*

American West: A Potpourri (Columbia: University of Missouri Press, 1977), 31–47.

18. Joel Garreau, *The Nine Nations of North America* (Boston: Houghton Mifflin, 1981), chaps. 7–10; Raymond D. Gastil, *Cultural Regions of the United States* (Seattle: University of Washington Press, 1975), chaps. 4–5. Garreau is fairly convincing in his depiction of a southwestern "Mexamerica," a West Coast "Ecotopia," and a midwestern "Breadbasket." But his depiction of the "Empty Quarter" reaching from the Great Basin to the Arctic is unconvincing as a region.

19. Webb, "American West: Perpetual Mirage"; Donald Worster, *Rivers of Empire: Water, Aridity, and the Growth of the American West* (New York: Pantheon, 1985); Donald Worster, "New West, True West: Interpreting the Region's History," *Western Historical Quarterly* 18 (April 1987): 141–156; and Marc Reisner, *Cadillac Desert: The American West and Its Disappearing Water* (New York: Viking, 1986).

20. Lowitt, *New Deal and the West*, chap. 14; Nash, *American West Transformed*, chap. 11; James T. Patterson, "The New Deal in the West," *Pacific Historical Review* 38 (August 1969): 317–327; Leonard Arrington, "The New Deal in the West: A Preliminary Statistical Inquiry," *Pacific Historical Review* 38 (August 1969): 311–316.

21. In addition to the works by Worster and Reisner cited in note 19, see on reclamation, Donald J. Pisani, *From the Family Farm to Agribusiness: The Irrigation Crusade in California and the West, 1850–1931* (Berkeley: University of California Press, 1984); Donald E. Green, *Land of the Underground Rain: Irrigation on the Texas High Plains, 1910–1970* (Austin: University of Texas Press, 1973); Norris Hundley, Jr., *Dividing the Waters: A Century of Controversy between the United States and*

Mexico (Berkeley: University of California Press, 1966); and Norris Hundley, Jr., *Water and the West: The Colorado River Compact and the Politics of Water in the American West* (Berkeley: University of California Press, 1975). Two exceptional histories are Elmo R. Richardson, *The Politics of Conservation: Crusades and Controversies, 1897-1913* (Berkeley: University of California Press, 1962); and Samuel P. Hays, *Conservation and the Gospel of Efficiency: The Progressive Movement, 1890-1920* (Cambridge, Mass.: Harvard University Press, 1959). Among numerous good works on modern Indian policy, see Francis Paul Prucha, *The Great Father: The United States Government and the American Indians*, 2 vols. (Lincoln: University of Nebraska Press, 1984); and Lawrence C. Kelly, *The Assault on Assimilation: John Collier and the Origins of Indian Policy Reform* (Albuquerque: University of New Mexico Press, 1983). Good beginnings on federal military expenditures and their impacts are James L. Clayton, "The Impact of the Cold War on the Economies of California and Utah, 1946-1955," *Pacific Historical Review* 36 (November 1967): 449-473; and Adam Yarmolinsky and Gregory D. Foster, *Paradoxes of Power: The Military Establishment in the Eighties* (Bloomington: Indiana University Press, 1983); "The Angry West vs. the Rest," *Newsweek*, December 17, 1979, 39; Hedrick Smith, *The Power Game: How Washington Works* (New York: Random House, 1988), 54.

22. Limerick, *Legacy of Conquest*, 17-32; Cronon, "Revisiting the Vanishing Frontier," 172.

23. Bernard Bailyn, *The Peopling of British North America: An Introduction* (New York: Alfred A. Knopf, 1986), 113; see also Bernard Bailyn, *Voyagers to the West: A Passage in the Peopling of America on the Eve of the Revolution* (New York: Alfred A. Knopf, 1986); Bailyn, "Challenge of Modern Historiography," 15; William H.

McNeill, *The Great Frontier: Freedom and Hierarchy in Modern Times* (Princeton N.J.: Princeton University Press, 1983), 3–25; William H. McNeill, *The Rise of the West: A History of the Human Community* (Chicago: University of Chicago Press, 1963); and William H. McNeill, *Arnold J. Toynbee: A Life* (New York: Oxford University Press, 1989), chaps. 9–10.

24. L. S. Stavrianos, *Global Rift: The Third World Comes of Age* (New York: Morrow, 1981). For similar insights, see Paul Kennedy, *The Rise and Fall of the Great Powers* (New York: Random House, 1987); and William Woodruff, *Impact of Western Man: A Study of Europe's Role in the World Economy, 1750–1960* (New York: St. Martin's Press, 1967). It is interesting to note that the great world-historian Arnold Toynbee took Turner quite seriously; see his *A Study of History*, 2 vols., abr. ed. by D. C. Somervell (New York: Oxford University Press, 1946), 1:465. Toynbee wrote an introduction for the 1964 revised edition of Webb's *The Great Frontier* (Austin: University of Texas Press, 1965) and was, in fact, a friend and admirer of Webb. A similarly broad perspective is offered by D. W. Meinig in his *Atlantic America, 1492–1800* (New Haven, Conn.: Yale University Press, 1986), and it will be interesting to see how his subsequent volumes in *The Shaping of America* will treat this specific region.

25. Theodore H. von Laue, *The World Revolution of Westernization: The Twentieth Century in Global Perspective* (New York: Oxford University Press, 1987); Immanuel Wallerstein, *The Politics of the World-Economy: The States, the Movements, and the Civilizations* (New York: Cambridge University Press, 1984), 2–10, 13–17, 37–46; Immanuel Wallerstein, *The Capitalist World-Economy* (New York: Cambridge University Press, 1979); and Immanuel Wallerstein, *The Modern World-System: Capitalist Agriculture and the Origins of the European World-*

Economy in the Sixteenth Century (New York: Academic Press, 1974).

26. Among the numerous works emerging on comparative frontiers, see especially Jerome O. Steffen, *Comparative Frontiers: A Proposal for Studying the American West* (Norman: University of Oklahoma Press, 1980); Howard R. Lamar and Leonard Thompson, eds., *The Frontier in History: North America and Southern Africa Compared* (New Haven, Conn.: Yale University Press, 1981); David H. Miller and Jerome O. Steffen, eds., *The Frontier: Comparative Studies*, vol. 2 (Norman: University of Oklahoma Press, 1979); W. Turrentine Jackson, "A Brief Message for the Young and/or Ambitious: Comparative Frontiers as a Field for Investigation," *Western Historical Quarterly* 9 (January 1978): 5–18; George Wolfskill and Stanley Palmer, eds., *Essays on Frontiers in World History* (Austin: University of Texas Press, 1981); George M. Fredrickson, *White Supremacy: A Comparative Study in American and South African History* (New York: Oxford University Press, 1981); H. C. Allen, *Bush and Backwoods: A Comparison of the Frontier in Australia and the United States* (East Lansing: Michigan State University Press, 1959); James Gump, "The Subjugation of the Zulus and Sioux: A Comparative Study," *Western Historical Quarterly* 19 (January 1988): 21–36; Earl Pomeroy, "The West and New Nations in Other Continents," in John Alexander Carroll, ed., *Reflections of Western Historians*, (Tucson: University of Arizona Press, 1969), 237–261; Walter Nugent, "Frontiers and Empires in the Late Nineteenth Century," in Michael Heyd et al., eds., *Religion, Ideology, and Nationalism in Europe and America: Essays in Honor of Yehoshua Arieli* (Jerusalem: Historical Society of Israel and the Zalman Shazar Center for Jewish History, 1986), 263–275; and Howard R. Lamar, "Comparing Depressions: The Great Plains and Canadian Prairie Ex-

periences, 1929-1941," in Nash and Etulain, eds., *Twentieth-Century West*, chap. 6.

27. John Naisbitt, *Megatrends: Ten New Directions Transforming Our Lives* (New York: Warner Books, 1982), chaps. 1-3. Two more rewarding appraisals of the contemporary economic situation are Robert B. Reich, *The Next American Frontier* (New York: Time Books, 1983); and Lester C. Thurow, *The Zero-Sum Solution: Building a World-Class American Economy* (New York: Simon and Schuster, 1985).

28. William G. Robbins, *American Forestry: A History of National, State, and Private Cooperation* (Lincoln: University of Nebraska Press, 1985); William G. Robbins, *Lumberjacks and Legislators: Political Economy of the U.S. Lumber Industry, 1890-1941* (College Station: Texas A&M University Press, 1982); William G. Robbins, "The Social Context of Forestry: The Pacific Northwest in the Twentieth Century," *Western Historical Quarterly* 16 (October 1985), 413-427; and William G. Robbins, "The Western Lumber Industry: A Twentieth-Century Perspective," in Nash and Etulain, eds., *The Twentieth-Century West*, chap. 8.

29. David M. Potter, *People of Plenty: Economic Abundance and the American Character* (Chicago: University of Chicago Press, 1954). I am indebted to William L. Lang for his insight in reading Potter in this manner in his essay "Using and Abusing Abundance: The Western Resource Economy and the Environment," in my edited volume *Historians and the American West*, chap. 12.

30. Limerick, *Legacy of Conquest*, 25-26.

31. Gerald Thompson, "Frontier West: Process or Place," *Journal of the Southwest* 29 (Winter 1987): 364-375.

32. McNeill, *Great Frontier*, 50-61; William Woodruff, *America's Impact on the World: A Study of the Role of the*

United States in the World Economy, 1750–1970 (New York: Wiley, 1975). The reversal of the West's colonial status after the New Deal and World War II is the primary theme of Gerald D. Nash's path-breaking *The American West in the Twentieth Century: A Short History of an Urban Oasis* (Englewood Cliffs, N.J.: Prentice-Hall, 1973), 136, 191.

33. Paul Johnson, *Modern Times: The World from the Twenties to the Eighties* (New York: Harper and Row, 1983), 727; Kirkpatrick Sale, *Power Shift: The Rise of the Southern Rim and Its Challenge to the Eastern Establishment* (New York: Random House, 1975); Peter Wiley and Robert Gottlieb, *Empires in the Sun: The Rise of the New American West* (New York: Putnam, 1982); Lamm and McCarthy, *Angry West*; K. Ross Toole, *The Rape of the Great Plains: Northwest America, Cattle, and Coal* (Boston: Little, Brown, 1976); and Neal R. Peirce and Jerry Hagstrom, *The Book of America: Inside 50 States Today* (New York: W. W. Norton, 1983), parts. 6–8.

34. Peter F. Drucker, "The Changed World Economy," *Foreign Affairs* 64 (Spring 1986): 768–791; Robert B. Reich, "The Economics of Illusion and the Illusion of Economics," *Foreign Affairs* 66, no. 3 (1987/88): 516–528; W. Michael Blumenthal, "The World Economy and Technological Change," *Foreign Affairs* 66, no. 3 (1987/88): 529–550; "The New West," *Wall Street Journal*, October 28, 1987.

35. "American West Has Collapsed Economically," *Buffalo* [New York] *News* (and other Knight-Ridder newspapers), April 19, 1987; Michael Malone, "The Collapse of Western Metal Mining: An Historical Epitaph," *Pacific Historical Review* 55 (August 1986): 455–464; "The Death of Mining," *Business Week*, December 17, 1984, 64–70; U.S. Congress, Office of Technology Assessment, *Technology, Public Policy, and the Changing Structure of Ameri-*

can Agriculture (Washington, D.C.: Government Printing Office, 1986), 16–18; Michael Brody, "The 1990s," *Fortune*, February 2, 1987, 22–24; Gurney Breckenfeld, "Where to Live—And Prosper," *Fortune*, February 2, 1987, 52–56; "Economic Diary," *Business Week*, April 13, 1987, 24; "A Savage Rocky Mountain Low That Won't Let Up," *Business Week*, October 31, 1988, 112–116.

36. The work referred to here by Lamar and Nugent is referenced in the preceding notes; the evolving studies by Olin and Robbins were presented at a session of the Western History Association annual convention at Wichita, Kansas, October 14, 1988.

37. Turner quotation is in "The Significance of History," in Billington, ed., *Frontier and Section*, 26.

CHAPTER 11. FRONTIERS AND EMPIRES
IN THE LATE NINETEENTH CENTURY

1. This is a revised version of an essay that appeared in Michael Heyd et al., eds., *Religion, Ideology and Nationalism in Europe and America: Essays in Honor of Yehoshua Arieli* (Jerusalem: Historical Society of Israel and the Zalman Shazar Center for Jewish History, 1986). I thank Professor Arieli for graciously consenting to its republication. I also thank Charles S. Peterson for encouragement and for incisive questions that brought about clarification of many points.

2. S. B. Saul, *The Myth of the Great Depression in England* (London and New York: Macmillan, 1969); Dan S. White, "Political Loyalties and Economic Depression in Britain, France, and Germany, 1873–1896," paper delivered at the American Historical Association meeting, New York City, December 1979.

3. Jeffrey G. Williamson, *Late Nineteenth-Century*

American Development: A General Equilibrium Theory (New York: Cambridge University Press, 1974), 93, chap. 5.

4. B. R. Mitchell, *European Historical Statistics 1750–1970* (New York: Columbia University Press, 1976), 335.

5. Ibid., 399.

6. Edward Meeker, "The Improving Health of the United States, 1850–1915," *Explorations in Economic History* 9 (Summer 1972): 353–373.

7. From the "50 and 100 Years Ago" columns, *Scientific American*, April and November 1984.

8. B. R. Mitchell, *International Historical Statistics: The Americas and Australasia* (Detroit: Gale Research, 1983), 657–658, 661–662. For the railway lines in operation, see Mitchell, *European Historical Statistics*, 583–584.

9. Mitchell, *European Historical Statistics*, 135. The per-decade totals of migrants leaving Europe are (in millions): 1851–1860, 2.8; 1861–1870, 2.8; 1871–1880, 3.2; 1881–1890, 7.8; 1891–1900, 6.8; 1901–1910, 11.4; 1911–1920, 6.8; 1931–1940, 1.2.

10. Mexico, impoverished by the free-trade policies of the Porfirio Díaz regime (1874–1911), and racked for the decade after that by revolution, was in no position to develop whatever frontier it had left, much of which had been swallowed by the United States in the war of 1846–1848 anyway. Like the South of the United States, Mexico already had an oversupply of poor people and an undersupply of jobs. Europeans had no reason to migrate there, either for farms or for wages.

11. Comparative frontiers have received many enlightening discussions in recent years. Two that have helped me most are William H. McNeill, *The Great Frontier: Freedom and Hierarchy in Modern Times* (Princeton,

N.J.: Princeton University Press, 1983), and Alistair Hennessy, *The Frontier in Latin American History* (Albuquerque: University of New Mexico Press, 1978).

12. Mexico had given way politically in Texas in 1836.

13. Hennessy, *Frontier*, 66–67.

14. Ibid., 65. See also James R. Scobie, *Revolution on the Pampas: A Social History of Argentine Wheat, 1860–1910* (Austin: University of Texas Press, 1964), 39.

15. See, for example, James Gump, "The Subjugation of the Zulus and Sioux: A Comparative Study," *Western Historical Quarterly* 19 (January 1988): 21–36.

16. On New Zealand and the reduction of the Maori, see Alfred W. Crosby, *Ecological Imperialism: The Biological Expansion of Europe, 900–1900* (New York: Cambridge University Press, 1986), 172–173, 265–266.

17. Isak Dinesen, *Out of Africa* (New York: Harcourt, Brace, Javanovich, 1952).

18. French Canada is an exception; whatever "frontier" it had was filled before 1950, and as was true of settled rural New England, its excess population migrated not to western farms but to nearby cities, often ones in the United States.

19. Helpful studies of Canadian population, migration, and frontiers include Yolande Lavoie, *L'Émigration des Canadiens aux États-Unis avant 1930: Mésure du Phénomene* (Montreal: University of Montreal Press, 1972); Warren E. Kalbach and Wayne W. McVey, *The Demographic Bases of Canadian Society*, 2d ed. (Toronto: McGraw-Hill of Canada, 1979); R. H. Coats and M. C. Maclean, *The American-Born in Canada: A Statistical Interpretation* (Toronto: Ryerson Press, 1943); Leon E. Truesdell, *The Canadian Born in the United States: An Analysis of the Statistics of the Canadian Element in the Population of the United States, 1850 to 1930* (New Haven, Conn.: Yale University Press, 1943); Chester Martin, *'Do-*

minion Lands' Policy (Toronto: Toronto University Press, 1973); Gerald Friesen, *The Canadian Prairies: A History* (Lincoln: University of Nebraska Press, 1984). Martin's book does for Canada what Paul W. Gates's *History of Public Land Law Development* (Washington, D.C.: Government Printing Office, 1968) does for the United States public domain. Friesen's book is a finely crafted, readable, comprehensive history of the prairie provinces.

20. Useful works on Brazilian demography, migration, and frontiers include Paul Hugon, *Demografia Brasileira: Ensaio de Demoeconômia Brasileira* (São Paulo: Editora Atlas, 1977); Lucy Maffei Hutter, *Imigração Italiana em São Paulo (1880–1889): Os Primeiros Contactos do Imigrante com o Brasil* (São Paulo: University of São Paulo, Institute of Brazilian Studies, 1972); Thomas Lynn Smith, *Brazil: People and Institutions*, 4th ed. (Baton Rouge: Louisiana State University Press, 1972); Thomas William Merrick and Douglas H. Graham, *Population and Economic Development in Brazil: 1800 to the Present* (Baltimore: Johns Hopkins University Press, 1979); Warren Dean, *Rio Claro: A Brazilian Plantation System, 1820–1920* (Stanford, Calif.: Stanford University Press, 1976); Thomas H. Holloway, *Immigrants on the Land: Coffee and Society in São Paulo, 1886–1934* (Chapel Hill: University of North Carolina Press, 1980); Manual Diegues Junior, *População e Propriedade da Terra no Brasil* (Washington, D.C.: União Pan-Americano, 1959.

21. For Argentine migration and frontiers, some of the best works are Ezequiel Gallo, *La Pampa Gringa: La Colonización Agrícola en Santa Fe (1870–1895)* (Buenos Aires: Editorial Sudamericana, 1982); Roberto Cortes Conde, *El Progresso Argentino, 1880–1914* (Buenos Aires: Editorial Sudamericana, 1979); James R. Scobie, *Revolution on the Pampas: A Social History of Argentine Wheat, 1860–1910* (Austin: University of Texas Press, 1964);

and—excellent for explicit comparisons—Carl E. Sollberg, *The Prairies and the Pampas: Agrarian Policy in Canada and Argentina, 1880–1930* (Stanford, Calif.: Stanford University Press, 1987).

22. Clodomir Vianna Moog, *Bandeirantes and Pioneers* (New York: G. Braziller, 1964), 92, 103.

23. In his excellent comparative history of white settlement in six Southern Hemisphere countries, Donald Denoon defines capitalism in a way that covers agriculture as well as mining and manufacturing: "Here it is taken as a mode of production in which the means of production are privately owned, and labour is performed by workers who sell their labour for wages." (*Settler Capitalism: The Dynamics of Dependent Development in the Southern Hemisphere* [New York: Oxford University Press, 1983], 8).

24. Birth- and death rates were very high compared with a late-twentieth-century industrialized society. On the disproportionately male population of French West Africa, see William B. Cohen, *Rulers of Empire: The French Colonial Service in Africa* (Stanford, Calif.: Hoover Institution Press, 1971): "Because of the deplorable health conditions the administrators could not bring their families with them and few men were willing to accept a career involving nearly lifetime separation from their families" (p. 23).

25. Raymond F. Betts, "Immense Dimensions: The Impact of the American West on Late Nineteenth-Century European Thought about Expansion," *Western Historical Quarterly* 10 (April 1979): 149–166, esp. 150, 152, 154.

26. For a recent discussion of German policy, see Klaus J. Bade, "Imperial Germany and West Africa: Colonial Movement, Business Interests, and Bismarck's 'Colonial Policies,'" in Stig Foerster, Wolfgang J. Mommsen, and Ronald Robinson, eds., *Bismarck, Europe, and Africa: The*

Berlin Conference, 1884–1885, and the Onset of Partition, (London: Oxford University Press, 1988), 121–147. For a summary of motives for imperialism, see Winfried Baumgart, *Imperialism: The Idea and Reality of British and French Colonial Expansion, 1880–1924* (New York: Oxford University Press, 1982), 39–46. A typology of imperialism with examples from the nineteenth century and the very recent past is Tony Smith, *The Pattern of Imperialism: The United States, Great Britain, and the Late-Industrializing World Since 1815* (New York: Cambridge University Press, 1981). V. G. Kiernan, *From Conquest to Collapse: European Empires from 1815 to 1960* (New York: Pantheon, 1982), is a handy narrative survey of European conquests.

27. McNeill, *Great Frontier*, 11, 17.

CHAPTER 12. LAYING SIEGE TO WESTERN HISTORY:
THE EMERGENCE OF NEW PARADIGMS

1. For Herbert Hoover's early career in international mining activities, see Joan Hoff-Wilson, *Herbert Hoover: Forgotten Progressive* (Boston: Little, Brown, 1975), 12–17, 21–23; David Burner, *Herbert Hoover: The Public Life* (New York: Alfred A. Knopf, 1979), 24–44; and George Nash, *The Life of Herbert Hoover: The Engineer, 1874–1914* (New York: W. W. Norton, 1983), 52–124. For a brief contemporary discussion of the global movement of people and capital, see Chris Raymond, "Global Migration Will Have Widespread Impact on Society, Scholars Say," *Chronicle of Higher Education,* September 12, 1990, A1, A6.

2. This argument is expressed best in Earl Pomeroy, *The Pacific Slope: A History of California, Oregon, Washington, Idaho, Utah, and Nevada* (New York: Alfred A.

Knopf, 1965), 8–22; Rodman W. Paul, *California Gold: The Beginning of Mining in the Far West* (Lincoln: University of Nebraska Press, 1965), 20–35; and Carlos A. Schwantes, *The Pacific Northwest: An Interpretive History* (Lincoln: University of Nebraska Press, 1989), 38–46.

3. Ann Markusen points out that with the construction of the transcontinental railroads, purchasing and banking regions "had the upper hand" in those interrelationships. (*Regions: The Economics and Politics of Territory* [Totowa, N.J.: Rowman and Littlefield, 1987], 91).

4. Hoover's internationalism is addressed in Burner, *Herbert Hoover*, 44–62.

5. For only a sampling of the recent journalism on the New Western History, see T. R. Reid, "Shootout in Academia over History of U.S. West," *Washington Post*, October 10, 1989; Richard Bernstein, "Among Historians the Old Frontier Is Turning Nastier with Each Revision," *New York Times*, December 17, 1989; Tom Wolf, "The Newest Historians Attack the Frontier," *High Country News*, January 1, 1990; Richard Bernstein, "The Old West," *New York Times Magazine*, March 18, 1990; Miriam Horn, "How the West Was Really Won," *U.S. News & World Report*, May 21, 1990; and Larry McMurtry, "How the West Was Won or Lost," *New Republic*, October 22, 1990. The two books most often mentioned in the genre of the New Western History are Donald Worster, *Rivers of Empire: Water, Aridity, and the Growth of the American West* (New York: Pantheon, 1985); and Patricia Nelson Limerick, *The Legacy of Conquest: The Unbroken Past of the American West* (New York: W. W. Norton, 1987). See also David M. Kennedy, " 'We Enjoy Pushing Rivers Around,' " *New York Times Book Review*, February 23, 1986; Clyde A. Milner II, " 'A Reconquered Frontier,' " A Review of Patricia Nelson Limerick, *The Legacy of Conquest: The Unbroken Past of the American West*," *Reviews*

in American History 17 (March 1989): 90–94; and Donald Worster et al., *"The Legacy of Conquest,* by Patricia Nelson Limerick: A Panel of Appraisal," *Western Historical Quarterly* 20 (August 1989): 303–322. Discussions of the "new" in Western History have been featured in prominent sessions at recent meetings of the Western History Association. See "The Twentieth-Century West: A Retrospective Panel Discussion" (Gene Gressley, Robert Hine, Howard Lamar, and Gerald Nash) and "Environmental History: A Panel Discussion" (William Cronon, Stephen Pyne, Susan Schrepfer, Richard White, and Donald Worster), both at the Western History Association's Twenty-Seventh Annual Conference, Los Angeles, October 9, 1987; and "What's Wrong and Right with Western History," at the Western History Association's Twenty-Ninth Annual Conference, Tacoma, October 13, 1989.

6. Walter Prescott Webb, *The Great Frontier* (Boston: Houghton Mifflin, 1952). For a discussion of Turner's contributions to the development of a set of legitimizing ideas for western history, see Brian W. Dippie, "The Winning of the West Reconsidered," *Wilson Quarterly* 14 (Summer 1990): 71–72.

7. Henry Nash Smith, *Virgin Land: The American West as Symbol and Myth* (Cambridge, Mass.: Harvard University Press, 1950), 304; and Donald Worster to the author, July 9, 1990.

8. Richard White made these remarks at the session "What's Wrong and Right with Western History."

9. For a general survey of these criticisms, see George Wilson Pierson, "American Historians and the Frontier Hypothesis in 1941," *Wisconsin Magazine of History* 26 (September 1942): 36–60, 170–185; George Rogers Taylor, ed., *The Turner Thesis Concerning the Role of the Frontier in American History,* rev. ed. (Boston: Heath, 1956); Richard Hofstadter and Seymour Martin Lipset, eds.,

Turner and the Sociology of the Frontier (New York: Basic Books, 1968); Ray Allen Billington, ed., *The Frontier Thesis: Valid Interpretation of American History?* (New York: Holt, Rinehart, Winston, 1968); and Ray Allen Billington, *The Genesis of the Frontier Thesis: A Study in Historical Creativity* (San Marino, Calif.: Huntington Library, 1971). Other sources that offer critical insights into the legacy of the frontier thesis include Lee Benson, *Turner and Beard: American Historical Writing Reconsidered* (Glencoe, Ill.: Free Press, 1960); Richard Hofstadter, *The Progressive Historians: Turner, Beard, and Parrington* (New York: Alfred A. Knopf, 1968); Jackson K. Putnam, "The Turner Thesis and the Westward Movement: A Reappraisal," *Western Historical Quarterly* 7 (October 1976): 377–404; Richard Jensen, "On Modernizing Frederick Jackson Turner: The Historiography of Regionalism," *Western Historical Quarterly* 11 (July 1980): 307–322; and David W. Noble, *The End of American History* (Minneapolis: University of Minnesota Press, 1985).

10. Fred A. Shannon, "A Post-Mortem on the Labor-Safety-Valve Theory," *Agricultural History* 19 (January 1945): 31–37; Smith, *Virgin Land*; and Earl Pomeroy, "Toward a Reorientation of Western History: Continuity and Environment," *Mississippi Valley Historical Review* 41 (March 1955): 579–600. See also Harry N. Scheiber, "Turner's Legacy and the Search for a Reorientation of Western History: A Review Essay," *New Mexico Historical Review* 44 (July 1969): 231–248; Jerome O. Steffen, "Some Observations on the Turner Thesis: A Polemic," *Papers in Anthropology* 14 (1973): 16–30; and Martin Ridge, "Frederick Jackson Turner, Ray Allen Billington, and American Frontier History," *Western Historical Quarterly* 19 (1988): 5–20. For two excellent recent assessments, see William Cronon, "Revisiting the Vanishing Frontier: The Legacy of Frederick Jackson Turner," *West-*

ern Historical Quarterly 18 (April 1987): 155–176; and Michael Malone, "Beyond the Last Frontier: Toward a New Approach to Western American History," *Western Historical Quarterly* 20 (November 1989): 409–428.

11. For sources that assess the exceptionalist theme in American history, see Frances FitzGerald, *Fire in the Lake: The Vietnamese and the Americans in Vietnam* (Boston: Little, Brown, 1972), 9; Laurence Veysey, "The Autonomy of American History Reconsidered," *American Quarterly* 31 (Fall 1979): 455–477; Michael Kammen, "The Historian's Vocation and the State of the Discipline in the United States," in Kammen, ed., *The Past Before Us: Contemporary Historical Writing in the United States*, (Ithaca, N.Y.: Cornell University Press, 1980), 22; James O. Robertson, *American Myth, American Reality* (New York: Hill and Wang, 1980), 7–8; Warren I. Susman, *Culture as History: The Transformation of American Society in the Twentieth Century* (New York: Pantheon, 1984), 3–26; Loren Baritz, *Backfire: A History of How American Culture Led Us into Vietnam and Made Us Fight the Way We Did* (New York: W. Morrow, 1985), 9–34; Noble, *End of American History*, 7; Eric Monkonnen, "The Dangers of Synthesis," *American Historical Review* 91 (December 1986): 1146–1157; Thomas Bender, "Wholes and Parts: The Need for Synthesis in American History," *Journal of American History* 73 (June 1986): 120–136; Thomas Bender, "Wholes and Parts: Continuing the Conversation," *Journal of American History* 74 (June 1987): 123–130; Carl N. Degler, "In Pursuit of an American History," *American Historical Review* 92 (February 1987): 1–12; and Richard Oestreicher, "Urban Working-Class Political Behavior and Theories of American Electoral Politics, 1870–1940," *Journal of American History* 74 (March 1988): 1257–1286.

12. William Howarth, "America's Dream of the Wide

Open Spaces," *Book World*, January 4, 1987, 4; and Peter Schrag, "Straddling the Fault," *Nation*, November 27, 1989, 638–640.

13. These comments are based on my own notes taken at the session "What's Wrong and Right with Western History."

14. Martin Ridge, "The American West: From Frontier to Region," *New Mexico Historical Review* 64 (April 1989): 138–139.

15. For Richard White's remarks, see "What's Wrong and Right with Western History," and Reid, "Shootout in Academia." For Michael Malone's comments, see Worster et al., *"Legacy of Conquest*, by Patricia Nelson Limerick," 313, and Malone, "Beyond the Last Frontier," 424–427.

16. Although the History Book Club selected *Legacy of Conquest* as an alternate Book of the Month selection, some reviewers have been highly critical of *Legacy*. For the shift in Bernstein's view, see his two essays: "Among Historians the Old Frontier Is Turning Nastier with Each Revision" and "Old West."

17. Limerick, *Legacy of Conquest*, 20–21, 30–31. For praise of Limerick as a writer, see McMurtry, "How the West Was Won or Lost," 32.

18. Reid, "Shootout in Academia," and Limerick, *Legacy of Conquest*, 20–21, 30–31. Limerick urges other scholars to take advantage of the wealth of excellent research in western history and to pursue, as she has, further efforts at synthesis. At the panel discussion on *Legacy*, she urged her colleagues to have the courage that Turner did in putting their ideas forward from "many different perspectives." See Worster et al., *"Legacy of Conquest*, by Patricia Nelson Limerick," 316–317, and Patricia Nelson Limerick, address to the annual meeting of the Pacific Northwest Conference of Historians, Tacoma, Washington, April 22, 1988.

19. David M. Kennedy, "Bells, Whistles, and Basics in American History Textbooks," *OAH Newsletter* 18 (May 1990): 12–13; and Dippie, "Winning of the West Reconsidered," 81. For the concern about the dangers of narrow specialization in American historical scholarship, see Herbert Gutman, *Work, Culture, and Society in Industrializing America* (New York: Alfred A. Knopf, 1977), xii; Karen J. Winkler, "Wanted: A History That Pulls Things Together," *Chronicle of Higher Education*, July 7, 1980, 3; Herbert Gutman, "Whatever Happened to History?" *Nation*, November 21, 1981, 521, 553–554; Eric Foner, "History in Crisis," *Commonweal*, December 18, 1981, 723–726; Bender, "Wholes and Parts: The Need for Synthesis in American History"; Monkonnen, "Dangers of Synthesis"; Spencer C. Olin, Jr., "Toward a Synthesis of the Political and Social History of the American West," *Pacific Historical Review* 55 (November 1986): 599–601; Degler, "In Pursuit of an American History"; and David Thelen et al., "A Round Table: Synthesis in American History," *Journal of American History* 74 (June 1987): 107–130. For a discussion on the need for a new conceptual framework for western American history, see William G. Robbins, "Western History: A Dialectic on the Modern Condition," *Western Historical Quarterly* 20 (November 1989): 429–450.

20. My argument here reflects in part exchanges of correspondence and conversations with Walter Nugent and Gerald Nash. For Donald Worster's comments, see "What's Wrong and Right with Western History." For further commentary on the "darker side" of western history, see Worster et al., *"Legacy of Conquest*, by Patricia Nelson Limerick," 304–306, 321–322; and Tom Wolf, "The Newest Historians Attack the Frontier," 14–15. See also Richard White, "American Environmental History: The Development of a New Historical Field," *Pacific Histori-*

cal Review 54 (August 1985): 334; and Howarth, "America's Dream of the Wide Open Spaces."

21. McMurtry, "How the West Was Won or Lost," 33; and Richard Etulain, "Fragmented Unities: Cultural Change and Continuity in the Modern West," paper delivered at the annual meeting of the American Historical Association, San Francisco, December 29, 1989, 24–26 (copy in the author's possession).

22. See Steve J. Stern, "Feudalism, Capitalism, and the World-System in the Perspective of Latin America and the Caribbean," *American Historical Review* 93 (October 1988): 836; Ian Tyrrell, *The Absent Marx: Class Analysis and Liberal History in Twentieth-Century America* (New York: Greenwood Press, 1986), 3–5; and Olin, "Toward a Synthesis." See also Olin's important paper on the subject delivered at the annual meeting of the Western History Association, Wichita, Kansas, October 13, 1988.

23. Cronon, "Revisiting the Vanishing Frontier," 174–175; and Richard White, *Roots of Dependency: Subsistence, Environment, and Social Change among the Choctaws, Pawnees, and Navajos* (Lincoln: University of Nebraska Press, 1983), xvii.

24. "What's Wrong and Right with Western History"; and Cronon, "Revisiting the Vanishing Frontier," 174.

25. Earl Pomeroy, "Introduction," in Josiah Royce, *California, from the Conquest in 1846 to the Second Vigilance Committee in San Francisco: A Study of American Character* (Santa Barbara, Calif.: Peregrine, 1970; reprint of 1886 edition), xvi–xvii; Robert Hine, *The American West: An Interpretive History*, 2d ed. (Boston: Little, Brown, 1984), 112; and Robert Hine, "The American West as Metaphysics: A Perspective on Josiah Royce," *Pacific Historical Review* 58 (August 1989): 267–292.

26. Harold Simonson, *Beyond the Frontier: Writers,*

Western Regionalism, and a Sense of Place (Fort Worth: Texas Christian University, 1989); and Harold Simonson, *The Closed Frontier: Studies in American Literary Tragedy* (New York: Holt, Rinehart, Winston, 1970).

27. Melvyn Dubovsky, *We Shall Be All: A History of the Industrial Workers of the World* (Chicago: Quadrangle Books, 1969); Roger Daniels, *The Politics of Prejudice: The Anti-Japanese Movement in California and the Struggle for Japanese Exclusion* (Berkeley: University of California Press, 1962); and Roger Daniels, *Asian America: Chinese and Japanese in the United States Since 1850* (Seattle: University of Washington Press, 1988).

28. Weber also contends that borderlands scholars were among the first to see the world-systems analysis, dependency theory, and core/periphery relations in a strictly North American setting. See David J. Weber, "Turner, the Boltonians, and the Borderlands," *American Historical Review* 91 (February 1986): 79. For a recent essay on borderlands literature, see Gerald E. Poyo and Gilberto M. Hinojosa, "Spanish Texas and Borderlands Historiography in Transition: Implications for United States History," *Journal of American History* 75 (1988): 393–416.

29. Donald Meinig, *The Shaping of America*, vol. 1, *Atlantic America, 1492–1800* (New Haven, Conn.: Yale University Press, 1987); and Donald Meinig, "Continental America, 1800–1915: The View of an Historical Geographer," *History Teacher* 22 (February 1989): 189–191, 198. For a study of the relationship between conquest and human geography, see Albert L. Hurtado, *Indian Survival on the California Frontier* (New Haven, Conn.: Yale University Press, 1988). Hurtado's work emphasizes the strategies adopted by California Indians to survive.

30. David J. Weber, *The Mexican Frontier, 1821–1846* (Albuquerque: University of New Mexico Press, 1982), 282. For pertinent studies of Mexico, see James D. Cock-

croft, *Mexico: Class Formation, Capital Accumulation, and the State* (New York: Monthly Review Press, 1983); and John Mason Hart, *Revolutionary Mexico: The Coming and Process of the Mexican Revolution* (Berkeley: University of California Press, 1987).

31. David Montejano, *Anglos and Mexicans in the Making of Texas, 1836–1986* (Austin: University of Texas Press, 1987), 1–5, 313–314. Vicki Ruiz points out that Montejano and others deny credibility to organizations like the Texas Rangers, a group she refers to as "two-bit vigilantes." Ruiz made these remarks at "Northern Lights: A Symposium on the Northern Plains," University of California, Davis, May 12, 1990.

32. Oscar Martinez, *Border Boom Town: Ciudad Juarez Since 1848* (Austin: University of Texas Press, 1978), 4–5; and Oscar Martinez, *Troublesome Border* (Tucson: University of Arizona Press, 1988). The latter work, a history of the contradictions, friction, and violence along the Mexican–United States border since 1848, also addresses issues associated with the cultural worlds of Spanish-speaking peoples.

33. Mario T. García, *Desert Immigrants: The Mexicans of El Paso, 1880–1920* (New Haven, Conn.: Yale University Press, 1981), 3–8; and Mario T. García, *Mexican-Americans, Leadership, Ideology, and Identity, 1930–1960* (New Haven, Conn.: Yale University Press, 1989). For Mexican Americans, García argues, the central historical experiences have been the Mexican Revolution and immigration.

34. Raul A. Fernandez, *The United States–Mexico Border: A Politico-Economic Profile* (Notre Dame, Ind.: University of Notre Dame Press, 1977), 4.

35. For a much-heralded social history that is disappointing in its broader analytical framework, see Richard Griswold del Castillo, *La Familia: Chicano Families in the*

Urban Southwest, 1848 to the Present (Notre Dame, Ind.: University of Notre Dame Press, 1984).

36. Thomas D. Hall, *Social Change in the Southwest, 1350–1880* (Lawrence: University Press of Kansas, 1989), 3, 12–13.

37. Ibid., 244.

38. John Thompson, *Closing the Frontier: Radical Response in Oklahoma, 1889–1923* (Norman: University of Oklahoma Press, 1986), 224–225. Thompson uses Walter Prescott Webb's concept of the Great Frontier to explain the economic exploitation that took place in Oklahoma and the radical response that ensued.

39. Sarah Deutsch, *No Separate Refuge: Culture, Class, and Gender on an Anglo-Hispanic Frontier in the American Southwest, 1880–1940* (New York: Oxford University Press, 1987), 8–12.

40. Meinig, "Continental America," 24–25.

41. Seymour Martin Lipset, *Continental Divide: The Values and Institutions of the United States and Canada* (Washington, D.C.: Canadian-American Committee, 1990), 91; and Fernandez, *The United States–Mexico Border*, 3. For a look at the contemporary debate regarding similarity and difference, see "Special Report: Portrait of Two Nations," *Maclean's* 103, no. 6 (1990): 37–88.

42. Vernon C. Foulke, "National Policy and Western Development in North America," *Journal of Economic History* 16 (December 1956): 463, 479. In contrast, Seymour Martin Lipset views the "frontier" experiences of the two nations as distinct from each other. The Canadian example emphasized a deeper respect for law and for national institutions, whereas individualism and disrespect for authority characterized the American side. See Lipset, *Continental Divide*, 51–52, 91–92. For two cross-border studies centering on the northern West, see Carlos A. Schwantes, *Radical Heritage: Labor, Socialism, and*

Reform in Washington and British Columbia (Seattle: University of Washington Press, 1979); and Norbert Mac-Donald, *Distant Neighbors: A Comparative History of Seattle and Vancouver* (Lincoln: University of Nebraska Press, 1987).

43. William J. McAndrew, " 'Weighing a Wild-Cat on the Kitchen Scales': Canadians Evaluate the New Deal," *American Review of Canadian Studies* 4 (1974): 23; and Lipset, *Continental Divide*, 52. For a discussion of the Turner thesis in Canada, see M. S. Cross, ed., *The Frontier Thesis in the Canadas: The Debate on the Impact of the Canadian Environment* (Toronto: Copp Clark, 1970), 104–125.

44. Martin Robin, *The Rush for Spoils: The Company Province, 1871–1933* (Toronto: McClelland and Stewart, 1972); M. Patricia Marchak, *Ideological Perspectives on Canada* (Toronto: Ryerson Press, 1975); and David Jay Bercuson, "Labour Radicalism and the Western Industrial Frontier," *Canadian Historical Review* 58 (1974): 154–175.

45. Harold Chorney, "Amnesia, Integration, and Repression: The Roots of Canadian Urban Political Culture," in Michael Dear and Allen J. Scott, eds., *Urbanization and Urban Planning in Capitalist Society* (New York: Methuen, 1981), 535, 539; and M. Patricia Marchak, *Green Gold: The Forest Industry in British Columbia* (Vancouver: University of British Columbia Press, 1983), 17–21. See also M. Patricia Marchak, *In Whose Interests: An Essay on Multinational Corporations in a Canadian Context* (Toronto: McClelland and Stewart, 1979).

46. Norman Clark, *Mill Town: A Social History of Everett, Washington* (Seattle: University of Washington Press, 1970), 233. For two accounts that celebrate economic development and the lumber industry's contributions to growth, see Edwin T. Coman, Jr., and Helen Gibbs, *Time,*

Tide, and Timber: A Century of Pope and Talbot (Stanford, Calif.: Stanford University Press, 1949); and Ralph W. Hidy et al., *Timber and Men: The Weyerhauser Story* (New York: Macmillan, 1963). Robert Ficken's *The Forested Land: A History of Lumbering in Western Washington* (Seattle: University of Washington Press, 1987), provides a more balanced view. For a recent brief survey of regional history that generally depicts the Northwest as a success story, see Gordon B. Dodds, *The American Northwest: A History of Oregon and Washington* (Arlington Heights, Ill.: Forum Press, 1986).

47. Richard White, *Land Use, Environment, and Social Change: The Shaping of Island County, Washington* (Seattle: University of Washington Press, 1980), 7.

48. William G. Robbins, *Hard Times in Paradise: Coos Bay, Oregon, 1850–1986* (Seattle: University of Washington Press, 1988).

49. Michael P. Malone, *The Battle for Butte: Mining and Politics on the Northern Frontier, 1864–1906* (Seattle: University of Washington Press, 1981), 216–217; and Malone, "Beyond the Last Frontier," 424–425.

50. David M. Emmons, *The Butte Irish: Class and Ethnicity in an American Mining Town, 1875–1925* (Urbana: University of Illinois Press, 1989); and Jerry Calvert, *The Gibraltar: Socialism and Labor in Butte, Montana, 1895–1920* (Helena: Montana Historical Society Press, 1988). The quotations are from David M. Emmons, "Social Myth and Social Reality," *Montana The Magazine of Western History* 39 (Autumn 1989): 9.

51. Paula M. Nelson, *After the West Was Won: Homesteaders and Townbuilders in Western South Dakota, 1900–1917* (Iowa City: University of Iowa Press, 1986); and Barbara Allen, *Homesteading the High Desert* (Salt Lake City: University of Utah Press, 1987), xii. For an exhaustively researched and innovative study of the way

Chinese immigrants took part in the development of agriculture in California, see Sucheng Chan, *This Bittersweet Soil: The Chinese in California Agriculture, 1860–1910* (Berkeley: University of California Press, 1986).

52. See the following works by Carlos A. Schwantes: "Protest in a Promised Land: Unemployment, Disinheritance, and the Origin of Labor Militancy in the Pacific Northwest, 1885–1886," *Western Historical Quarterly* 13 (1982): 373–390; "The Concept of the Wageworkers' Frontier: A Framework for Future Research," *Western Historical Quarterly* 18 (January 1987): 39–55; *Radical Heritage*; and *Coxey's Army: An American Odyssey* (Lincoln: University of Nebraska Press, 1985).

53. Schwantes, *Pacific Northwest*, 14–16, 382–385. More recently, at a three-day symposium, "The Centennial West," in Billings, Montana (June 22–24, 1989), Schwantes argued that the "Centennial States" (Washington, Idaho, Montana, North Dakota, South Dakota, and Wyoming), with the exception of "Pugetopolis" at the far western edge of the region, were characterized by low population, abundant natural resources, and largely colonial economies. The West, according to Schwantes, was far less stable and more destructive than the one expressed in the Turnerian vision; in the northern West, outside forces in the form of capital contributed to the "fracturing" of communities. (These remarks are based on the author's notes.)

54. Deutsch, *No Separate Refuge*; and Peggy Pascoe, *Relations of Rescue: The Search for Female Moral Authority in the American West, 1874–1939* (New York: Oxford University Press, 1990). For other recent works, see Paula Petrik, *No Step Backward: Women and Family on the Rocky Mountain Mining Frontier, Helena, Montana* (Helena: Montana Historical Society Press, 1987); Karen J. Blair, ed., *Women in Pacific Northwest History: An An-*

thology (Seattle: University of Washington Press, 1988); Susan Armitage and Elizabeth Jameson, eds., *The Women's West* (Norman: University of Oklahoma Press, 1987); Carol Fairbanks, *Prairie Women Images in American and Canadian Fiction* (New Haven, Conn.: Yale University Press, 1986); Joan M. Jensen and Darlis A. Miller, eds., *New Mexico Women: Intercultural Perspectives* (Albuquerque: University of New Mexico Press, 1986); and Patricia Zavella, *Women's Work and Chicano Families: Cannery Workers of the Santa Clara Valley* (Ithaca, N.Y.: Cornell University Press, 1987).

55. See the following: Donald Worster, *Dust Bowl: The Southern Plains in the 1930s* (New York: Oxford University Press, 1979); Brian W. Blouet and Frederick C. Luebke, eds., *The Great Plains in Transition: Environment and Culture* (Lincoln: University of Nebraska Press, 1979); and Richard C. Luebke, "Nebraska: Time, Place, and Culture," in James H. Madison, ed., *Heartland: Comparative Histories of the Midwestern States,* (Bloomington: Indiana University Press, 1988), 232–238.

56. Spencer C. Olin, Jr., "The View from the Top: Orange County's Political Elites Since World War II," paper presented at the annual meeting of the Pacific Coast Branch, American Historical Association, Seattle, August 21, 1984 (copy in the author's possession); Olin, "Toward a Synthesis," 599–611; Rob Kling, Spencer C. Olin, Jr., and Mark Poster, eds., *Post-Suburban California: The Social Transformation of Orange County Since World War II* (Berkeley: University of California Press, 1991); and Susan Church, "The Post-Industrialists," *UCI Journal* 4, no. 6 (1985): 3, 5.

57. Andrew Gulliford, *Boomtown Blues: Colorado Oil Shale, 1885–1985* (Boulder: University Press of Colorado, 1989), 13. The classic study of a mining-town boom and bust in the nineteenth century is Malcolm Rohrbough's

Aspen: The History of a Silver Mining Town, 1879–1893 (New York: Oxford University Press, 1986).

58. Walter Nugent, "Frontiers and Empires in the Late Nineteenth Century," *Western Historical Quarterly* 20 (1989): 393–408; and Walter Nugent, "The People of the West Since 1890," in Gerald D. Nash and Richard W. Etulain, eds., *The Twentieth-Century West: Historical Interpretations*, (Albuquerque: University of New Mexico Press, 1989), 35–70.

59. Carl Abbott, "The Metropolitan Region: Western Cities in the New Urban Era," in Nash and Etulain, eds., *The Twentieth-Century West*, 71–98. For more recent and provocative works on the urban West, see Peter Wiley and Robert Gottlieb, *Empires in the Sun: The Rise of the New Urban West* (New York: Putnam, 1982); Carl Abbott, *The New Urban America: Growth and Politics in the Sunbelt Cities* (Chapel Hill: University of North Carolina Press, 1981); Joe R. Feagin, *Free Enterprise City: Houston in Political and Economic Perspective* (New Brunswick, N.J.: Rutgers University Press, 1988); and Bradford Luckingham, *Phoenix: The History of a Southwestern Metropolis* (Tucson: University of Arizona Press, 1989).

60. Nash and Etulain, eds., *The Twentieth-Century West*; Gerald D. Nash, *The American West in the Twentieth Century: A Short History of an Urban Oasis* (Englewood Cliffs, N.J.: Prentice-Hall, 1973); Clyde A. Milner II, ed., *Major Problems in the History of the American West* (Lexington, Mass.: Heath, 1989); and Michael P. Malone and Richard W. Etulain, *The American West: A Twentieth-Century History* (Lincoln: University of Nebraska Press, 1989).

61. Malone and Etulain, *American West*, 272–294.

62. Bernstein, "Old West."

63. The phrase belongs to William Appleman Williams and is in William G. Robbins, "William Appleman Wil-

liams: 'Doing History Is Best of All. No Regrets,'" in Lloyd Gardner, ed., *Redefining the Past: Essays in Diplomatic History in Honor of William Appleman Williams* (Corvallis: Oregon State University Press, 1986), 6.

THE CONTRIBUTORS

BRIAN W. DIPPIE is professor of history at the University of Victoria in Canada. He is the author of *Custer's Last Stand: The Anatomy of an American Myth* (Missoula: University of Montana, 1976), *Looking at Russell* (Fort Worth, Tex.: Amon Carter Museum, 1986), *Remington and Russell: The Sid Richardson Collection* (Austin: University of Texas Press, 1982), *The Vanishing American: White Attitudes and U.S. Indian Policy* (Middletown, Conn.: Wesleyan University Press, 1982; reprint, Lawrence: University Press of Kansas, 1991), and *Catlin and His Contemporaries: The Politics of Patronage* (Lincoln: University of Nebraska Press, 1990). He is the editor of *"Paper Talk": Charlie Russell's American West* (New York: Knopf, 1979) and *Nomad: George A. Custer in Turf, Field, and Farm* (Austin: University of Texas Press, 1980).

PATRICIA NELSON LIMERICK is professor of history at the University of Colorado at Boulder. She is the author of *Desert Passages: Encounters with the American Deserts* (Albuquerque: University of New Mexico Press, 1985) and *The Legacy of Conquest: The Unbroken Past of the American West* (New York: W. W. Norton, 1987).

MICHAEL P. MALONE is professor of history at Montana State University. He is the author of *C. Ben Ross and the New Deal in Idaho* (Seattle: University of Washington Press,

279

1970), *Montana: A History of Two Centuries* (with Richard Roeder; Seattle: University of Washington Press, 1976), *Battle for Butte: Mining and Politics on the Northern Frontier, 1864–1906* (Seattle: University of Washington Press, 1981), and *The American West: A Twentieth-Century History* (with Richard W. Etulain; Lincoln: University of Nebraska Press, 1989). He is the editor of *The Montana Past: An Anthology* (with Richard Roeder; Missoula: University of Montana Press, 1969) and *Historians and the American West* (Lincoln: University of Nebraska Press, 1983).

CLYDE A. MILNER II is professor of history at Utah State University. He is the author of *With Good Intentions: Quaker Work among the Pawnees, Otos, and Omahas in the 1870s* (Lincoln: University of Nebraska Press, 1985) and the editor of *Churchmen and the Western Indians, 1820–1920* (with Floyd O'Neil; Norman: University of Oklahoma Press, 1988) and *Major Problems in the History of the American West* (Lexington, Mass.: D. C. Heath, 1989).

WALTER NUGENT is professor of history at the University of Notre Dame. He is the author of *The Tolerant Populists: Kansas, Populism, and Nativism* (Chicago: University of Chicago Press, 1963), *Creative History: An Introduction to Historical Study* (Philadelphia: Lippincott, 1967), *The Money Question during Reconstruction* (New York: W. W. Norton, 1967), *Money and American Society, 1865–1880* (New York: Free Press, 1967), and *Structures of American Social History* (Bloomington: Indiana University Press, 1981).

PEGGY PASCOE is professor of history at the University of Utah. She is the author of *Relations of Rescue: The*

Search for Female Moral Authority in the American West, 1874–1939 (New York: Oxford University Press, 1990).

CHARLES E. RANKIN is editor of *Montana The Magazine of Western History* and director of publications for the Montana Historical Society. He is currently writing a history of journalism in the Rocky Mountain West between 1850 and 1920.

WILLIAM G. ROBBINS is professor of history at Oregon State University. He is the author of *Lumberjacks and Legislators: Political Economy of the U.S. Lumber Industry, 1890–1941* (College Station: Texas A&M University Press, 1982), *American Forestry: A History of National, State, and Private Cooperation* (Lincoln: University of Nebraska Press, 1985), and *Hard Times in Paradise: Coos Bay, Oregon, 1850–1986* (Seattle: University of Washington Press, 1988). He is the editor of *Regionalism and the Pacific Northwest* (with Robert J. Frank and Richard G. Ross; Corvallis: Oregon State University Press, 1983) and *A Celebration of Work* (Lincoln: University of Nebraska Press, 1990).

GERALD THOMPSON is former editor of *The Historian* and professor of history at the University of Toledo. He is the author of *The Army and the Navajo* (Tucson: University of Arizona Press, 1976) and *Edward F. Beale and the American West* (Albuquerque: University of New Mexico Press, 1983).

ELLIOTT WEST is professor of history at the University of Arkansas at Fayetteville. He is the author of *The Saloon on the Rocky Mountain Mining Frontier* (Lincoln: University of Nebraska Press, 1979) and *Growing Up with the Country: Childhood on the Far Western Frontier* (Albu-

THE CONTRIBUTORS

querque: University of New Mexico Press, 1989). He is
the editor of *Essays on Urban America* (with Margaret
Francine Morris; Austin: University of Texas Press, 1975)
and *Essays on Walter Prescott Webb* (with Kenneth R.
Philp; Austin: University of Texas Press, 1976).

RICHARD WHITE is professor of history at the University of
Washington. He is the author of *Land Use, Environment,
and Social Change: The Shaping of Island County, Washington* (Seattle: University of Washington Press, 1980)
and *The Roots of Dependency: Subsistence, Environment,
and Social Change among the Choctaws, Pawnees, and
Navajos* (Lincoln: University of Nebraska Press, 1983).

DONALD WORSTER is Hall Distinguished Professor of History
at the University of Kansas. He is the author of *Nature's
Economy: A History of Ecological Ideas* (Cambridge: Cambridge University Press, 1977), *Dust Bowl: The Southern
Plains in the 1930s* (New York: Oxford University Press,
1979), and *Rivers of Empire: Water, Aridity, and the
Growth of the American West* (New York: Pantheon Press,
1985). He is the editor of *Ends of the Earth: Perspectives
on Modern Environmental History* (Cambridge: Cambridge University Press, 1988).

INDEX